Treating High-Risk Offenders with Personality Disorder

Individuals who have personality disorder and commit serious, violent offences present a particular challenge in terms of rehabilitation and risk management. Drawing from the experiences of those working within the Millfields Unit specialist service for high-risk male offenders with personality disorder, this book provides readers working in forensic personality disorder services, whether in hospital or in prison, with a primer on the theory underpinning a successful treatment model and demonstrates how to put it into practice.

Written by staff in dialogue with their patients, the innovative approach explored within this book brings together psychodynamic thinking and offending behaviour theory to create a more holistic way of addressing the suffering caused, both to themselves and others, by these complex individuals. Chapters explore:

- the rationale and theoretical underpinnings of the psychodynamically informed therapeutic community approach
- the process of selecting, assessing and admitting a patient
- how to form a therapeutic alliance in the face of challenging presentations
- the potentially volatile process of change
- the importance of transitions and aftercare
- staff selection and training at beginner and higher levels
- working as part of a multidisciplinary team.

An essential read for forensic mental health clinicians and allied health professionals, this book will be instrumental for those already dedicated to working with this target population. It will challenge certain stigmas by demonstrating that an informed treatment approach carries with it a good chance of successful rehabilitation and can also be highly rewarding.

Celia Taylor is Consultant Forensic Psychiatrist with West London NHS Mental Health Trust and a Fellow of the Royal College of Psychiatrists. She previously was Lead Clinician at Millfields Unit, a national medium secure service for high-risk male offenders with severe personality disorder.

Brittni Jones is Director of BE Psychology Ltd; Chartered Clinical Psychologist and Psychodynamic Psychotherapist. She is currently also Therapeutic Community Specialist, supporting the review of the accreditation of Therapeutic Communities. She was previously Lead Psychologist at Millfields Unit.

Treating High-Risk Offenders with Personality Disorder

What Can Work When Prison Doesn't

Edited by Celia Taylor
and Brittni Jones

Routledge
Taylor & Francis Group

LONDON AND NEW YORK

Designed cover image: Getty Images

First published 2026
by Routledge
4 Park Square, Milton Park, Abingdon, Oxon OX14 4RN

and by Routledge
605 Third Avenue, New York, NY 10158

*Routledge is an imprint of the Taylor & Francis Group, an informa
business*

British Library Cataloguing-in-Publication Data
A catalogue record for this book is available from the British
Library

ISBN: 978-1-032-71731-9 (hbk)
ISBN: 978-1-032-70921-5 (pbk)
ISBN: 978-1-032-71730-2 (ebk)

DOI: 10.4324/9781032717302

Typeset in Times New Roman
by KnowledgeWorks Global Ltd.

Contents

Acknowledgements

This book would not have been possible without all the people – staff and patients – who made Millfields such a special place for over 19 years. We would particularly like to thank the nine former members of staff who contributed as chapter authors, and the nine former patients who gave their time to be interviewed or provide written accounts of their experience in the unit for inclusion throughout the book. Your varied perspectives and experiences represent the Millfields community that we wanted to honour and preserve.

We would also like to acknowledge the invaluable expertise of Dr Rob Hale, who helped the staff team to become wiser and more thoughtful clinicians, and to thank him for his consultation on this book. Finally, we would like to thank one former patient who contributed significant time to proofreading and providing further consultation on chapters from prison.

Although this book was born from an ending, we hope it will be part of many new beginnings.

Contributors

Miguel Acha Gimenez Social Therapist, East London NHS Foundation Mental Health Trust, UK

Miguel Acha moved from Spain to the United Kingdom to obtain a BSc in Criminology and Psychological Studies. His role in Millfields Unit was a Life Skills Recovery Worker, and he is still employed in this capacity at East London NHS Foundation Mental Health Trust. He has published on the topics of creativity and problem solving.

Jack Blake Resident Doctor in Psychiatry, North West School of Psychiatry, UK

Jack Blake's role in Millfields Unit was that of Social Therapist. He went on to become a doctor and is now completing his specialist training in psychiatry in the Northwest of England. He is an Executive Board member of the International Association for Forensic Psychotherapy.

Dean Bristow Specialist Practitioner, North London NHS Foundation Mental Health Trust, UK

Dean Bristow's role in Millfields Unit was Life Skills Recovery Worker. He now works as a Specialist Practitioner in the Enfield Personality Disorder Pathway, North London NHS Foundation Mental Health Trust, as well as being a registered Integrative Psychotherapist in private practice. He is working towards an MSc in Psychodynamic Psychotherapy.

Jessica Collier Art Psychotherapist, HMP Bronzefield, UK

Jessica Collier's role in Millfields was that of Art Psychotherapist. She continues to work clinically with incarcerated women and leads a team of art psychotherapists working across prisons in the South East of England. She lectures to postgraduate students on forensic art psychotherapy at a number of universities, has published widely on forensic art psychotherapy with women, and was the inaugural co-editor in chief of the International Journal of Forensic Psychotherapy.

Will Irvine Mental Health Practitioner, Haringey Personality Disorder Service, North London NHS Foundation Mental Health Trust, UK

Will Irvine's role in Millfields Unit was that of Social Therapist. His background is in the arts and voluntary work with mental health charities. He is currently a Mental Health Practitioner with the Haringey Personality Disorder Service and completing his training as a psychodynamic psychotherapist.

Jinnie Jefferies Co-director, London Centre for Psychodrama, UK

Jinnie Jefferies' role in Millfields was as an external staff trainer in the Therapeutic Community approach, which she specially adapted for the service. She was for many years head of Psychodrama and staff trainer at HMPS Grendon, and is the founder and co-director of the London Centre for Psychodrama.

Brittni Jones Clinical Psychologist and Psychodynamic Psychotherapist in private practice, London, UK

Dr Brittni Jones is a Clinical Psychologist and Psychodynamic Psychotherapist and was the Psychology Lead and Therapeutic Community Specialist at Millfields Unit. She now works in private practice and contributes to the advisory board for the 'Community of Communities', the accrediting body for Therapeutic Communities in the United Kingdom.

Alex Maguire Music Therapist and Psychotherapist

Alex Maguire's role at Millfields was that of group and individual Psychotherapist. Prior to that he was for over twenty years the Senior Music Psychotherapist at Broadmoor High Security Hospital, where he specialised in the treatment of violent offenders in high dependency and intensive care settings. He is currently Music Therapist and Psychotherapist in a Therapeutic Community-informed outpatient service for patients with emotionally unstable personality disorder, as well as a tutor on a postgraduate Music Therapy training programme in London.

Phil Minoudis Co-Chair of the London Pathways Partnership and Head of Forensic Personality Disorder Psychology at East London NHS Foundation Mental Health Trust, UK.

Phil Minoudis was the Lead Psychologist in Millfields, before moving on to become Co-Chair of the London Pathways Partnership and Head of Forensic Personality Disorder Psychology at East London NHS Foundation Mental Health Trust. He has published widely on personality disorder and offending.

Helen Scott Senior Occupational Therapist, West London NHS Mental Health Trust, UK

Helen Scott was the Millfields Unit Lead Occupational Therapist. She is now also an Advanced Practitioner in Sensory Integration, and currently works as the Lead Occupational Therapist in The Orchard, a service for high risk female offenders in West London NHS Mental Health Trust.

Celia Taylor Consultant Forensic Psychiatrist, Specialist Community Forensic Team, West London NHS Mental Health Trust, UK

Celia Taylor is a Consultant Forensic Psychiatrist and was for 19 years the Lead Clinician of Millfields Unit, one of three national medium secure inpatient treatment services for high-risk male offenders suffering from personality disorder. She was also a member of the London Pathways Partnership Steering Group and of the National Probation Service's London 'Stuck Cases' IPP panel. Dr Taylor is currently employed in West London NHS Foundation Trust's Specialist Community Forensic Service.

Preface

This book has been written in the wake of the closure of a very successful, innovative and unusual medium secure service for high-risk male offenders who suffer from severe personality disorder in England: Millfields Unit. We know it was successful through published quantitative evidence of risk reduction and improvements in psychological wellbeing, and through the testimonials of the many patients who found their therapy to be transformative. Likewise, numerous staff described their professional and personal growth as life-changing and went on to undertake further training, or to work in this very specialist but enormously rewarding field.

The service started life as part of the UK government's Dangerous and Severe Personality Disorder programme, and admitted its first patient in 2005. In 2001, it was absorbed into what is now called the Offender Personality Disorder pathway and assumed a nationwide catchment area. This change acknowledged the expertise and role of Millfields Unit as a national specialist service, but also prevented provision to hospital-based patients and focussed the service on supporting the criminal justice system through admitting and then returning patients to the prison environment post-treatment.

The treatment model, which was that of an adapted therapeutic community (TC) based on psychodynamic thinking, was also evidence-based, as has been affirmed by more recent research. It took several years for the Millfields model to mature and to become embedded into the culture of the unit, and adjustments and adaptations continued to be made in light of organisational and policy changes: this kept the service alive and in touch with external realities. It is in the nature of TCs that they allow for a much greater involvement of all their members in the running of the service, albeit within safe limits. This in itself is anxiety-provoking to senior managers who have adapted to a 'never event' culture which focusses on avoiding risks at all costs; the danger is, however, that performance or 'quality' ratings are prioritised over treatment. Within such a system, it is understandable that anything – or anyone – which might upset the reputation of the host organisation is feared. This insecurity tends to be split off and projected into those who represent real (or imagined) threats: people with personality disorder, and indeed, the TC, which sits uneasily within a doctrinaire bureaucracy. These dynamics and pressures and their consequences can overwhelm any service which seeks to 'break the mould' and attempts to work with some of the most disturbed patients; unfortunately this was the experience of Millfields in its eventual closure in 2022.

The purpose of this book is to describe the Millfields treatment model in all its elements, not necessarily so that a replica service can be set up, but so that other professionals working with this group of very damaged but at the same time highly risky people can utilise elements of it in their own places of work. It has been written by experienced staff from a number of different disciplines, who all participated in and understood the approach.

The first two chapters describe the nature and origin of the patient's difficulties, or how and why severe personality disorder develops and its link with serious offending. Subsequent chapters outline the rationale and theoretical underpinnings of the model, and its component parts: community meetings, small psychotherapy groups, offence focussed work, substance misuse, art psychotherapy and the importance of the unstructured spaces in the day. The art psychotherapy chapter in particular explores the evolution of the therapist's understanding alongside that of the patient's. Equally important parts of the work included, first, 'rehabilitation' or helping the patients to develop the skills needed to function in society, usually for the first time in their lives; and second, was what has been called 'deprisonisation', or mitigating the impact of long-term incarceration, often in brutal environments. This theme is developed further in a chapter on the importance of transitions and aftercare.

Selection for treatment, risk assessment and formulation are also discussed in detail, all of which need to be approached with skill, humility and adequate, detailed information. How to form a therapeutic alliance is discussed as a task that requires patience, and a depth of understanding as to why these patients will seek to punish and reject those who care for them. This alliance is perhaps the key element in fostering change, which also has a dedicated chapter, as it is crucial to get this right and not be pulled into a cycle of hostility and recrimination.

None of this work can take place without willing, interested and informed staff, at all levels of seniority, who have the necessary personal attributes. These include the capacity to reflect, emotional resilience, and an aptitude for listening to different perspectives without rancour when challenged – whether by patients or by colleagues. Dedicated chapters describe the importance of ensuring protected spaces for staff support, clinical supervision and reflective practice, and the impact of this work on individuals, teams and organisations. Finally, common but complex pitfalls are discussed, which need to be mitigated and worked through, given the wide scepticism and stigma that is still, sadly, attached to people with personality disorder, even by mental health professionals. We hope that this book will go a long way to change this mindset in favour of respect and positive regard.

The most important people in the service were, of course, the patients, and a great effort has been made to ensure that their voices, in their own words, run throughout the book. Consent has been given for individual quotes and the inclusion of artwork, although we have ensured that no patient can be identified by any of their input. Other case examples contain anonymised material that has been amalgamated from several individual examples.

As Millfields was a service for men, we have referred throughout this chapter to patients with the pronouns he/him. Of course, women can also have personality disorders and present with risk, and many of the principles in this book would also apply to them. Within health services, the term 'patient' is commonly used, whilst within prisons it would be 'prisoners', and within residential TCs more often it is 'residents'. We use these terms interchangeably throughout the book, depending often on the focus of the chapter.

Brittni Jones and Celia Taylor

Chapter 1

The origin and nature of the patient's difficulties

Jack Blake and Celia Taylor

Parental influences

Personality disorders have a complex aetiology, stemming from a combination of detrimental early experiences and inherited traits that can predispose the individual to their development. The origin of personality disorders is, in essence, a result of the response of the individual to the environment and the response of the environment to the individual: nature interacting with nurture. Although research is limited, the evidence we have suggests that there is a significant genetic influence on temperamental characteristics such as risk-taking (Nicolaou and Shane, 2019) and childhood attention deficit hyperactivity disorder (ADHD) symptoms, both of which are common in the backgrounds of these patients. ADHD is associated with inattention, impulsivity and hyperactivity, and has a heritability as high as 74% (Faraone and Larsson, 2019). A genetic predisposition to impulsivity and aggression appears to be rooted in the functions governed by the neurotransmitter serotonin (Pavlov, Chistiakov and Chekhonin, 2012). Research has also shown that so-called 'callous, unemotional traits', such as low empathy, lack of guilt and a shallow affect, are significantly influenced by genetics (Moore *et al.*, 2019). These are risk factors for future psychopathic traits and antisocial behaviour, and can help to identify at-risk children. Unsurprisingly, many such children will also experience difficulties with making friends, which, alongside often traumatic family backgrounds and difficulties in education, can draw these children either into further social exclusion or antisocial peer groups such as gangs.

Usually, the most important environmental influence is that of the primary caregiver. Many of our patients' parents had themselves experienced traumas such as violence or sexual abuse, predisposing them to both lifelong mental health difficulties and repeating abusive behaviours with their own children (Lünnemann *et al.*, 2019). Their parenting style is influenced not only by what happened to them in early life, but also how poorly these events have been processed and assimilated, with inevitable long-term consequences on personality development. Either predictably abusive, or persistently unpredictable and chaotic, responses on the part of the caregiver create for the child a world full of confusion and threat, amply sufficient to lay the foundations in the next generation for problematic ways

DOI: 10.4324/9781032717302-1

of relating to the self and others. Frank mental illness in the caregiver, sometimes accompanied by emotional volatility and hostility, can compound the situation.

Also influential is what happened to the mother at the time of the child's conception and intra-uterine development. Intimate partner violence (IPV) from the father in the prenatal period can see maladaptation to stress via chronically raised levels of the stress hormone cortisol, to which the growing foetus is also exposed. Such violence can adversely impact on the mother's attachment to her unborn baby, which in turn influences birth outcomes – this includes effects on the growth and development of the newborn infant (Zare *et al.*, 2022). A mother who is the victim of what is often ferocious violence will be unpredictable in her care responses to the infant at best, and unavailable at worst. This is deeply frustrating, frightening and incomprehensible: from a very young age, the child learns that his basic needs might not be met.

Childhood

The story of a patient's childhood is an essential part of understanding how 'nurture' (including the response to his 'nature', such as temperament or ADHD symptoms in early life) has contributed to the person we meet. His story will reveal the complexity of his battles in early life and how they have played out later on, especially in terms of harms caused. In this section, we will describe some of the typical difficulties our patients encounter at each milestone. It is important to note that, although we suggest some experiences that these patients hold in common, this is by no means a set formula, and meaningful individual variation always exists.

> "I came to terms with skeletons that I'd been carrying around for decades. Childhood trauma, relational difficulties, paranoia and so on".

Abuse, neglect and the impact on attachment

Gilligan (1996) was for many years the Director for Mental Health of the Massachusetts prison system. He found that the most violent men had been subject to extremes of neglect, abuse and humiliation:

They have seen their closest relatives – their fathers and mothers and sisters and brothers – murdered in front of their eyes, often by other family members. As children, these men were shot, axed, scalded, beaten, strangled, tortured, drugged, starved, suffocated, set on fire, thrown out of windows, raped, or prostituted by mothers who were their 'pimps'; their bones have been broken, and they have been locked in closets or attics for extended periods.

(p. 45)

Such an environment inexorably leads to the development of an insecure or avoidant attachment style, where the child experiences little or no psychological safety, and cannot learn to regulate his emotions. Insecure early attachments, in particular, undermine and distort the ability to mentalise – in other words, the ability to make sense of the mental states of self and others (Bateman and Fonagy, 2010). The child grows up to view others as inherently dangerous, or even deliberately cruel, and develops a mind-set in which self-protection overrides any empathy or altruism. Focussed purely on survival in such a 'dog-eat-dog' world, he will be prepared to use, humiliate and defraud others with impunity (Narvaez, 2014). As Van den Berg and Oei (2009) point out, "to survive, which is what people with very unsafe attachments have to do, the obvious 'choice' is to enter into instrumental relations whose goal is the acquiring of power".

As importantly, the child who is subject to relentless rejection, mocking or terror, incorporates deeply into his sense of self an identity predicated on shame and self-loathing (Fonagy *et al.*, 2003). By the time he is an adult, he will have unconsciously disavowed these intensely painful emotions along with the hated 'weakness' they imply. Gilligan (1996) has called this the 'death of the self' – a loss of any capacity to feel love, guilt or remorse, reflected in the cruelty these men inflict on their victims. Gilligan describes how any perceived threat to their masculinity – any sign of being disrespected (or 'dissed', as these men often say) – is experienced as existential: a matter of life and death. A violent response is therefore not merely justified, it is essential. This hatred of weakness goes part-way to explaining otherwise incomprehensible, vicious attacks on the very elderly or disabled. Shengold (1989, p. 114) described a similar concept that he called 'soul murder': the destruction of "a child's capacity for joy and inhibiting the power to care and to love".

"My fear of weakness and inability to deal with things".
– Former Millfields patient

The callous and unfeeling behaviour of those with psychopathic traits can be understood, therefore, as an emotional adaptation to severe parental maltreatment (Skeem *et al.*, 2007). Long-term stress leads to excessively high cortisol levels until, over time, the feedback loop that normally suppresses excess production of cortisol is over-ridden, and the capacity to discriminate between threat levels disappears. Everything seems dangerous, resulting in a constant state of fear, or nothing does, resulting in depression and nihilism. Teicher writes that, "Maltreatment is a chisel that shapes a brain to contend with strife, but at the cost of deep, enduring wounds" (2002; p. 13).

In the purely antisocial patient, there is often an idealisation of the mother and an unconscious repression of the rage and sense of betrayal connected with her failure (however understandable, given that she is also often a victim) to protect him from the violent father. This animosity is often an unrecognised factor in later violence towards women. Alternatively, fear of the father, combined with a longing for his affection and validation, can see the patient following in his father's example of habitual violence. Such dynamics can fuel the split between the over-indulgent but impotent mother and the hyper-strict but containing father.

It is important to stress the infant's need for attachment: from an evolutionary standpoint, the infant needs his mother to survive (Ainsworth, 1979). It is the unconscious defence of repression that makes it possible for him to maintain this attachment when care is unpredictable, absent or accompanied by cruelty and abuse. As the child develops a separate identity to its mother, and an increased sense of independence, he is put in touch with some of the painful aspects of his earlier experiences, which can manifest as the misogyny we describe.

Experiences in care

Many patients will have been placed in care when parental abuse has been discovered. Unfortunately, related to this experience, our patients often had a life-long distrust of our social workers, as representatives of the profession that 'failed' to rescue them sooner, or placed them in foster families or children's homes where they experienced further abuse. These unmanageable children tend to have been moved multiple times – often, eventually, to secure adolescent units. It is not uncommon for them to abscond and run back home: a profoundly insecure attachment does not mean there is no attachment at all. Understandably, patients struggle to differentiate between the parents who failed them and the professionals, and perhaps, later surrogate families or environments that are unable or unwilling to provide the care that could help to repair early adverse experiences.

Experiences in education

The patients had also been moved from school to school. The classroom environment is often our first experience of authority in society, outside the nuclear family. Teachers can be thought of as taking on some of the parental responsibilities during the day, particularly in the area of discipline. School, however, is a physically safer space in which to display rebellious behaviour, and many of our patients had been repeatedly suspended and then expelled for fighting, stealing or truancy. Alternatively, some boys will have been taken out of school by their families and taught via intimidation, coercion and extortion – perhaps accompanied by rare praise and rewards – how to be a successful criminal. The deleterious impact on learning sews the seeds of what can be a life-long shame over poor basic skills such as literacy or mathematics. Our patients also often had a history of bullying their peers and being shunned as a consequence, leading to an identification with being bad and unwanted.

Exclusion from mainstream education almost inevitably escalates to placement in specialist schools for children with emotional and behavioural difficulties. It is a shocking fact that some of our patients were exposed in these very schools to further physical maltreatment and sexual exploitation. A few of them were contacted during their inpatient stay by bodies such as the Independent Inquiry into Child Sexual Abuse, which was pursuing a public investigation into these historical crimes.

Sexual abuse

Many of our patients will have had their sexual boundaries violated as children, sometimes violently and sadistically, over a prolonged period of time. Given their propensity to go on to commit sexual offences, it is worth exploring the relationship between childhood sexual abuse and adult sexual offending in more detail. We know that sex offenders are more likely to have been sexually abused than non-sex offenders, (e.g. Jespersen, Lalumière and Seto, 2009), and various authors have explored the developmental factors that could explain this association. Marshall, Serran and Cortoni (2000) in particular have located the origins in a prior insecure or avoidant parent/child attachment, which interferes with the child acquiring the resilience and sense of self-worth that comes from knowing he is loved and lovable. This leaves the child vulnerable to predatory sexual approaches by adults. The adults concerned can 'spot' these children: they are the ones who have 'internalised' their distress and become fearful, anxious and withdrawn, or alternatively have 'externalised' it and become thieves (Bowlby, 1944), fire-setters and the like (Tyler, 2002).

Confusingly for the child, sexual abuse can meet some of his desperate need for attention, with the perpetrator becoming a source of love in his life, while he assumes that any negative consequences must be due to his own deficiencies: a deep sense of self-blame is both common and long lasting (Coffey *et al.*, 1996). This disorientating experience can lead to intense shame, and become a driver for narcissistic rage and violence later in life. Alternatively, exposure to violent or sadistic sex during the formative years can see it being incorporated into the child's own sexual identity and expression. Masturbation to such themes becomes his predominant way of managing emotions such as distress and rage (Marshall, Serran and Cortoni, 2000), setting the stage for future sexual aggression as an adult. The risk is greatly increased in the presence of baked-in victim-blaming attitudes, and sheer anger, towards women (Pithers *et al.*, 1989).

Our clinical impression is that childhood sexual abuse by a female perpetrator is a particularly damaging source of shame for men: they are less likely ever to have confided that it happened, and are very prone to suffering "long-term difficulties with substance misuse, misuse, self-harm, suicidal thoughts, depression, rage, strained relationships with women ... and a discomfort with sex" (Denov, 2003).

Consequences of early adverse experiences

> "Sometimes I still really doubt things, but I now know that is part of my personality disorder, how I perceive people and places. I was paranoid, and it's not a nice way to live".
>
> – Former Millfields patient

It comes as no surprise that intimate relationships for these men can be one of the most difficult areas to manage. Our patients may have had many, intense relationships with many partners, sometimes overlapping with one another, sometimes resulting in children to whom they long to be good fathers, but almost inevitably fail. Those with borderline features are unable to manage distance within relationships, feeling overwhelmed when close to their partner, and abandoned – as well as enraged – when she tries to leave. Research has shown this to be one of the most dangerous moments in terms of risk to her life (e.g. Nicolaidis *et al.*, 2003). The more antisocial men enact serial violence as a means of control. Often partners involved with these patients suffer both physically and emotionally, as a result of their impulsivity, anger and emotional dysregulation (e.g. Collison and Lynam, 2021). Feelings of failure and rejection in relationships can lead to intense shame and become a driver for narcissistic rage and violence later in life.

Trauma and personality

> "I started to understand why I was so angry, and in the process my anger dissipated. It was all about humiliation and anger about being hurt".
>
> – Former Millfields patient

Herman (1992) described the adult sequalae of prolonged childhood abuse as Complex Post-Traumatic Stress Disorder. Features include poor regulation of affect, alterations in consciousness such as depersonalisation and dissociation, difficulty with interpersonal relationships and identity confusion. Just as corrosive is the accompanying loss of a sense of agency and meaning in life (Livesley, 2003). Very often, symptoms of acute post-traumatic stress disorder, such as anxiety, intrusive memories, nightmares and flashbacks persist into adult life. There is a considerable overlap in symptoms between complex post-traumatic stress disorder and borderline personality disorder.

Mentalisation and epistemic trust

A failure in developing mentalisation, or a distortion of it, can see the patient mis-perceiving others as intending to cause them harm when they do not (Bateman and Fonagy, 2004). This pervasive, mistrustful – essentially paranoid – world-view, when combined with violence as a way of solving problems, can give insight into their later offending. More recently, it has been described in terms of a failure to develop 'epistemic trust' (Fonagy *et al.*, 2019) or trust relating to knowledge and how it is acquired. The term refers to a person's willingness to accept new informa-tion from others as usually dependable, generalisable and relevant. Healthy levels of epistemic trust allow us to relax our innate, self-protective 'epistemic vigilance' and are essential for close human relationships (Fonagy and Allison, 2014). Our patients usually had the opposite stance towards the world. Often, feelings of persecution, fostered from a young age, followed them as a kind of self-fulfilling prophecy. In other words, their narratives about others were confirmed in the way they thought and acted. A common attitude, for example, was one of outrage at be-ing convicted for the one crime – out of many – that they allegedly did not commit. This then justified mistrusting the entire criminal justice system and those working within it as liars.

Lifelong difficulties

Systematic research into 'Adverse Childhood Experiences' (ACEs; Felitti *et al.*, 1998) shows them to be indisputably associated with both short- and long-term poor physical and mental health outcomes. Furthermore, there is a 'dose-response' effect (Lacey and Minnis, 2020), in that the more ACEs the child suffers, the worse his prospects in later life. Against this background, it is possible to map out the developmental trajectory of antisocial personality disorder and serious offending. A famous study by Robins (1966) followed children referred to a clinic because of early conduct problems into adulthood. It showed that the presence of persis-tent, generalised aggression and unruly behaviour predicted problems that endured through adolescence and into later life. These problems included not just antisocial behaviour, but severe difficulties in education, relationships, parenting and work. This trajectory is exacerbated at each stage by negative influences and by the indi-vidual 'doubling down' or forging an identity as an offender and an outsider. The common pattern is expulsion from school, joining a gang (or, indeed, being re-jected even by criminal peers), early crime, getting into trouble with the police and, multiple appearances in court and finally, being incarcerated. The individual will have internalised a criminal identity and attitudes, together with a sense of failure in the eyes of society for all the 'normal' goals he has not achieved: a long-term job, stable housing, marriage and a family.

Offenders with more borderline traits (often combined with antisocial ones), have generally experienced early loss of, or rejection by, an attachment figure, neglect and severe abuse. Often one parent has his or her own mental health difficulties. The temperament of these borderline individuals is different to that of the more antisocial patients, in that emotional pain tends to be processed internally and then communicated differently. Zanarini and Frankenburg (1997) have described this as "the transformation of unbearable feelings of rage, sorrow, shame, and/or terror into unremitting attempts to get others to pay attention to the enormity of the emotional pain that one feels". This transformation leads to acts such as deliberate self-harm as a communication (which is often misunderstood), or much more dangerous ones such as arson. Many of our patients convicted of this offence later described it as 'a cry for help'.

Final thoughts

Some final thoughts on abuse: although the different types tend to co-occur, it is our clinical experience that neglect, in the long-term, leaves a void that is very difficult to fill, and outcomes in therapy can be poor. Thus, one patient illustrated this in his art psychotherapy group by making a clay 'man' figure with a hole in the stomach area big enough to see right through. On an emotional level, the neglected child internalises the clear message that he is useless and unworthy, and assumes he will fail in life's essential goals such as making friends, finding work and being loved by a partner (Egeland et al., 2002). Somewhat surprisingly, neglect in infancy can constitute an important part of the pathway to later acting out and aggression (English et al., 2005; Kotch et al., 2008).

In relation to emotional abuse, studies show that it is an important, independent predictor of later psychiatric symptomatology (Cecil et al., 2017), over and above other types of maltreatment, perhaps because it implies a deliberate, sadistic motivation on the part of the abuser. Emotional abuse is also an important predictor of revictimisation, even more so than other kinds of maltreatment (Gama et al., 2021). Experiences of having been the victim were an important contributor to our patients' propensity to victimise others. These are therefore important factors to tease out into the conscious mind and process in therapy.

References

Ainsworth, M.S. (1979) 'Infant–mother attachment', *American Psychologist*, 34(10), p. 932. http://dx.doi.org/10.1037/0003-066X.34.10.932

Bateman, A. and Fonagy, P. (2010) 'Mentalization based treatment for borderline personality disorder', *World Psychiatry*, 9(1), p. 11. http://dx.doi.org/10.1002/j.2051-5545.2010.tb00255.x

Bateman, A.W. and Fonagy, P. (2004) 'Mentalization-based treatment of BPD', *Journal of Personality Disorders*, 18(1), pp. 36–51. http://dx.doi.org/10.1521/pedi.18.1.36.32772

Bowlby, J. (1944) 'Forty-four juvenile thieves: their characters and home-life', *The International Journal of Psychoanalysis*, 25, pp. 19–52.

Cecil, C.A., Viding, E., Fearon, P., Glaser, D. and McCrory, E.J. (2017) 'Disentangling the mental health impact of childhood abuse and neglect', *Child Abuse & Neglect*, 63, pp. 106–119. http://dx.doi.org/10.1016/j.chiabu.2016.11.024

Coffey, P., Leitenberg, H., Henning, K., Turner, T. and Bennett, R.T. (1996) 'Mediators of the long-term impact of child sexual abuse: perceived stigma, betrayal, powerlessness, and self-blame', *Child Abuse & Neglect*, 20(5), pp. 447–455. http://dx.doi.org/10.1016/0145-2134(96)00019-1

Collison, K.L. and Lynam, D.R. (2021) 'Personality disorders as predictors of intimate partner violence: a meta-analysis', *Clinical Psychology Review*, 88, p. 102047. http://dx.doi.org/10.1016/j.cpr.2021.102047

Denov, M.S. (2003) 'To a safer place? Victims of sexual abuse by females and their disclosures to professionals', *Child Abuse and Neglect*, 27(1), pp. 47–61. http://dx.doi.org/10.1016/S0145-2134(02)00509-4

Egeland, B., Yates, T., Appleyard, K. and Van Dulmen, M. (2002) 'The long-term consequences of maltreatment in the early years: a developmental pathway model to antisocial behavior', *Children's Services: Social Policy, Research, and Practice*, 5(4), pp. 249–260. http://dx.doi.org/10.1207/S15326918CS0504_2

English, D.J., Upadhyaya, M.P., Litrownik, A.J., Marshall, J.M., Runyan, D.K., Graham, J.C. and Dubowitz, H. (2005) 'Maltreatment's wake: the relationship of maltreatment dimensions to child outcomes', *Child Abuse and Neglect*, 29(5), pp. 597–619. http://dx.doi.org/10.1016/j.chiabu.2004.12.008

Faraone, S.V. and Larsson, H. (2019) 'Genetics of attention deficit hyperactivity disorder', *Molecular Psychiatry*, 24(4), pp. 562–575. http://dx.doi.org/10.1038/s41380-018-0070-0

Felitti, V.J., Anda, R.F., Nordenberg, D., Williamson, D.F., Spitz, A.M., Edwards, V. and Marks, J.S. (1998) 'Relationship of childhood abuse and household dysfunction to many of the leading causes of death in adults: the adverse childhood experiences (ACE) study', *American Journal of Preventive Medicine*, 14(4), pp. 245–258. http://dx.doi.org/10.1016/j.amepre.2019.04.001

Fonagy, P. and Allison, E. (2014) 'The role of mentalizing and epistemic trust in the therapeutic relationship', *Psychotherapy*, 51(3), pp. 372–380. http://dx.doi.org/10.1037/a0036505

Fonagy, P., Luyten, P., Allison, E. and Campbell, C. (2019) 'Mentalizing, epistemic trust and the phenomenology of psychotherapy', *Psychopathology*, 52(2), pp. 94–103. http://dx.doi.org/10.1159/000501526

Fonagy, P., Target, M., Gergely, G., Allen, J.G. and Bateman, A.W. (2003) 'The developmental roots of borderline personality disorder in early attachment relationships: a theory and some evidence', *Psychoanalytic Inquiry*, 23(3), pp. 412–459. http://dx.doi.org/10.1080/07351690230934904d

Gama, C.M.F., Portugal, L.C.L., Gonçalves, R.M., de Souza Junior, S., Vilete, L.M.P., Mendlowicz, M.V., Figueira, I., Volchan, E., David, I.A., de Oliveira, L. and Pereira, M.G. (2021) 'The invisible scars of emotional abuse: a common and highly harmful form of childhood maltreatment', *BMC Psychiatry*, 21(1), p. 14. http://dx.doi.org/10.1186/s12888-021-03134-0

Gilligan, J. (1996) *Violence: Our deadly epidemic and its causes*. New York: GP Putnam.

Herman, J.L. (1992) 'Complex PTSD: a syndrome in survivors of prolonged and repeated trauma', *Journal of Traumatic Stress*, 5(3), pp. 377–391. http://dx.doi.org/10.1002/jts.2490050305

Jespersen, A.F., Lalumière, M.L. and Seto, M.C. (2009) 'Sexual abuse history among adult sex offenders and non-sex offenders: a meta-analysis', *Child Abuse and Neglect*, 33(3), pp. 179–192. http://dx.doi.org/10.1016/j.chiabu.2008.07.004

Kotch, J.B., Lewis, T., Hussey, J.M., English, D., Thompson, R., Litrownik, A.J., Runyan, D.K., Bangdiwala, S.I., Margolis, B. and Dubowitz, H. (2008) 'Importance of early neglect for childhood aggression', *Pediatrics*, 121(4), pp. 725–731. http://dx.doi.org/10.1542/peds.2006-3622

Lacey, R.E. and Minnis, H. (2020) 'Practitioner review: twenty years of research with adverse childhood experience scores–advantages, disadvantages and applications to practice', *Journal of Child Psychology and Psychiatry*, 61(2), pp. 116–130. http://dx.doi.org/10.1111/jcpp.13135

Livesley, W.J. (2003) *Practical management of personality disorder*. New York: Guilford Press.

Lünnemann, M.K.M., Van der Horst, F.C.P., Prinzie, P., Luijk, M.P.C.M. and Steketee, M. (2019) 'The intergenerational impact of trauma and family violence on parents and their children', *Child Abuse and Neglect*, 96, p. 104134. http://dx.doi.org/10.1016/j.chiabu.2019.104134

Marshall, W.L., Serran, G.A. and Cortoni, F.A. (2000) 'Childhood attachments, sexual abuse, and their relationship to adult coping in child molesters', *Sexual Abuse: A Journal of Research and Treatment*, 12, pp. 17–26. http://dx.doi.org/10.1177/107906320001200103

Moore, A.A., Blair, R.J., Hettema, J.M. and Roberson-Nay, R. (2019) 'The genetic underpinnings of callous-unemotional traits: a systematic research review', *Neuroscience and Biobehavioral Reviews*, 100, pp. 85–97. http://dx.doi.org/10.1016/j.neubiorev.2019.02.018

Narvaez, D. (2014) *Neurobiology and the development of human morality: evolution, culture, and wisdom (Norton Series on interpersonal neurobiology)*. New York: W.W. Norton & Company.

Nicolaidis, C., Curry, M.A., Ulrich, Y., Sharps, P., McFarlane, J., Campbell, D., Gary, F., Laughon, K., Glass, N. and Campbell, J. (2003) 'Could we have known? A qualitative analysis of data from women who survived an attempted homicide by an intimate partner', *Journal of General Internal Medicine*, 18, pp. 788–794. http://dx.doi.org/10.1046/j.1525-1497.2003.21202.x

Nicolaou, N. and Shane, S. (2019) 'Common genetic effects on risk-taking preferences and choices', *Journal of Risk and Uncertainty*, 59, pp. 261–279. http://dx.doi.org/10.1007/s11166-019-09316-2

Pavlov, K.A., Chistiakov, D.A. and Chekhonin, V.P. (2012) 'Genetic determinants of aggression and impulsivity in humans', *Journal of Applied Genetics*, 53, pp. 61–82. http://dx.doi.org/10.1007/s13353-011-0069-6

Pithers, W.D., Beal, L.S., Armstrong, J. and Petty, J. (1989) 'Identification of risk factors through clinical interviews and analysis of records', in Laws, D.R. (ed.) *Relapse prevention with sex offenders*. New York: The Guilford Press, pp. 77–87.

Robins, L.N. (1966) *Deviant children grown-up: a sociological and psychiatric study of sociopathic personalities*. Baltimore, MD: Williams and Wilkins.

Shengold, L. (1989) *Soul murder: the effects of childhood abuse and deprivation*. New Haven, CT: Yale University Press.

Skeem, J., Johansson, P., Andershed, H., Kerr, M. and Louden, J.E. (2007) 'Two subtypes of psychopathic violent offenders that parallel primary and secondary variants', *Journal of Abnormal Psychology*, 116, pp. 395–409. http://dx.doi.org/10.1037/0021-843X.116.2.395

Teicher, M.H. (2002) 'Scars that won't heal: the neurobiology of child abuse', *Scientific American*, 286(3), pp. 68–75. http://dx.doi.org/10.1038/scientificamerican0302-68

Tyler, K.A. (2002) Social and emotional outcomes of childhood sexual abuse: A review of recent research. *Aggression and Violent Behavior*, 7(6), pp. 567–589.

Van den Berg, A. and Oei, K. (2009) 'Attachment and psychopathy in forensic patients', *Mental Health Review Journal*, 14(3), pp. 40–51. http://dx.doi.org/10.1108/13619322200900020

Zanarini, M.C., Barison, L.K., Frankenburg, F.R., Reich, D.B. and Hudson, J.I. (2009) Family history study of the familial coaggregation of borderline personality disorder with axis I and nonborderline dramatic cluster axis II disorders. *Journal of Personality Disorders*, 23(4), 357–369. http://dx.doi.org/10.1521/pedi.2009.23.4.357

Zanarini, M.C. and Frankenburg, F.R. (1997) 'Pathways to the development of borderline personality disorder', *Journal of Personality Disorders*, 11(1), pp. 93–104. http://dx.doi.org/10.1521/pedi.1997.11.1.93

Zare, E., Ghaffari, M., Nahidi, F., Nasiri, M. and Masjedi, A. (2022) 'Relationship between domestic violence in pregnancy and maternal fetus attachment', *Iranian Journal of Psychiatry and Behavioral Sciences*, 16(1). http://dx.doi.org/10.5812/ijpbs.111406

Chapter 2

Personality disorder and serious offending

Celia Taylor

Violence in personality disorder

The association between personality disorder and offending has been demonstrated by the many studies looking at the prevalence of the condition in sentenced prison inmates. A consistent finding over the years has been that it is considerably higher than in the general population. Figures vary from 60% to 70% both in the United Kingdom and internationally (e.g. Coid *et al.*, 2002; Fazel and Danesh, 2002; Singleton *et al.*, 1998). Amongst male offenders, much of this is attributable to high rates of antisocial personality disorder (ASPD), where criminality is built into the definition, e.g. "failure to conform to social norms with respect to lawful behaviours, as indicated by repeatedly performing acts that are grounds for arrest" (Diagnostic and Statistical Manual of Mental Disorders – 5th Edition; American Psychiatric Association, 2013, p. 659). The same is true of violence: "Irritability and aggressiveness, as indicated by repeated physical fights or assaults" (Diagnostic and Statistical Manual of Mental Disorders – 5th Edition, p. 659). Offenders with ASPD tend to have lived criminal lifestyles from a young age, to be impulsive, reckless and deceitful, and to be unable – or unwilling – to take responsibility for their own lives or those of their dependents.

Sometimes, however, personality disorder is associated with more unusual but much more serious crimes, which are difficult to understand and treat, let alone predict, both in the first instance and in terms of the risk of recidivism. Sometimes this is due to the type of victim, for example a parent, a child, or a stranger with a very particular look; in the latter case, the crime can be meticulously planned around a certain person. Sometimes it is due to the extreme nature of the violence, which might be vastly excessive, prolonged or risky to others who are not directly involved. Any individual professional is likely to encounter only a handful of such rare cases in his or her career, so we find ourselves falling back on our clinical skills, on case reports and, above all, on thorough exploration of the offence with the offender, victims (if still available) and witnesses. Bearing in mind that there can be some overlap, we will illustrate some of these unusual offences, of both the more antisocial and the more psychopathic type, through our learning from the individuals referred and/or admitted to Millfields.

DOI: 10.4324/9781032717302-2

Parricide: a special type of violence

Over the course of nineteen years, we treated just a handful of patients who had killed their father or mother. Parricide is the general term for the killing of a parent, with the terms matricide and patricide applying to the killing of the mother or the father, respectively. Parricide is an unusual offence: fewer than 3% of all homicides in England and Wales involve parricide (Holt, 2017). Sons are by far the most frequent perpetrators, and they kill their mothers slightly more often than they kill their fathers. Parricide has been referred to as 'the schizophrenic crime' (Gillies, 1965), because it accounts for around a quarter of homicides committed by psychotic individuals (Holt, 2017). However, studies of non-psychotic offenders have highlighted the central importance of long-term childhood maltreatment, often with a particular, sadistic quality. A study looking at adolescent parricides (Corder *et al.*, 1976) found a pattern of sons having experienced purposeful, routine cruelty at the hands of their parent. This can be so extreme that it has been described as tantamount to torture. In some countries, 'battered child syndrome' is admitted as a defence against murder in these situations (e.g. Malmquist, 2010). It has long been known that childhood abuse is a very common historical finding in offenders with severe personality disorder (e.g. up to 80% of patients in forensic mental health settings; Roberts *et al.*, 2008). Observing this phenomenon should not distract from the culpability of these individuals for their offences: most people who are severely abused do not go on to harm or kill others.

In *Dark Legend: A Study in Murder* (1941), Wertham postulated a variation of Freud's Oedipus conflict, the Orestes Complex, in which the son harbours an attachment to, but also a deep-seated hatred of, his mother. Wortham linked this ambivalence to an eventual 'Catathymic Crisis', in which these highly ambivalent feelings ultimately manifest themselves in homicidal rage. In Homer's story, Clytemnestra murdered her husband Agamemnon in retribution for his sacrifice of their daughter Iphigenia, to obtain favourable winds for a voyage to Troy. However, Clytemnestra was at the same time being unfaithful to Agamemnon with her lover Aegisthus. Years later, when Agamemnon's son Orestes returned from a journey to discover what his mother had done, in a state of mental anguish, he avenged his father's betrayal and death by killing his mother and her lover. The theme seems to be one of the castrating mother, in the sense that she scorns and derides masculinity in a way that cannot be borne. In his study of a series of these men, Wortham found that, generally, they had no history of delinquency, were excessively attached to their mothers and often committed the homicide in her bedroom. Excessive force – so-called overkill – is frequently a feature.

In our experience, this description was eerily accurate. The sons we encountered who had killed their mothers had suffered from prolonged, denigrating psychological maltreatment, with the mother using calculated, physical, psychological and occasionally sexual methods of domination. The father was usually absent from the home, or dominated by and submissive towards his wife. In this family milieu, the relationship between mother and her often somewhat immature and dependent son is close but claustrophobic (Green, 1981). One patient, whose story we have altered here to preserve his anonymity, was told by his mother over such a long period that he was weak, inadequate and innately inferior, that he had incorporated her appraisal of him into his very identity. She would also whip him with her belt or inflict deep scratches on his face. As an adult, he moved out of the family home, only to find himself drawn back again. She then found novel ways of inflicting humiliation, this time by mocking his use of prostitutes, which she found out about when she searched his room. He refused to defend himself, until his prolonged and rigid self-control broke down into homicidal rage. The precipitating factor was her taking off her belt during a row, and he responded with catastrophic violence that far exceeded what was needed to kill her. He felt completely numb and then relieved in the immediate aftermath. Like many, despite his festering resentment, he had had no prior conscious thought of killing his mother and ex-perienced his explosion of violence as coming 'out of the blue'. By the time he entered treatment, he had spent years in prison, paralysed by internal persecutory feelings of intolerable guilt, the legacy of an extremely harsh superego and unable to speak about what he had done. During his therapy, his capacity at least partially to forgive himself was assisted by the forgiveness of one of his brothers. His other two siblings were unable to come to terms with the loss of both their mother and the grandmother to their future children.

Diamond (2006, p. 192) has argued that a characteristic of "these deeply dam-aged individuals that they do indeed experience guilt: not of the neurotic variety, but rather, ontological or *existential guilt*. Whenever any human being commits some act that violates his or her primary values or fundamental nature; when we somehow dishonour or desecrate our own being or the being of others … there develops, often subconsciously … a natural, existential anger with one's self; an inner outrage at failing to follow our most noble, not basest, impulses. And it is pre-cisely this innate inclination toward good that, when thwarted, generates … painful gnawing guilt feelings". These guilt feelings can be greatly exacerbated in that the surrounding culture tends to idealise mothers, and clinical experience shows that this is even more true of men in prison (Taylor, 2018).

Men who kill their fathers – commit patricide – have been less well studied, but the existing research allows us to develop a tentative profile. In this instance, rather than the 'castrating' mother, the father is experienced as a threat to the son's very life, physically or psychologically. While the killing of the father has echoes of Freud's Oedipus Complex (1973), the threat in these cases is literal: the nature of the abuse has often left the boy child fearing death. Heide (2017) categorised these offenders either into the 'severely abused' type, who kill to end the abuse – to survive, in our examples – or the 'enraged' type, who kill out of deeply rooted rage over historical abuse that is triggered by some present-day provocation. Amongst the patients we admitted to Millfields, one who provides an example of the 'severely abused type', had an alcoholic father with connections to notorious armed gangs in his home country. The man possessed ceremonial daggers, with which he forced his children into 'play fights'. When he reached adolescence, our patient stabbed his father in the back, in terror that he would eventually kill them. He himself joined a gang that fought other gangs in the streets, armed with machetes. His offences carried at least the potential for a re-enactment of his crime, by fighting others for dominance of their territory.

Another patient, whose story is altered here to preserve his anonymity, provides an example of the 'enraged' type: his father was a sadistic, cruel man, who "never showed me any affection, respect or even ordinary kindness". His mother abandoned her husband and children, after which he became a severely avoidant recluse: 'basically a slave' to his father. He 'walked on eggshells', could not make eye contact with others and frequently felt suicidal. When he saw his father was about to hit his sister during a row, he 'snapped' and beat him to death with a garden spade. Interestingly, the truth about the extreme tensions within this family was not apparent to the outside world: neighbours later described the dead father as a gentle, quiet man. Our patient described how they "pretended to be a happy family, but in fact there was never any peace at home". He felt only relief: a huge burden he had carried since childhood was lifted.

Writing about adolescents, Malmquist (2010) describes how central both shame and humiliation can often be to parricide: we found the same in our adult offenders. Like guilt, shame carries with it an unbearable toxicity, leading to feelings of self-loathing. A point is reached whereby killing one's tormentor seems to be the only alternative to suicide, the only way to transform a state of powerlessness into being an agent of power. The rage that accompanies shame finally breaks through, leaving a sense of calm relief and moral justification after the act has been committed: it was the response to a narcissistic wound so great that it felt near fatal to the self (Malmquist, 2010).

Sexual offending in personality disorder

Many studies have shown high rates of personality disorder amongst prisoners who have committed sex offences, e.g. 67.4% (Arbanas, 2022) and 53.6% (Eher, Rettenberger and Turner, 2019). While many sex offenders have surprisingly low reconviction rates of around 14% (Hanson and Morton-Bourgon, 2005), individuals with a personality disorder have, by definition, a number of risk factors that make them more likely to reoffend. These include adverse childhood experiences and antisocial features such as impulsivity, difficulties managing anger and unstable relationships. These features also mean they are also more likely to drop out of treatment; those who do are about twice as likely to reoffend (Craissati et al., 2009; Marques et al., 2005).

Sexual assault and rape were therefore common offences for Millfields patients to have committed. The most serious of these offenders, and the most likely to offend repeatedly, were those who had a history of violence independent of any sexual crimes, in the context of antisocial and borderline personality traits (Schroeder et al., 2013). From them, we often heard about extreme childhood abuse: examples included their mothers pimping them out to multiple strange men, or repeatedly engaging in sexual intercourse with their sons, even from the age of three or five. This lays the foundation for entirely conscious, deep rage and hatred, especially if the abuse features overt sadism and humiliation: one man referred to his mother as a 'fucking little slut'; "the most evil person I know … cruel and vicious … she was evil personified". Beneath this loathing one often finds a longing, which is rarely acknowledged, for their mothers to have loved them as sons. Sometimes there was incest in the wider family, with the patient finding out as an older child or adult that his father was his grandfather, or his uncle had raped his mother. This sets up a situation where the mother, seemingly, cannot bear this child in particular, as he is a constant reminder of her own trauma. It was not uncommon for our patients to have been forced to watch violent or otherwise non-consensual pornography at a young age. The evidence shows that such early exposure is probably not a sole cause of later sexual offending, but it does 'add fuel to the fire' in men with other predisposing factors (Malamuth, 2018).

Very often, sexual, emotional and physical torment continued in care homes and with foster parents; one patient gave evidence, while he was at Millfields, to a national inquiry in this regard, including telling them that he "would not have been surprised if children had died" in his particular home. These men were de-scribed as being 'out of control' as children, unable to make friends or to contain their aggression, let alone to learn. More than one described himself as "unable to fit in anywhere, a complete outsider". He would deliberately sabotage potential friendships by angering or disgusting others, 'playing up' as he thought to people's negative impressions of him; by preventing people from getting to know him or getting close to him, he kept himself safe from rejection. This then reinforced his feelings of being rejected himself and fuelled 'righteous' anger: "I never wanted for food or money … I could just take what I wanted" – including, in his case, sex. In some instances, 'taking' involved vicious stabbings or beatings, later justified by saying that the victim was actually a paedophile. In fact, the murder of a presumed paedophile was a not uncommon offence for these patients to have committed. Sometimes this assumption was a tragic error: one patient murdered a man who had toys in his living room, which were in fact there for when his nieces and nephews visited.

For these men, violent sexual assault was sometimes motivated by wanting the woman – or, in some instances, the man – 'to feel like I did' when they were being abused. Some of them continued to be very violent within the prison system, lead-ing to years spent in segregation almost as a choice: the four walls of the empty room can serve as the ultimate, and the only, safe container. These individuals are not to be under-estimated and will usually need to spend a long period in a Close Supervision Centre[1] or High Secure Hospital before it is safe for them to enter a therapeutic community (TC).

Another dynamic we came across in some high-risk sex offenders was that of nihilism. One patient's formulation described his 'drive towards destructiveness and death', both in his suicidal gestures and in his homicidal fantasies. We found notes written by him about the latter, naming female staff in such a way as to make them feel profoundly uncomfortable and unsafe. Another man, in the lead-up to his index offence, had started not to care about what happened to him. He said that he had thought about what he was going to do for a long time, until, finally, he was 'beyond the fantasy'. Freud (1915) long ago described a human drive, which he named Thanatos, whose aim is the reduction of psychic stress to its lowest possible point, which is death. It is first directed inward as a self-damaging tendency and is later turned outward in the form of aggression and sadism. In these men, the countervailing life instinct Eros, had been subsumed into something much more powerful and destructive.

The more sadistic – and psychopathic – sex offenders were skilled at forming relationships with women, which over time became controlling and cruel. Surprisingly often, this included a history of forming relationships with female prison or hospital staff, through exploiting their natural empathy and likely personal experiences of childhood boundary violations. Some of those thus targeted paid the high price of being convicted of offences themselves (e.g. for smuggling a mobile phone into a prison), or of being struck off their professional register. One man exhibited an extreme need for control and coercion, in order to shore up his fragile narcissistic defences and fears of being shown up as worthless. He did this by seducing women into a relationship, which he gradually transformed into a manipulative means of control. He would sexually humiliate or degrade his many partners, requiring their compliance in order to 'prove their devotion' to him. His anger and insecurity were split off and projected into these women, who represented real (or imagined) threats. As a result, he could justify his actions, be immune from conscious feelings of guilt, and a renounce responsibility for his actions. Put another way, projective identification (a defense mechanism that involves unconsciously attributing parts of oneself to another person; Klein, 1996) served to locate and externalise the weak and worthless part of himself into women, whom he was then justified in hating. On the ward, he frequently accused staff of being responsible for his multiple boundary breaches, effectively by saying, "Now look what you made me do". Having been sexually molested in particularly humiliating ways by an uncle, he identified with the aggressor (Ferenczi, 1988) – his abuser – and repeated his abuse as the perpetrator rather than the victim; this became a way of managing and defending himself against intense feelings of vulnerability and shame. Such individuals invariably have psychopathic traits, which make them extremely challenging to treat without robust security of the physical, procedural and especially relational kind, and frequent space for reflective practice to explore the impact on staff in real time.

Two Millfields patients were identified as being so over-preoccupied with sex that they were unable to concentrate on their therapy. One, for example, was distracted by thoughts of sex much of the time. He was masturbating six or seven times each day and would spend his small group staring at the female facilitator's breasts. Some of his fantasies involved significant violence and degradation towards women, particularly those of Asian appearance. He was greatly helped by the prescription of a Selective Serotonin Reuptake Inhibitor (SSRI) antidepressant as a form of antilibidinal medication (Igoumenou, 2020). This is a controversial intervention, but used judiciously and with informed consent, can not only make psychological work possible but also greatly reduce the chances of there being future victims. We did not use hormonally based antilibidinal medication, but such treatment is available in the United Kingdom and internationally.

Unpredictable and unexplainable?

Very few patients who were referred to Millfields had no history of childhood trauma at all, but there were a few. Admittedly, there were too few to constitute anything like a representative sample, and none had living relatives from whom we could gather collateral information about their early years. Nonetheless, they characteristically came from unbroken, middle class homes where they had experienced a stable and ostensibly loving upbringing by their parents. They might describe a rather harsh father or somewhat distant mother, or they might recall feeling that their brothers or sisters were the preferred children, but these common family dynamics are faced by millions of other very ordinary children. It seemed to us that to label such events as 'traumatic' would have diminished the harrowing experiences of the vast majority of those who came to the unit. As adults, all achieved good jobs, although not stable relationships – again, something that characterises a good proportion of the population. Indeed, by this measure, they did not fulfil all the diagnostic criteria for personality disorder, since overt early disturbance was absent. Two did suffer from depression as adults. In all these cases, their later offending seemed to come out of the blue and, according to their accounts, caused bewilderment and deep shame in the rest of the family.

Examples of these individuals included a highly conscientious man who beat his wife to death when she tried to leave him; a man who started stalking a professional, against whom he made death threats and a rape allegation that nearly succeeded in conviction; and a man with an early foot fetish who took a woman captive, tied her up and, after several hours, killed her because she remained – in his mind – 'too calm'.

It was difficult to understand the developmental roots of such acts, which no doubt were somewhat different in each case, which left us in the realm of informed speculation. It seemed that early personality disturbance can remain hidden until much later in life, when the person is faced with life circumstances or a life event that precipitates toxic destructiveness. If something goes badly wrong during infancy, there will be no concrete memories or identifiable events that can be spoken or thought about later. Early lack of adequate attunement seems to be a factor, but it is usually too subtle to be detected. In a systematic review, Rocha *et al.* (2020) found strong support for the notion that the quality of the mother's sensitivity and responsiveness to her baby greatly influences later language, cognitive and social development. Repeated restrictive or punitive actions do not teach the child self-control, or that agency and spontaneity are welcome. It is easy to imagine that repeatedly misinterpreting or ignoring the child must lead to deep confusion, frustration and eventually rage. This, in turn, will impact on mother's responsiveness, as will her own experiences of depression, anxiety and the like.

All of our patients with seemingly 'normal' childhoods offended in the context of a deep, psychically catastrophic, narcissistic wound. Pathological narcissism is likely to develop in the very early stages of childhood: if the child feels rejected, unloved or mocked, he will learn that affection and approval are contingent on being someone else, the child the mother wants him to be. In other words, he will develop a 'false self'. In this sense, as pointed out by Diamond (2006), the pathological narcissist does not love himself at all: instead, he has "buried his or her true self-expression in response to early injuries and replaced it with a highly developed, compensatory, 'false self'". Diamond (2006) cites Kohut's (1972) writings on the distinct psychological quality of narcissistic rage:

> The need for revenge, for righting a wrong, for undoing a hurt by whatever means, and a deeply anchored, unrelenting compulsion in the pursuit of all these aims, which gives no rest to those who have suffered a narcissistic injury – these are the characteristic features of narcissistic rage in all its forms and which sets it apart from other kinds of aggression.

For our men, the original narcissistic injury and the depth of the pain it caused, seems to have been buried deep in the unconscious until triggered by an event that called on the wrong to be righted, at any cost.

Note

1 Close Supervision Centres (CSCs) are small, specialist units located within six of the high security prisons. https://hmiprisons.justiceinspectorates.gov.uk/hmipris_reports/close-supervision-centres/

References

American Psychiatric Association (2013) Diagnostic and statistical manual of mental disorders – 5th edition. Washington, DC: American Psychiatric Association.

Arbanas, G. (2022) 'Personality disorders in sex offenders, compared to offenders of other crimes', *The Journal of Sexual Medicine*, 19(11), p. S39.

Coid, J., Bebbington, P., Jenkins, R., Brugha, T., Lewis, G., Farrell, M. and Singleton, N. (2002) 'The national survey of psychiatric morbidity among prisoners and the future of prison healthcare', *Medicine, Science and the Law*, 42(3), pp. 245–250.

Corder, B.F., Ball, B.C., Haizlip, T.M., Rollins, R. and Beaumont, R. (1976) 'Adolescent parricide: a comparison with other adolescent murder', *The American Journal of Psychiatry*, 133(8), pp. 957–961. doi: 10.1176/ajp.133.8.957

Craissati, J., Falla, S., McClurg, G. and Beech, A. (2002) 'Risk, reconviction rates and pro-offending attitudes for child molesters in a complete geographical area of London', *Journal of Sexual Aggression*, 8(1), pp. 22–38. doi: 10.1080/13552600208413330

Diamond, S.A. (2006) 'Violence as secular evil: forensic evaluation and treatment of violent offenders from the viewpoint of existential depth psychology', in *Forensic psychiatry: influences of evil* (pp. 179–206). Totowa, NJ: Humana Press. doi: 10.1007/978-1-59745-006-5_9

Eher, R., Rettenberger, M. and Turner, D. (2019) 'The prevalence of mental disorders in incarcerated contact sexual offenders', *Acta Psychiatrica Scandinavica*, 139(6), pp. 572–581. doi: 10.1111/acps.13024

Fazel, S. and Danesh, J. (2002) 'Serious mental disorder in 23,000 prisoners: a systematic review of 62 surveys', *The Lancet*, 359(9306), pp. 545–550. doi: 10.1016/S0140-6736(02)07740-1.

Ferenczi, S. (1988) 'Confusion of tongues between adults and the child: the language of tenderness and of passion', *Contemporary Psychoanalysis*, 24(2), pp. 196–206. doi: 10.1080/00107530.1988.10746234

Freud, S. (1915) *Instincts and their vicissitudes*. Collected Papers, IV. London: Hogarth Press.

Freud, S. (1973) 'Three essays on the theory of sexuality', in Strachey, J.(ed.) *Standard edition of the complete psychological works of Sigmund Freud*. London: Hogarth Press Ltd.

Gillies, H. (1965) 'Murder in the west of Scotland', *The British Journal of Psychiatry*, 111(480), pp. 1087–1094. doi: 10.1192/bjp.111.480.1087

Green, C.M. (1981) 'Matricide by sons', *Medicine, Science and the Law*, 21(3), pp. 207–214. doi: 10.1177/002580248102100309

Hanson, R.K. and Morton-Bourgon, K.E. (2005) 'The characteristics of persistent sexual offenders: A meta-analysis of recidivism studies', *Journal of Consulting and Clinical Psychology*, 73(6), pp. 1154–1163.

Heide, K.M. (2017) 'Parricide encapsulated', in Brookman, F., Maguire, E.R., and Maguire, M. (eds.) *The handbook of homicide*. Hoboken, NJ: Wiley, pp. 197–211. doi: 10.1002/9781118924501.ch12

Holt, A. (2017) 'Parricide in England and Wales (1977–2012): an exploration of offenders, victims, incidents and outcomes', *Criminology & Criminal Justice*, 17(5), pp. 568–587. doi: 10.1177/1748895816688332

Igoumenou, A. (2020) 'The use of medication for the treatment of sex offenders: ethical issues and controversies', *Ethical issues in clinical forensic psychiatry*, pp. 51–83. doi: 10.1007/978-3-030-37301-6_4

Klein, M. (1996) 'Notes on some schizoid mechanisms', *The Journal of Psychotherapy Practice and Research*, 5(2), p. 160.

Kohut, H. (1972) 'Thoughts on narcissism and narcissistic rage', *The Psychoanalytic Study of the Child*, 27(1), pp. 360–400. doi: 10.1080/00797308.1972.11822721

Malamuth, N.M. (2018) 'Adding fuel to the fire'? Does exposure to non-consenting adult or to child pornography increase risk of sexual aggression?', *Aggression and Violent Behavior*, 41, pp. 74–89. doi: 10.1016/j.avb.2018.02.013

Malmquist, C.P. (2010) 'Adolescent parricide as a clinical and legal problem', *Journal of the American Academy of Psychiatry and the Law Online*, 38(1), pp. 73–79.

Marques, J.K., Wiederanders, M., Day, D.M., Nelson, C. and Van Ommeren, A. (2005) 'Effects of a relapse prevention program on sexual recidivism: final results from California's Sex Offender Treatment and Evaluation Project (SOTEP)', *Sexual Abuse: A Journal of Research and Treatment*, 17, pp. 79–107. doi: 10.1177/107906320501700108

Meloy, J.R. and Reavis, J.A. (2007) 'Dangerous cases: when treatment is not an option', *Severe personality disorders: Major issues in everyday practice*, pp. 181–195. doi: 10.1017/CBO9780511544439.012

Roberts, A., Yang, M., Zhang, T. and Coid, J. (2008) 'Personality disorder, temperament, and childhood adversity: findings from a cohort of prisoners in England and Wales', *The Journal of Forensic Psychiatry & Psychology*, 19(4), pp. 460–483. doi: 10.1080/14789940801936597

Rocha, N., dos Santos Silva, A.C.F., Dos Santos, F.P. and Dusing, M.M. (2020) 'Impact of mother–infant interaction on development during the first year of life: a systematic review', *Journal of Child Health Care*, 24(3), pp. 365–385. doi: 10.1177/1367493519864742

Schroeder, M., Iffland, J.S., Hill, A., Berner, W. and Briken, P. (2013) 'Personality disorders in men with sexual and violent criminal offense histories', *Journal of Personality Disorders*, 27(4), pp. 519–530.

Singleton, N., Meltzer, H., Gatward, R., Coid, J. and Deasy, D. (1998) *Psychiatric morbidity among prisoners in England and Wales*. London: The Stationery Office.

Taylor, C. (2018) 'Treating violent men: the significance of the mother–son relationship', in Foster, A. (ed.) *Mothers accused and abused*. London: Routledge, pp. 42–60.

Wertham, F. (1941) *Dark legend: A study in murder*. New York: Doubleday.

Chapter 3

Rationale and theoretical underpinnings of the adapted therapeutic community approach

Brittni Jones

Introduction

As this book introduces the principles of the adapted therapeutic community (TC) model with high-risk offenders with personality disorder, many theories, practices and ideas will be presented. With so much information, there is a risk of losing sight of the proverbial wood for the trees. Rigidly or blindly following practices and customs can distort or miss the point of them, resulting in a service which is ineffective or even harmful. This chapter will therefore first explore the core ethos of TC, followed by the theories, evidence base and principles that support and structure the treatment model.

The core of the TC

If one were to draw up a list of the most popular movies or television and book series of the last few decades, many of these would be able to tell something about the fundamental values of a TC. For example, at first glance the television series 'Friends' and the 'Harry Potter' films and books look quite different in content. However, looking beyond the coffee and magic, both are centred around a group of people facing challenges together, and places where the main characters are known by their community, and there is a sense of acceptance, goodwill and belonging. Whether it is 'Hogwarts' or 'Central Perk', the place, its culture, and the people inside it (in other words, the *community*) are key features of the story which draw people to them.

Of course, these are idealised versions of places that can be found in everyday life. But, helpfully, consideration of these fantasy places and their elements can give an insight into what a TC is striving to be. A TC is a place where everyone knows your name, it is noticed if you are not there or if you are going through something difficult, and there is a reasonable certainty that conflicts or mistakes can be worked through. These elements do not always exist in real life, but they are the high standards that make these stories so popular and which TCs emulate.

These qualities are also what functional and stable families provide, and the experience and internalisation of this safety and acceptance is something that is

DOI: 10.4324/9781032717302-3

important to our development as humans. If enough goes well with this in early life, we can venture forth in the world with an internalised sense of self-worth and self-efficacy, which in turn can help sustain us through periods of pain and hardship. However, if for whatever reason this process goes wrong, we miss out on this important internal infrastructure, which sets us up for difficulties in the way that we relate to ourselves and others in later life. Childhood trauma, and particularly parental abuse or neglect, can result in the building of a malignant internal structure, one which comes with a sense of worthlessness, victimhood, or a constant state of vigilance and threat. This is the basis for many personality disorders, and the way a person responds to these internal structures, sometimes referred to in psychotherapies as 'core beliefs', 'schemas' (Barazandeh *et al.*, 2016) or 'internal working models' (Knox, 1999) can often help to explain serious offending.

Many psychotherapies attempt to target and change these internal structures, and the relationship between the client and the therapist may or may not be brought into this endeavour as a way of achieving that change. However, the TC seeks first and foremost to provide the *experience* of an environment and community that behaves like the family should have, and can therefore deconstruct old beliefs and ways of living, and build new ones. This provides what is called a *living learning environment*, a place for unlearning and relearning through experience (Haigh, 2013).

> "[The most helpful aspect of Millfields was] the level of support, from the moment I arrived and all the way through. I was treated differently and given a gentle introduction … It was a community and I'd never felt that before. I could open up and gain confidence. I could relate to the others, even though they had lived a very different lifestyle. I had never had that in my life. I had a good lead up to OTT (Orientation to Therapy group), with time to integrate and learn about things; I could ease myself in. I very much appreciated my initial psychology assessment sessions: they helped to build up a picture of me. The process was thorough and not rushed or skimmed over. There was no favouritism, but rather egalitarianism. We could talk to who we wanted to. The social therapists took the time, which was a huge bonus that I had never had in my life before. Here [in prison] the officers don't see you. Obviously, Millfields was much more comfortable, but here it's 'them and us'. In Millfields you could bring things up. You had a degree of autonomy, and we were equal – it was liberating. There was a sense of purpose".
>
> – Former Millfields patient

History and theoretical underpinnings

The idea of the TC links clearly with human social experience which, for better or worse, will be known by us all. As such, it is certainly not rocket science. However, as a model or way of thinking when working with those who are experiencing psychological difficulties, it is for many still a radical approach. Rather than the traditional model of psychiatry or psychological intervention, where a treatment is done to a patient by a skilled authority or clinician, in TCs the authority is given to the group and its members, patients and clinicians/staff included together. It is this community that becomes both patient and treatment, or as Rapoport (2001) put it, it is the 'community as doctor'.

The term 'Therapeutic Community' was coined by Thomas Main through his involvement, alongside other psychiatrists and psychoanalysts such as Bion, Foulkes and Maxwell Jones, in treating soldiers with psychological difficulties during the second World War (Pearce and Haigh, 2017, p. 21). The fact that this idea came about with this very specific group of patients is worth reflecting on. Perhaps for the first time, the patients were exclusively a group of people who, prior to mental breakdown, had a function and strength as soldiers, and there was an obviously traumatic trigger of war that preceded their psychological distress. This was different to the usual patients, often women, whose functionality or roles prior to breakdown were less recognised and valued, who were presumed to be weak rather than strong, and whose distress often seemed disproportionate to triggering events or even unexplainable. We now know that there is much more to consider regarding experiences of trauma and an individual's response to it. At the time of the Second World War, however, these clear factors in what seemed to be a different patient group helped push beyond the usual explanation of mental distress, in which an individual is considered to have an intrinsic mental weakness or fault which results in 'illness'.

In the traditional way of thinking about mental health treatment, the clinician seeks to do something to the patient which will fix or reduce the symptoms or the mental disorder. At the start of the treatment of the soldier patients, this is indeed the model that was initially followed, with Bion noting that sedation was the main tool of treatment and that it achieved a reduction in 'neurotic' symptoms, but did not address the underlying problems or restore function. Recognising the capacities of the patients prior to breakdown, Bion had the idea to create an environment which stimulated the patients' sense of personal responsibility and authority and drew them back to acting on their own behalf. The idea was that this would trigger their former sensibilities and strengths, bringing them out of a state of breakdown and back to healthy functioning. These ideas and their implementation became known as the 'Northfield Experiments' (Harrison and Clarke, 1992).

These experiments, and how they led on to the development of the TC models and ideas we know today, is an interesting history which cannot be covered in further detail in this chapter. What has become more recognised over time is that all patients have strengths and capacities that can be harnessed towards improved wellbeing when their sense of value, connection, authority and responsibility are nurtured. There is also a greater understanding of the cumulative impact of all forms of trauma (i.e. not just extreme experiences such as war) on mental health. How early experiences of trauma, and the breakdown or absence of supportive attachments in childhood, impact on a person throughout their life and contribute to serious mental distress and offending (see Chapters 1, 2 and 13) for a more detailed exploration of these ideas). Essentially, what was discovered to be useful about a TC for soldiers also applies to people more generally.

Evidence for TCs

In non-forensic mental health settings, TCs are increasingly falling out of favour due to perceived higher costs and time commitments for interventions. However, within forensic or care home environments, where the costs of residency are inherent, TCs have been increasingly embedded and growing in numbers since the 1980s. The most recent meta-analysis of treatment programmes for 'severe personality disorder' by Warren et al. (2003) concluded that TCs had the most promising evidence base. It is understandably challenging for existing TCs to produce gold-standard evidence of effectiveness (i.e. randomised controlled trials with control groups), although many have produced good evidence of effectiveness (Shuker, 2010), including the Millfields unit on which this book is based (Wilson et al., 2014) and TCs within prisons (Richardson and Zinny, 2020; Shuker, 2008). There is also good evidence within prisons that TCs provide safe environments that improve the quality of life of residents and reduce rates of self-harm and suicide (Newberry, 2009, cited in Shuker, 2010). The principles and practices of TCs have also led to movements such as the 'enabling environments' standards that promote trauma-informed and relational practices within all services even if it is not possible or desirable to operate as a full TC (Royal College of Psychiatrists, 2015).

People with complex, entrenched difficulties arguably need the more intensive therapeutic experience that TCs provide, where they have the opportunity and the support to learn through experience. For many, this will be the first time they have had the experience of a supportive and healthy community and been given the authority and responsibility to reflect on themselves and develop. Essentially, the TC is providing a 'corrective experience' to counteract and unlearn the destructive lessons from residents' past experiences (Yalom and Leszcs, 2005, p. 27). This is beyond what discreet and specific therapeutic interventions can provide alone, though more specific interventions can be incorporated into the wider TC treatment as required (see Chapter 9).

TC principles

The living learning environment requires several key elements in the culture of the community: attachment, communalism, democratisation, openness, culture of enquiry, permissiveness, reality confrontation, responsibility and empowerment (Pearce and Haigh, 2017, pp. 53–61). Within TCs, these are often referred to as the 'TC principles', or the 'pillars' or 'values' of the community, and they align well with what are known as 'trauma-informed care' principles of safety, trustworthiness, choice, collaboration and empowerment (The Institute on Trauma and

Trauma-Informed Care, 2022). They may also be referred to using different terms and some may not be specifically named as pillars within the community (e.g. attachment) but nevertheless are required for the functioning of the TC. These principles will be defined and explained in this chapter and will often be referred to in following chapters.

Attachment

Attachment is a concept developed by Bowlby and Ainsworth that has become an essential element in our understanding of human relationships and mental wellbeing (Bretherton, 1992). Attachment begins in childhood when we are reliant on our caregivers for survival and remains a key factor in how we operate in the world as we gain the capacity to look after and govern ourselves. When we have 'secure' attachment in childhood, we have learnt that our caregivers are mostly reliable and benevolent, and we build confidence that we are loveable and worthwhile as people. At the same time, we gain trust that there are other good people in the world, that we can explore it with increasing autonomy, and that we can face challenges and solve the inevitable problems that arise, knowing that we can return to the care and protection of our safe base of caregivers when we need to.

However, for many people generally, and especially for those with personality disorders, the experience with caregivers has been unreliable or, worse, harmful. This can lead to insecure attachment styles: 'avoidant' in which a person attempts to cut-off from others entirely and be wholly self-sufficient; 'preoccupied/anxious' in which a person makes frantic efforts to get closer and win the care of attachment figures; and 'disorganised' in which a person is frightened of attachment figures and freezes, or approaches and then retreats (Lyddon and Sherry, 2001). These attachment styles are relevant to the understanding of personality disorder and offending.

The experiential learning in a TC is dependent on residents forming an increasingly secure attachment to the community, as this is the method by which they change their patterns of relating to themselves and others that have led to risk and mental suffering. To do this, they need to have an experience of the community being reasonably reliable, trustworthy and benevolent. One way that TCs deliver this reliability is through the structure of the day and the treatment programme – that for the most part, groups and activities run on time and as expected, and that staff and residents all respect and participate in this routine. It is expected that staff and senior residents will set an example for others in their upholding of boundaries and the structure of the day, and that they will provide notice and explanation for their absences from groups whenever possible.

It is also expected that residents and staff (within professional boundaries) will model bringing themselves to the community and being open to the support and views of others. This could be messages of validation or concern, receiving feedback on how they have come across, differing viewpoints on issues discussed, or, particularly for staff, challenges on the boundaries or rules set for the TC. For many residents, their experience of communications like these in their childhood, or in environments such as prisons prior to their admission to the TC will have been defensiveness, rejection, denial or aggression. As a result, they have often learned not to trust others and to favour actions such as violence over communication and negotiation to meet their needs. With this in mind, the TC needs to provide the experience of communication and negotiation being welcomed and rewarded. Over time, this should lead to increasing levels of trust and mutual support between individual residents and the wider community, allowing them to change their way of relating generally and therefore reduce risk, and improve their wellbeing and ability to live a meaningful and prosocial life outside of institutions.

"I really grew as a person at Millfields. Certain therapies were so important in my recovery, also in settling back into the community. The people around me for those 5 yrs became a family, and as time went on I got better. Art psychotherapy was extremely useful but also very challenging. I came to terms with skeletons that I'd been carrying around for decades. Childhood trauma, relational difficulties, paranoia … Adjusting to living a new life in the community came from community leave, overnight stays at my high supported accommodation and many other experiences stemmed from the treatment I'd received at Millfields. Many, many years later I still, almost subconsciously sometimes use to this day".

– Former Millfields patient

Communalism

Attachment between patient and therapist is a component of most psychotherapeutic models. However, within a TC, the aim is that residents will form bonds with all members of the TC. The reasons for this are multiple: firstly, that this group represents both the family and the outside community, helping residents both to unlearn early patterns as well as develop the skills necessary to relate to and live within wider society on their release. Equally important, it also helps the staff team and wider community to avoid falling into intense, unhelpful relational patterns that are part of the residents' personality and risk.

This means that most of what happens within the community is done as a community, including treatment groups. It is also important for experiential learning that unstructured, day-to-day activities such as meals, tasks/chores (e.g. cleaning) and celebrations are also carried out as a community (see Chapter 10). It can be counterproductive to require the attendance of residents at these activities, which are intended to be informal and fun, especially when they have often had negative experiences of them in their lives prior to joining the TC. However, it is expected that they will be consistently encouraged and supported to attend and become more open to new experiences over time. This reflects a culture of shared commitment to learning that TCs aim to develop for all members.

> "I think some of the other patients I grew to like, quite a lot in some cases. I had such a laugh at times, on a Friday…we played Wii, pool, chatted and used the courtyard. I used to laugh so much with [psychologist]. I miss her a lot".
> – Former Millfields patient

Democratisation and flattened hierarchy

As much as possible, decisions are made as a community through discussion and consensus or voting. This differs from typical institutional settings where the prison governor or officer, or the hospital clinician, makes the decisions, and the prisoner or patient is expected to comply. For many people who have negative experiences of authority in their lives (as many residents will have had), this usual standard of management or treatment can bring up strong feelings or mistrust and an automatic response of resistance or rebellion. The TC environment therefore seeks to provide a different model of leadership or authority – one where there is supportive containment alongside shared decision-making and responsibility.

For most TCs, decisions will usually centre around activities, schedules, roles and events. Within some TCs, voting decisions can go as far as whether to admit or remove members, but this will also require the considered input of staff to ensure these decisions are well thought through and not harmful. When staff do intervene in a community decision or impose rules from the institution to address safety or security concerns, they should be fully explained within the community and challenges should be heard (even if they cannot change the outcome). Chapters 19 and 20 will explore some of the pitfalls and complexities with this, particularly within forensic environments.

> "It was helpful to have staff who would listen to you and put you on the right road, no judgement, patience and calmness. At the same time it was helpful to have staff who couldn't have the wool pulled over their eyes. In prison you are always judged and put to the side. You don't get honest and fair people. When you went to Millfields and you got treated differently, you realised that not everyone is bitter and twisted. That there are people in the system who are willing to help. It is important to be treated with a bit of respect, but also to be treated fair and square. When you do something wrong people should say that you shouldn't be doing things like that".
> – Former Millfields patient

Openness and culture of enquiry

The principle of openness and the 'culture of enquiry' supports communalism in TCs because they mean that, as much as possible, everything that happens in the community is either done as a community or disclosed to all and open for discussion. Psychotherapy is generally delivered in groups through Community Meetings (Chapter 4) or smaller treatment groups (Chapters 5–8). When individual treatment is needed for a discreet issue (e.g. Cognitive Behavioural Therapy for Obsessive Compulsive Disorder), then it is summarised and fed back to the wider TC in a community meeting, alongside the smaller group therapies (Chapter 9). Usually within TCs there is also a process for individual residents to share their formulation/understanding of themselves, their personality and relational patterns, and their risk with the community (Chapter 14). In forensic TCs, this includes the disclosure of the offence each resident is in custody for, which is repeated each time a new person (staff or patient) joins the TC. These aspects of openness and communalism are non-negotiable, as they are essential for fostering attachment and trust. The community cannot function as the method of treatment if it is not privileged the information of the 'doctor'.

The aim of TCs is to build a 'culture of enquiry', wherein members are open to examining and resolving problems together. This means that general problems, dilemmas and difficulties that arise between individuals should be brought into treatment groups and community meetings for discussion. Sometimes a 'crisis meeting' should be called to bring the community together to address an urgent issue (see Chapter 4). This can include disagreements or conflict between individuals, as well as concerns about a community member's wellbeing, risk or behaviour. If the concerns are between staff members, it is often not appropriate to raise them in a community group with residents. However, the principle still applies, and they should be brought to a staff support or reflective practice group for staff to work on the issue as a group (Chapter 18).

> "It was helpful having a reflective environment where you could get feedback from others. It gave me insight into how I struggle and why. It was helpful to look at the role I am playing in the group … being allowed to be in a social environment, which allowed me to observe my behaviour".
>
> – Former Millfields patient

Permissiveness

Joining a TC is a highly stressful and demanding experience, even for those without complex mental health problems or personality disorders. Staff running accredited TCs in the United Kingdom are encouraged to attend intensive 'mini TCs', usually held over the course of three days, to experience what it is like to be a resident. Feedback from attendees is often that the experience is exhausting and provokes high levels of anxiety – even though it is short-lived and well organised (Lees *et al.*, 2015; 2020; Rawlings, 2017). Most can identify with the challenges of joining a new group and navigating the dynamics that arise, whether they are thinking about a school class, workplace, friendship group, or family. If these prior experiences have been negative or traumatic, anxieties will inevitably be higher, and the ways of coping that were developed to manage or even survive will be activated.

For this reason, new residents joining the TC cannot be expected to behave in ways that are immediately helpful or healthy, either for themselves or others. Many will be mistrustful and anxious, and struggle with being open about themselves and discussing their issues in groups. They will often perceive feedback given to them to be attacking and believe that exposing vulnerability signals weakness and invites attack. The natural flight, fight, freeze reaction in the face of threat will lead to behaviours such as walking out of meetings, avoidance, defensiveness or verbal abuse. Many residents will also have learned to use aggression and violence to communicate and will not have developed healthier ways of negotiating with others. In other words, they will display the psychological factors and behaviours that led to their diagnosis, risk and offending, all of which they are seeking treatment for within the TC.

TCs therefore need a mechanism for accepting a certain level of negative behaviour, within reasonable limits, in order to give residents the opportunity to learn and develop new ways of living and relating. This is the concept of 'permissiveness', the tolerance of a certain level of old behaviours and mistakes, in the service of experience learning.

Whilst on the surface permissiveness can seem to be a common-sense principle – you cannot expect someone being treated for any condition to immediately be cured just by entering the hospital – it is a complex idea, which in the context of TCs is often a source of controversy, continuous questioning and dilemmas. In practice, it can be challenging to determine the limits of permissiveness. Physical violence must always be a non-negotiable limit, but are any other behaviours never permissible? What if a community member appears to be uninterested or incapable of learning and change? Are taking responsibility and showing remorse required? If the TC is 'too permissive' with some members, then what is the impact on the rest of the community? What is the right balance between the needs of individuals and the needs of the community as a whole? The reality is that these dilemmas and discussions are inevitable and normal within TCs, particularly those within forensic environments, so the aim is not to eradicate them, but to get as good as possible at discussing and resolving them as a community. See Chapter 20 for a more detailed analysis of the pitfalls and challenges that can arise and how they can be addressed.

"[It was helpful] having time to mess up or not mess up, but nonetheless to make the decision and then live with the consequences. Millfields helped me understand who I was and what I was. Learning about [personality disorder] and how to help myself. Feeling safe; you could take the chance to let your guard down and see how it plays out".

– Former Millfields patient

Reality confrontation

To learn and develop as people, we need information on how we 'are' in the world, especially if we have ways of relating to ourselves and others that are damaging or holding us back from reaching our full potential. This information, and how it reaches us, is 'reality confrontation', and TCs cannot function or manage risk without it.

At a basic level, reality confrontation takes place when the community seeks to give feedback to an individual, and that person is willing to receive and consider that feedback. It is the moment when the community, or some members of the community, say to another member that he is coming across as rude, aggressive or unhelpful, that he has crossed a boundary with his behaviour, or that there are concerns that he may be harming himself or using substances. The word 'confrontation' makes this process sound potentially accusatory or aggressive, but it is important that it be done in the spirit of the TC, with respectful and thoughtful feedback, given in the spirit of shared learning.

When anxiety runs high in a TC, there can be a pull towards avoidance. For example, in forensically based TCs, people who inform on each other are often blacklisted for 'grassing', and targeted with violence, even though boundary or security breaches can have severe consequences for a person's progression to release from custody. For this reason, residents can be extremely reluctant to talk openly about more serious rule-breaking, such as drug use or possessing contraband. Residents may also be avoidant of giving or receiving feedback if they do not trust in their own or the other person's ability to resolve matters without physical violence, as they will be aware that breaking this boundary will result in them going back to prison. Equally, the threat of violence and aggression is frightening, intimidating and potentially humiliating if not responded to with equal aggression, so the members most willing to make those threats will often not get as much reality confrontation as they should.

Just as we do not expect perfection from residents, we also do not expect TCs to perfectly address these dynamics. What is expected is that the principles of openness, the culture of enquiry, permissiveness and reality confrontation will be continually reinforced, to work through and beyond this anxiety and the conspiracy of silence that can develop.

"The community meetings were important for taking responsibility, hearing and giving opinions, hearing how things affect others. Community meetings helped me to understand how to be civilised and patient and treat people with respect, follow rules".

– Former Millfields patient

"It was helpful when people pointed out my mistakes to get me to learn from it. Turning a blind eye was not helpful – pointing out rule breaking in meetings directly and openly was helpful".

– Former Millfields patient

Responsibility

Alongside the previous principles, and providing a specific balance to permissiveness, it is expected that all members (staff and residents) are willing to take increasing responsibility over time, not just for their own actions but also for the community itself. At a basic level, everyone is expected to attend and participate in the formal treatment programme as well as the informal activities. This includes taking personal responsibility for lapses in participation, or negative or unhelpful behaviour, as well as taking part in discussions, giving and receiving feedback, and helping to resolve problems and make decisions.

It also involves taking on specific roles of responsibility within the TC, either through volunteering or a democratic process. For residents, there are the roles of chair and vice chair of community and crisis meetings, which collectively hold responsibility for leading the meetings, ensuring all voices are heard and boundaries are upheld, and managing the agenda, timekeeping and minute-taking (see Chapter 4). There are also often various roles or jobs within the community, such as cleaners for various areas, librarian, gardener, etc. for which there should be a regular process for reviewing performance and re-appointment. For staff, there should also be appointable roles and shared responsibilities, regardless of discipline. This can include chairing or taking minutes of staff meetings, providing collective feedback in community meetings, upholding boundaries, and organising and contributing to community events or celebrations.

> "I also had the chance to do other things that gave me a sense of purpose, especially in the anti-racism working group. I was trusted. Doing teaching with [another resident]. Also working in the Oasis and the other jobs. Getting time off the ward – being in the Unit could feel constricting. Integrating with other people. Using other skills was rewarding, in tandem with therapy. These things improved my sense of worth from a point that was low, low down ... I was very far down when I first started".
>
> – Former Millfields patient

Empowerment

Empowerment balances with responsibility, giving both an incentive to learn and to live differently, as well as providing opportunities to develop the skills needed for a life outside of custody. With responsibility and democratisation, members are given a rare opportunity to have their voices heard within the institution, and to have the power to shape their community. For staff who are often used to operating within strict professional hierarchies, and residents who are used to environments in which they are forced to comply with the institutional regime and rules, this can be a tricky dynamic to navigate. The potential power can often be exciting, but when real dilemmas arise and the potential consequences for people are serious, there will often be a wish from community members to give up power and its responsibility and assign it to someone in a traditional position of authority.

On a personal level, residents are empowered to take responsibility for their treatment goals, progress reviews and onward pathway. Institutional requirements such as risk assessments, care plans, treatment reviews (e.g. ward rounds and 'care programme approach' or CPA meetings in hospital environments), diagnostic assessment and formulations are conducted with involvement of the resident himself as well as the wider community. At times residents will need staff and the community to encourage them to take things further (e.g. put them forward for community leave), and at other times residents will benefit from hearing concerns that they should slow down.

> "[At Millfields] I learned about taking responsibility. I am an ex-armed robber. I know about cars and safes and it's scary to sit here with pennies in my pocket knowing how I used to deal with that. I had to make the change and Millfields gave me that".
>
> – Former Millfields patient

Summary

This chapter has covered the basics of the ethos and principles of TCs. It is worth reiterating that, underlying the principles, there is the core culture of the TC as a group where individual members are noticed, remembered and thought about, and where there is a collective agreement to uphold the TC principles in service of shared learning and progress. This is an extraordinarily challenging endeavour, and it is therefore important that all members – staff and residents – know what they are signing up for and agree to participate.

References

Barazandeh, H., Kissane, D.W., Saeedi, N. and Gordon, M. (2016) 'A systematic review of the relationship between early maladaptive schemas and borderline personality disorder/traits', *Personality and Individual Differences*, 94, pp. 130–139. doi:10.1016/j.paid.2016.01.021.

Bretherton, I. (1992) 'The origins of attachment theory: John Bowlby and Mary Ainsworth', *Developmental Psychology*, 1992, 28(5), pp. 759–775. https://10.1037/0012-1649.28.5.759

Haigh, R. (2013) 'The quintessence of a therapeutic environment', *Therapeutic Communities*, 34(1), pp. 6–15. doi:10.1108/09641861311330464

Harrison, T. and Clarke, D. (1992) 'The Northfield experiments', *British Journal of Psychiatry*, 160, pp. 698–708. doi:10.1192/bjp.160.5.698

Knox, J. (1999) 'The relevance of attachment theory to a contemporary Jungian view of the internal world: internal working models, implicit memory and internal objects', *Journal of Analytical Psychology*, 44, pp. 511–530. doi:10.1111/1465-5922.00117

Lees, J., Haigh, R., Bruschetta, S., Chatterji, A., Dominguez-Bailey, V., Kelly, S., Lombardo, A., Parkhe, S., Pereira, J.G., Rahimi, Y. and Rawlings, B. (2021) 'Transcultural transferability of transient therapeutic communities: the living-learning experience workshops', *Therapeutic Communities: The International Journal of Therapeutic Communities*, 42(1), pp. 27–42. doi:10.1108/TC-06-2019-0006

Lees, J., Haigh, R., Lombardo, A. and Rawlings, B. (2016) 'Transient therapeutic communities: the "living-learning experience" trainings', *Therapeutic Communities: The International Journal of Therapeutic Communities*, 37(2), pp. 57–68. doi:10.1108/TC-05-2015-0016

Lyddon, W. and Sherry A. (2011) 'Developmental personality styles: An attachment theory conceptualization of personality disorders', *Journal of Counseling & Development*, 79(4), pp. 405–414. doi:10.1002/j.1556-6676.2001.tb01987

Pearce, S. and Haigh, R. (2017) *Theory and practice of democratic therapeutic community treatment*. London: Jessica Kingsley Publishers.

Rapoport, R.N. (2001) *The community as a doctor: new perspectives on a therapeutic community (International behavioural and social sciences, classics from the Tavistock Press)*. London: Routledge.

Rawlings, B. (2017) 'Training for democratic therapeutic community staff: a description and evaluation of three experiential workshops', *Therapeutic Communities: The International Journal of Therapeutic Communities*, 38(1), pp. 10–22. doi:10.1108/TC-11-2016-0023

Richardson, J. and Zinni, V. (2020) 'Are prison-based therapeutic communities effective? Challenges and considerations', *International Journal of Prisoner Health*, 17(1), pp. 42–53. doi:10.1108/IJPH-07-2020-0048

Royal College of Psychiatrists (2015) *Enabling environments standards*. Available at: https://www.rcpsych.ac.uk/docs/default-source/improving-care/ccqi/quality-networks/enabling-environments-ee/ee-standards-2015.pdf?sfvrsn=abdcca36_4#:~:text=The%20Enabling%20Environment%20project%20aims,to%20be%20positive%20for%20health (accessed 25 October 2024).

Shuker, R. (2008) 'Treatment outcome following intervention in a prison-based therapeutic community: a study of the relationship between reduction in criminogenic risk and improved psychological wellbeing', *British Journal of Forensic Practice*, 10(3), pp. 33–44. doi:10.1108/14636646200800018

Shuker, R. (2010) 'Forensic therapeutic communities: a critique of treatment model and evidence base', *Howard Journal of Crime and Justice*, 49(5), pp. 463–477. doi:10.1111/j.1468-2311.2010.00637.x

The Institute on Trauma and Trauma-Informed Care (2022) *Trauma-informed organizational change manual*. Available at: http://socialwork.buffalo.edu/trauma-manual (accessed 22 October 2025).

Warren, F., Preedy-Fayers, K., McGauley, G., Pickering, A., Geddes, J.R., Kingsley, N. and Dolan, B. (2003) *Review of treatments for severe personality disorder*. Home Office Research. Available at: https://bulger.co.uk/prison/reviewtreatsseverePD.pdf (accessed 24 January 2025).

Wilson, K., Freestone, M., Hardman, F., Blazey, F. and Taylor, C. (2014) 'Effectiveness of modified therapeutic community treatment within a medium-secure service for personality-disordered offenders', *Journal of Forensic Psychiatry and Psychology*, 25(3), p. 243. doi:10.1080/14789949.2014.908317

Yalom, I.D. and Leszcs, M. (2005) *The theory and practice of group therapy*. 5th edn. New York: Basic Books.

Chapter 4

Community meetings

Jack Blake

Introduction

Community meetings are the beating heart of the therapeutic community (TC): the essential space in which all staff and patients attend and work through issues together. Unlike community meetings in more traditional psychiatric services where the focus is solely on patient involvement and empowerment on specific issues, the community meeting in a TC is a protected, psychoanalytically informed therapy group in which deeper psychological work is also expected to take place. The community meeting in a TC is therefore a blend between a large psychotherapy group, and a structured, institutional meeting with a meeting agenda, defined roles and rules. Community meetings also play a vital role in building the culture of the TC through reinforcement of the core values and providing living-learning opportunities, as well as integrating the work done in unstructured spaces, small groups or individual therapy. This chapter will explore the functions and principles of community meetings as well as the accompanying challenges in maintaining safety and effectiveness.

What is a large group?

To understand community meetings and how they function within TCs, it is important to first consider the nature of large psychoanalytically informed groups. These are spaces where people are usually arranged in a circle, with a loose aim that they sit together and speak about what comes to mind. In the purest psychoanalytic form, there is freedom for the group to follow a collective train of thought, freed from structural constraints apart from a set time when the group begins and ends. In other words, the framework for thought is dictated by the group rather than an institution presiding over the group, unlike a board meeting where a structured agenda is followed with a clear hierarchical arrangement of its members or indeed a psychoeducational therapy group where there is a set agenda for what will be discussed (Schwartz and Wolf, 1961). There will normally be one or two facilitators, but their contributions are more to the group process than the content. A large psychoanalytic group can be conceptualised as a stage for thinking.

DOI: 10.4324/9781032717302-4

The community meeting – rationale and structure

In a TC, the large group is the community meeting, which all staff and patients are expected to attend when they are present. This means that the community meeting will often have twenty to thirty people in attendance, where the small groups have a maximum capacity of ten, including facilitators. At Millfields, community meetings were held three times a week, as opposed to small groups which were held twice a week and other groups or individual work which was often once a week. This shows that the community meeting was at the heart of the TC, essential for maintaining therapeutic culture and the living learning experience (see Chapter 3). It can also be thought of as the barometer of the TC's ambience and the interpersonal dynamics at play.

Crucially, the community meeting prevents work being split off within individuals by encouraging and requiring disclosure and further exploration of this work within the wider community. This is essential because, for many with personality disorder, particularly the borderline type, they have existed in splits most of their lives, often giving the 'good' aspects of themselves to idealised people in their lives and the 'bad' parts to those who are denigrated (a process which is also often an element of their offending behaviour). This can lead to splits within the staff team and ineffective treatment due to 'blind spots' on both sides, as well as significant suffering, confusion and risk for patients. By bringing together all aspects of the patients and their relationships into the community meeting, patients can be supported to understand and address this splitting process as well as integrate the different aspects of themselves (de Zulueta, 2006, p. 148; Klein, 1946).

As part of the living learning environment, the community meeting is also where dynamics between members of the TC are brought for further exploration and therapeutic work. This reduces the chances of therapeutic material being lost and, ultimately, ensures that important aspects of the men's relational patterns and risk do not remain unaddressed. It is the constant testing of therapeutic work and repeated opportunities for learning that both highlights a patient's progress and promotes further healthy changes, all of which is particularly enabled by community meetings.

A large group like the community meeting can be conceptualised as a collective thought process, contributed to by each member. These group processes in turn influences the individual members' thinking. This can be a positive process when the therapeutic culture and sense of safety and containment in the TC is strong, but it can also be destructive when conditions are less favourable. The phenomenon of Groupthink (Janis, 1972) where a group does not scrutinise its own decision-making process, is pervasive in a unit treating men with high levels of antisocial traits. This is not owing solely to their typical anti-establishment stance, and would feel rather contradictory if it were, but it is rather in keeping with their shared experiences and ability to relate to one another. Within a forensic TC, Groupthink can lead to resistance to collaborative work towards healthy change, as the men may become entrenched in a collective sense of mistrust or 'us and them' culture.

Community meetings are formalised groups where attendance by all is formalised and expected. However, this does not impinge the existence and formation of sub-groups that can potentiate fractures of the large group and pervert the work. Where there is a perceived lack of safety, be that physical or psychological, groups can appear more nuclear, with more rigid and stronger agreed principles and boundaries – seeing an increase in tension and stifling of thought. This can be particularly pronounced when there is a section of the community engaged in antisocial behaviour or rule breaking, such as using illicit mobile phones or drugs. These behaviours reduce the sense of safety and containment in the TC, particularly when staff are either unaware or unable to address them. On the other hand, tensions and anxieties about 'grassing' or submitting to authority can arise when staff discover or suspect what is happening and start asking questions or putting in safety measures or restrictions in response.

It is the community meeting that can help to challenge these fractures and, with the therapeutic goals held in mind, better orientate the TC towards the overarching treatment goal for all: promoting a prosocial, empathic way of relating to others and ultimately reducing the patients' risk of reoffending. Community meetings, by design, will help to elucidate the thinking in the group and tend away from Groupthink by facilitators. They offer commentary, interpretation and challenge, and broaden the participation of the group – allowing space for new perspectives and ways of dealing with problems.

What does a community meeting look like?

The community meeting is a large group in which the role of facilitation and contribution lies with each member. As such, it is an embodiment of the culture and values of a TC, with an emphasis on a flattened hierarchy and personal responsibility for change and participation. Depending on the personal relevance of an issue raised in a community meeting, particular members of the TC could take on very different roles. For example, a conflict that arises between a few patients and members of staff would see all involved directly contributing based on their individual experience, whereas other members of the community who are not personally involved will take on the role of facilitators. Thus, the role of facilitation becomes more dynamic than in a typical psychoanalytic group – staff or patients can facilitate a particular issue, contribute directly, or both. There is de facto facilitation by members of the community who are less related to the issue, and those who take on this role more frequently also tend to be staff members or patients with more experience of the TC values.

With this increased flexibility on facilitation and such a large membership, there is a need for some established boundaries, roles and expectations to ensure the community meeting provides sufficient containment and safety, and that it addresses what it should.

Chair and vice chair

> "The process wasn't perfect, but what is. Certain aspects of treatment benefit-ted me greatly: art therapy, chairing and vice chairing community meetings, learning how to get on with others, managing paranoid thoughts to the best of my ability, anger management and one to one psychotherapy were just some parts of the process and experience of being a patient at Millfields".
>
> – Former Millfields patient

Every 4 months, a chair and vice chair are elected by the community. Members are asked to nominate who they think should take on these roles and patients are able to nominate themselves. (Indeed, it is sometimes made a treatment target that patients take on the chair or vice chair role, particularly if they need to practice as-sertive communication or the benevolent use of authority.) The two who are elected are then responsible for the meeting agenda and chairing the community meeting. They will note down issues that need 'time' in the meeting (e.g. a decision that needs to be made about an upcoming event, or a conflict between members), and balance the space needed for these issues with standing agenda items such as feed-back from other therapeutic work. Likewise, when an issue is being discussed, the chair and vice chair play a key role in ensuring that not just the dominant voices are heard. At times, this could include inviting particular community members to speak or asking people to take turns or raise their hands to speak.

The vice chair and chair work together in their task to maintain the structure of the community meeting, usually with the chair naming issues for discussion, invit-ing people to speak, or reinforcing rules and boundaries, and the vice chair sup-porting this task by writing down brief notes of what has been discussed, keeping a record of agenda items, or pointing out members who appear to need support to contribute. However, unlike the facilitator of a large group, the chair and vice chair do not have to focus solely on their roles and keep their issues out of the room. They are rather maintaining the structure through promoting the principles agreed upon by the community. If there is an issue that directly involves the chair and vice chair and they are unable to maintain their role effectively as a result, it is useful to ask another member of the community to temporarily take on the role in their place whilst the matter is discussed.

Owing to the dynamic roles TC members are expected to take, there are several structures built into the community meeting that must be maintained:

Establishing the rules

The chair reads the rules of the community meeting out at the beginning of each meeting. These rules are agreed by the whole community and should be reviewed periodically to ensure that they remain relevant and comprehensive. The rules generally set a precedent for behaviour in the meeting, for example asking members to attend on time, for drinks or food not to be consumed, mobile phones to not be in the meeting, language to be kept respectful, violence and aggression to never be used, and people to take some time out where they feel unable to contain themselves. It is important to again highlight that these rules apply equally to staff and patients.

Meeting agenda

The agenda for the meeting is kept by the chair and vice chair who carry a physical book with them. Members may either approach the chairs outside of the meeting or there is space within the meeting to request issues to be 'put down for time'. The length of time you will need to discuss a topic is usually allocated and the urgency and juxtaposition of topics considered. For example, the chair and vice chair may decide that two emotive, interpersonal difficulties may not be effectively discussed within one meeting and therefore reserve one of the issues for a following meeting.

Keeping time

Members must have taken their seats prior to the meeting starting and the meeting must be started and ended on time, all of which helps to maintain the meeting structure and provide a sense of containment and safety for the group (Rice and Rutan, 1981).

Crisis meetings

Important risk issues and conflicts can arise at any time, and sometimes the TC membership needs to come together to address these urgently rather than wait for the next scheduled community meeting. In these cases, the chair or vice chair will either call a crisis meeting themselves or facilitate the request for a crisis meeting from another member of the community or the staff group. At Millfields, crisis meetings were held for 30 minutes, with the option to extend for a further 10 minutes if needed. The rules of the community meeting and the roles of the chair and vice chair applied equally to crisis meetings, and staff also should hold a debrief following the crisis meeting to ensure that any risks are adequately addressed.

Therapeutic culture and values

Ultimately, having the community meeting regularly and at the heart of the TC allows integration of the wider work of the TC with its members and facilitation of the core TC principles. These are discussed in more depth in Chapter 3 but will also be covered here to demonstrate the particular role of the community meeting.

Democracy

The community meeting is the venue in which decisions about the community are taken. This is done by a democratic process where people can express their views and then vote on the outcome, whenever appropriate and possible. The security level of the TC will dictate the level of autonomy it can have (e.g. Millfields was in a medium secure hospital, and therefore some decisions and rules set by the institution were non-negotiable). However, decisions were deferred to the community whenever possible. This promotes responsibility-taking alongside empowerment, encouraging members to make decisions that will support and improve the community for everyone as well as themselves. Some examples of decision that can be made by the community could be when to hold events or activities and how to use the budget for these, how to improve the ward environment, and which members to put forward to represent the unit at wider hospital functions or on interview panels. The community can also vote to put individual patients up for a 'commitment review' if their engagement is not satisfactory or if they have broken boundaries, and they can give a view as to whether a patient should retain or lose their place in the TC (although the staff do need to have the ability to overrule this decision if destructive dynamics are at play).

Communalism

The space is shared by all its members and decisions pertaining to the whole community are made by the community. All staff and patients are expected to participate in these meetings and 'put down for time' to discuss any issues they might have. Not only does this allow for further flattening of the hierarchy, but it can also allow more senior members and staff to role model the use of the space. This communicates an important message, because it shows that use of the space, and time required in it, does not correlate negatively with one's progress in treatment – quite the opposite. Those who use the space effectively are likely to be engaged in their treatment and progressing through it.

Permissiveness

The community can be surprisingly permissive and thoughtful towards its members who are at the beginning of their journey in the TC and therefore can be expected to make more mistakes and struggle with developing healthier ways of coping and behaving. More experienced members of the community will remember their own difficulties in letting go of old ways of relating or thinking, and how hard it was to see things from a different perspective. Where a new patient is displaying particularly strong views towards another member of the community, or struggles to take another's point of view, crucial to understanding the reality of a situation, the community may help to close the topic and return to it in another point in that person's treatment when they are more able to do this work. The community meetings bear the footprints of its members which remain there for reference at any time.

Reality testing

Drawing on their personal experiences, patients are the most powerful tool at disposal of the community for challenging unhelpful or offence-paralleling beliefs or behaviours. Even newer patients who may be unable to see their own risks and limitations, are often quite astute in identifying these aspects in others and giving effective feedback from a position of experience. In turn, this process of seeing themselves in others can help them develop insight and motivation for change. The reciprocity of this dynamic is what allows a mutual suffering and healing process within the group.

What is it like to be in the community meeting?

> "Those meetings were important for taking responsibility, hearing and giving opinions, hearing how things affect others. Community meetings helped me to understand how to be civilised and patient and treat people with respect, follow rules".
>
> – Former Millfields patient

At Millfields, community meetings were held for an hour and a half on Mondays and Fridays, and on Wednesdays, it was 45 minutes as it incorporated the ward round (an institutional requirement). The staff in the meeting were from a variety of disciplines, and in the community meeting, their membership in the community took precedence over their discipline. This enables the community members to come alongside one another when trying to support the work of the TC, and in this task some self-disclosure from staff may be helpful. For example, they could relate to a patient who is anxious about taking leave outside the hospital by disclosing their own discomfort or frustration on public transportation at times and how they have learned to manage this.

However, the role of staff must be clear, and a flattening of the hierarchy does not mean a reversal of the therapeutic alliance or complete lateralisation of relationships. The patients will be expected to talk about how their difficulties, including their offending behaviour. This can include conflict with staff, and these staff members should be prepared to talk about the role they played in this conflict, being prepared to apologise where they got things wrong, or conversely, assert their differing perspective or challenge unacceptable behaviour. Although the patients can incite very strong feelings within the staff group, it is essential that more personal or uncontained experiences or emotions for staff members are taken to the post-community meeting debrief for staff only, or into group or individual clinical supervision (see Chapter 18).

Traditional psychiatric models see the level of transparency the community expects between members regarding their treatment as in conflict with their policies surrounding confidentiality. As a result, community meetings in TCs feel very different to those in more traditional services. Upon entering a TC voluntarily, patients agree to a shared confidentiality, which means that anything discussed in the community, is kept within the community. This is highlighted by the standing agenda items to feedback work from other therapeutic spaces such as small groups and individual therapy, as well as with the 'offence disclosures' that take place anytime there is a new member of the community (see Chapter 7).

For TCs in hospital settings, there is often the need to follow local procedures and legal statutes such as regular ward rounds and care programme approach (CPA) meetings. Rather than these being split off from the TC, it was helpful at Millfields to incorporate these meetings into the TC in a way which would make them meaningful and contribute to the therapeutic culture of the unit.

Ward rounds were held communally and incorporated into the community meeting. The patients were divided into two groups and would have ward rounds on alternative weeks. Simultaneously, for one hour and fifteen minutes, the staff group and patient group would meet separately and write feedback to the patient in question regarding their progress towards their treatment targets. The staff group would also consider requests from the patient such as approval for new possessions to be brought in, increases in leave outside of the hospital, or new visitor requests. The two groups would then meet in the community meeting and a nominated patient and staff member for that week would take it in turns to read the feedback on each patient. At the end of all feedback, there would then be time for each patient to request clarification or discuss the ward round feedback. Where the issue was too complex to discuss in the short amount of time available, it could be added to the agenda for a later community meeting. The ward round was thus another important tool in generating therapeutic material and helping patients to move towards a reflective position where they can take responsibility for themselves in the community. In conducting the ward round this way, the TC also maintained the principles of its treatment in not allowing work to be hidden, and the community being the agent of change (see Chapter 3). This process can also mitigate against the charm, deception and splitting that can lead to risks being unaddressed or overestimation of the positive effects of the therapy.

> "The ward round was excellent: we should be sharing; it's very important. It gave the whole room information".
>
> – Former Millfields patient

A final aspect to consider about the structure of the community meeting is regarding guests invited to the meeting. It is important that such a novel treatment model in the forensic system has a facility for allowing professionals to observe and learn from it, and at Millfields this was achieved through a monthly 'visitors day' for professionals. This was an educational experience for visitors, as well as a chance for the patients to interact with people external to the community, giving them an opportunity to take ownership of their treatment and to speak to the visitors about the challenges and benefits of therapy. Prior to visitation, the community's permission is sought, and the agenda considered for that day. It is likely that emotive, potentially volatile or deeply personal topics are left for when the community meeting feels safer with its regular members.

What difficulties tend to arise in the community meetings?

> "The Monday and Friday community meetings could get quite toxic between individuals. Some weren't trying to work things through, and open warfare developed".
>
> – Former Millfields patient

> "Some of the patients overreacted to feedback given to them in the group meetings. I think before people arrive, they should have it pumped into their heads that you're going to get feedback. Staff should look at for people defending each other and people should be confronted on their behaviour: 'You did something wrong, we still like you, but you can come forward and talk about it and we'll work with you'".
>
> – Former Millfields patients

Where the community meetings are running entirely smoothly, and the community is without conflict, it is likely that important work is being avoided. It is intrinsic to a TC treating men with interpersonal difficulties and failures in epistemic trust (Fonagy and Allison, 2014) that there will be attempts to corrupt, subvert TC structures and attack the collective therapeutic alliance. This is why all admissions to the unit are carefully timed and the community dynamic considered when introducing new group members. Whilst newer members of the TC, even with the best of intentions, are likely to be resistant to change and mistrustful of the community at the beginning of their treatment, over time and with support of more experienced members, they increasingly engage in a prosocial manner and in turn set a good example for further new members. It is this distribution of senior and newer patients that allows the community to safely contain the destructive elements that are inherent with this patient group.

The ethos of the TC is in assertive as well as empathic challenges of destructive behaviour or perspectives, as well as openly exploring deeply personal areas of vulnerability and risk. This is an unusual way of working and can thus be a provocative and uncomfortable style for new patients and staff. Members can feel 'called out', 'grassed on', 'mugged off' or disrespected, and it is important that they learn the difference between 'a telling off' and constructive feedback or challenges; the former designed to reprimand the behaviour, the second for reflection.

There can be verbal attacks and, rarely, physical attacks where patients become deeply defensive and enraged in response to feedback. These are most often when an interaction on the ward has been volatile, left someone feeling vulnerable or exposing a part of themselves that is incredibly painful and defended. Without healthy defences from this pain, the patients can become overwhelmed by feelings of guilt, shame, humiliation which can see them losing control of their emotions. For the violent offender, this often manifests as anger and aggression, and they must be encouraged to take a break from the meeting if this risk escalates.

Developing the capacity to stay calm and respond reasonably to feedback and challenges can help patients manage future challenges. For example, a former patient described his parole hearing as a five-hour long ordeal. The forensic psychiatrist on the panel asked him some very searching questions, and the patient had to back up his answers with examples of how he had put his learning into practice. The panel was very impressed with his ability to communicate his progress under such pressure. The patient felt that his experience in community meetings had given him the skills he needed to face this challenge.

The flattened hierarchy and shared authority and responsibility of members can help to manage challenges that arise. Patients have been known to take over de-escalation and even promoting discussions around delaying speaking about issues until a later date. Speaking from shared experience, their feedback can also land better than that of staff. They are also able to assess, with staff, whether they feel an issue has been authentically discussed or whether a particular patient is 'inauthentically engaging' (Blake and Taylor, 2022). They often find inauthentic engagement intolerable, and the level of collusion the community is perceived to have with this can infuriate community members and see sub-groups forming and fracturing the community.

It is often the senior patients who are instrumental in challenging work that is inauthentic and providing a model for others to engage in therapy in a more meaningful manner. This modelling is a way of showing rather than telling a patient how they might benefit from an alternative mindset or coping strategy. This is a less confrontational way in which patients show one another how a different approach to the same problem can bring about a more favourable outcome – for example, that they are better understood and therefore more able to achieve what they want in life if they explain themselves calmly rather than resorting to demands, threats, or violence. Conversely, just telling these men what to do often evokes defensiveness, mistrust and resistance to change.

As previously introduced, these patients are susceptible to Groupthink. Conspiracies often develop around staff motivations for decisions or treatment towards a particular patient. Transparency helps to allay these concerns, but that is not always possible due to security or risk concerns. Security measures are often a contentious point, as the TC cannot always be fully open with patients about why these are put in place or change policies that are unpopular. Sometimes, patients must be returned to prison following major boundary violations or serious corruption of the therapeutic environment. If these individuals are left too long in the TC or given too much warning of their departure, risks can escalate, and they can be destructive in the treatment of others. Depending on the severity of their sentence, there may be security stipulations in place that necessitate a swift, unpredictable discharge. This sees them not having a proper closure, the patients not being briefed and the patient being suddenly whisked away to prison with sometimes just an hour's notice. This is to stop them arranging for methods to escape during the transfer and their communication is thus blocked once they are told. They are closely monitored from the moment they are told. Such events feed into the community and where the conspiracies held about the staff are widespread, the engagement in the community meetings can be thwarted. As a result, the TC will need time and space for processing and reparations following events like these.

The community meeting is not just a space for thinking; it is also for feeling. Any tensions in the community or major divides between sub-groups are easily felt, but not so easily addressed, particularly when they are subtle. When the community is less able to work with these destructive elements, this can be felt in the community meeting as it begins to feel more stilted. It can run more akin to a business meeting rather than a psychotherapy group, with members seeming to just 'going through the motions'. As such, the community meeting can be thought of as the barometer for the community, reflecting the overall health and culture.

With any issue in the TC, be that individual or community wide, adherence to the community pillars helps to maintain the health and work of the community. So with the previous example, an open discussion around a 'business like' feel to the community is part of the 'living learning experience' of the TC. One is urged to think of any mishap, disturbance or any other difficulty experienced in the TC as therapeutic material, and the community meeting is the core space in which this material can be introduced and worked with, making it a vital component of the therapeutic journey.

Summary

The community meeting is an essential aspect of the TC, where the core psychotherapeutic pillars of the TC as put into action and the 'living learning' culture of the TC is formed and maintained. There are many challenges to authentic and safe engagement in community meetings, and staff and senior patients play a critical role in maintaining the boundaries and values as well as modelling prosocial and healthy ways of communicating and resolving interpersonal difficulties.

References

Blake, J.C. and Taylor, C. (2022) 'Examining influencers of treatment engagement by patients in an NHS medium-secure hospital treating high-risk offenders with personality disorder', *Therapeutic Communities: The International Journal of Therapeutic Communities*, 43(2), pp. 134–148.

de Zulueta, F. (2006) *From pain to violence*. Chichester: Whurr Publishers Limits (John Wiley & Sons.

Fonagy, P. and Allison, E. (2014) 'The role of mentalizing and epistemic trust in the therapeutic relationship', *Psychotherapy*, 51(3), pp. 372–380. doi:10.1037/a0036505

Janis, I.L. (1972) *Victims of groupthink: A psychological study of foreign-policy decisions and fiascos*. Boston: Houghton Mifflin.

Klein, M. (1946) 'Notes on some schizoid mechanisms', in *Envy and gratitude (1975)*. London: Hogarth.

Rice, C.A. and Rutan, J.S. (1981) 'Boundary maintenance in inpatient therapy groups', *International Journal of Group Psychotherapy*, 31(3), pp. 297–309. doi:10.1080/00207284.1981.11491709

Schwartz, E.K. and Wolf, A. (1961) 'Psychoanalysis in groups: some comparisons with individual analysis', *The Journal of General Psychology*, 64(1), pp. 153–191. doi:10.1080/00221309.1961.9920434

Chapter 5

Small groups

Brittni Jones

Introduction

The experience of being a therapeutic community (TC) member can be a seemingly contradictory mix of intense, deeply personal work, and everyday, often tedious, community discussions and negotiations. This can be likened to being in a family or relationship – a mix of meaningful connection and raw emotion, and the familiar and repetitive rhythm of daily life. As such, both sides of this experience are necessary and part of the work of the TC. Nevertheless, despite how frustrating they can be, there is a risk of the familiar and everyday problems or tasks dominating group spaces. This is particularly true of community meetings where decisions and disagreements should be discussed and resolved as a community (see Chapter 4). Whilst this is important work, the psychotherapeutic task of exploring the deeper individual experience must be equally prioritised, and facilitating small group space is a way of ensuring this happens.

What are small groups?

TC small groups are typically structured and facilitated in a way which is more in line with traditional psychodynamic group psychotherapy. Within most TCs, they are held once or twice a week (at Millfields, it was twice a week), have six to ten resident members, and two facilitators. Depending on the size of the TC, there could be several different small groups, of which each resident will be a member of one for the entirety of his treatment (i.e. small groups are considered part of the 'core' TC treatment, alongside community meetings).

Small groups are open and rolling, in that new residents of the TC will join, and residents who are moving on from the TC will leave the group when this time arises. This should mean that the group membership is largely stable, with only small and slow changes over time. The two facilitators should also be a stable and skilled pair who commit to, as much as possible, being present when the groups are running (i.e. only taking holidays during therapy breaks or non-group days). This is important, because the small group should provide a consistent and safe space in which to explore personal issues.

DOI: 10.4324/9781032717302-5

Rationale and purpose of small groups

Human beings are fundamentally social, and our existence in relation to others can and should be a rich source of feelings of connection, purpose and belonging. However, our experiences in families, schools, peer groups, communities, workplaces, culture and society, past and present, all have a profound impact on how we perceive ourselves and others in relationships and groups. For many residents, these experiences will have been negative, and relationships generally and groups specifically will be associated with feelings of isolation, exclusion, rejection and fear. Experiences such as abuse, neglect, bullying, exclusion, discrimination or persecution damage our sense of trust and safety in others and can make groups feel fundamentally threatening.

Understandably, residents develop different defence mechanisms to protect themselves within relationships and groups, many of which are adaptive when they are in genuinely threatening and hostile groups, but outside of these are destructive and limiting. These can include becoming completely cut-off from others (e.g. avoidant attachment style, Schizoid, Antisocial or Avoidant personality features), or intensely focussing on others in order to bolster their own sense of worth (e.g. preoccupied attachment style, Borderline, Narcissistic or Dependent personality features). Many residents will both intensely desire and fear deeper connections, getting into confusing 'push, pull' dynamics with others which often results in confusion and pushes people away, further reinforcing residents' fears (see Chapters 2 and 13 for more discussion of these personality types and their relevance to offending).

Individual therapy involves exploring these experiences, making sense of what happened, and helping to change and resolve the unhelpful ways of relating to ourselves and others. Often this can include recognising, understanding and learning from dynamics that arise in relation to the therapists, as these will often mirror what happens in relationships outside of therapy. However, this way of learning about oneself in a therapeutic relationship can be amplified in powerful ways within a therapeutic group. This is because the relationships that are developed in group therapy, with the group as a whole, the therapists and other group members, will have numerous parallels with relationships with people outside of therapy. Group members also have opportunities for learning from other group members with shared experiences, practising social skills and new ways of relating, and giving and receiving support.

Theory and practice

Psychodynamic group psychotherapy is a model of treatment on its own and cannot be covered in full here. For more reading on this subject, Kleinberg's book (2012) on the subject is recommended. It is important that those responsible for the supervision and facilitation of small groups are qualified to deliver this therapy, as well as knowledgeable about how group psychotherapy is adapted to the TC environment. Group facilitators or leaders are necessary to help the group observe and process what is happening between people in the group (including the facilitators themselves!). This is a complex task, requiring knowledge of the individuals and their formulations as well as of interpersonal and group processes, and the clinical skills to make use of their observations and knowledge in a way which will be constructive to the group. It also requires the self-reflective capacity to make sense of one's own emotional reactions and participation in dynamics.

Within forensic services, it is not always possible for all facilitators (of which there are normally two in any small group) to be fully trained in psychodynamic group psychotherapy. However, they should receive regular supervision and training to support them in their role. In particular, facilitators should be aware of dynamics and conflicts that can arise in small groups with offenders with personality disorders, as well as the theory addressing common issues for members. These will be explored in further detail in this chapter.

Therapeutic group principles

Faced with a complex group of residents with different formulations and ways of relating to one another, facilitators can be overwhelmed by the responsibility of leading a small group and ensuring that it is therapeutic. It is therefore helpful for them to be informed regarding the theory and evidence regarding which factors make a psychotherapy group effective. One of the most helpful in this setting is Yalom's therapeutic factors (Yalom and Leszcs, 2005, pp. 1–17) which include: group cohesiveness, universality, interpersonal learning, imparting of information, catharsis, imitative behaviour, simulation of the primary family, self-understanding, instillation of hope and existential factors.

Many of these factors feed into one another. For example, *group cohesiveness* is the sense of belonging to a group that is valued and worth investing in, and this is aided by a sense of being 'in it together' and not alone in one's suffering (*universality*), as well as by group members helping and supporting one another (*altruism*) and the ability to express emotions in a safe environment (*catharsis*). Group members may identify with one another and senior members may model healthier ways of thinking or behaving (*imitative behaviour*), and through this, group members can develop a better *self-understanding* and learn new ways of relating to themselves and others and resolving conflicts or getting their needs met (*interpersonal learning*). The group may develop the dynamic of patient's early family lives, helping them to identify and change the unhelpful patterns of relating that developed from those experiences (*simulation of primary family*). And all of this can help group members feel able to take responsibility for their lives (*existential factors*) and *instil hope* for change.

"Being in East India was like being escorted, reflecting about your life and other people's lives. A weird experience to have other people knowing about my experience. It helped me processing about my history and get more confident and positive ... Group work can bring out many things but later should be controlled (better contained)".

– Former Millfields patient

If group facilitators can keep these factors in mind, they can spot when one of the factors is particularly present (or, indeed, absent), and guide the group to promising areas of therapeutic value. For example, when a group member is on the receiving end of the interest and support of several others, this can be noted by the facilitator and the experience of both receiving and giving support can be explored. This exploration can highlight the benefits of the process and help the group see the value in sharing their experiences as well as in being curious and reflective about the experiences of others.

On the other hand, if there is a notable absence of group cohesion, altruism, and identification or imitative behaviour, then facilitators can identify important factors in why the group may not be functioning therapeutically and work on improving these aspects of the group. For example, they may need to highlight the similarities in members' experiences and feelings, or the ways in which they may be able to learn from each other. Alternatively, if there is a lack of or change in the sense of safety in the group, then facilitators may need to work on upholding the boundaries or frame of the group (e.g. starting and ending on time, being respectful of one another, refraining from aggression).

Stages of group development

Similarly, facilitators benefit from being familiar with Tuckman's stages of group development (1965): forming, storming, norming and performing. As TC groups are 'rolling', with members leaving and joining at different stages, there is normally not a 'beginning' or 'end' to the small group (apart from at the start or end of the service of course). However, the small group does need to adapt to new members joining at different stages, and this will have a significant impact on the therapeutic factors and dynamics of the group. This can be unsettling to all group members, including facilitators, and it is therefore important that facilitators are aware of the stages that all groups go through in this process so that they can normalise and help the group navigate this challenge.

Without this normalisation, group members may feel that the group is somehow defective or ruined by the loss of senior members or the inclusion of recent joiners. More longstanding group members may forget that new members are not immediately familiar with the culture of the group or may not immediately be able to rise to the challenge of trusting the group with their feelings or stories, and new members of the group will need support to understand how to make use of the group (*forming*). As the group settles in and members become more open with one another, conflicts and dynamics may arise that require working through (*storming*) to get to a place where the group feels more cohesive and trusting (norming), and finally where the most complex therapeutic work can take place (*performing*). Facilitators and group members generally can benefit from understanding that this is a normal process in groups of all kinds so that the 'success' or 'failure' (or comfort/discomfort) of the group is not projected into individual members.

Epistemic trust and reality confrontation

As introduced in Chapter 3 on the theory and practice of TCs, reality confrontation is a central pillar of the TC, and as such it is also a central pillar of the small group. Fundamentally, all personality and mental health problems are a mismatch between what a person perceives or feels about themselves or others, and what is actually happening in their external world. Looking at the treatment process through this lens, any psychotherapy is about helping to bring a person's internal experience more in line with external reality, which TCs refer to as reality confrontation.

For most residents, the way they perceive themselves and the world was born from an external reality which was actually threatening, and therefore their reactions and behaviour were logical and adaptive in that place and time. For example, it makes sense to mistrust parents who abuse or neglect you, and to conclude that you are better off looking after yourself. However, problems arise when they are unable to adapt or change their way of thinking or behaving to different circumstances. For example, they could make the assumption that because parents could not be trusted, nobody in a position of authority or care can. This assumption will be reinforced by any further experience of mistreatment by people in authority such as teachers, police or prison officers. However, they are often unable to recognise and will reject any person who is offering them genuine care or opportunities to develop, and therefore not only miss out on opportunities for positive change, but create a self-fulfilling prophecy that furthers their suffering and entrapment. This can also be referred to as 'epistemic mistrust', wherein they actively resist any alternative information or ways of perceiving the world and stick rigidly with their pre-formed ideas (Fonagy et al., 2015).

The group environment holds powerful potential for helping residents break free from this 'prison of the mind'. Group members can often more easily see this process at play when it is displayed by others, which in turn helps them to reflect on themselves. They can also witness the change process in others, and particularly for senior group members, follow their example and see tangible rewards for taking this risk. For many, receiving feedback from peers can be more impactful than from a therapist who they may mistrust or see as too different to themselves. However, over time they can also begin to trust the facilitators, seeing them as a positive source of measured leadership and care in the group.

Mentalisation

Through this process of reality confrontation and trying out new ways of relating, group members are developing the skills to more accurately 'mentalise', in other words to understand the mental states that lead to behaviour in themselves and others (Bateman and Fonagy, 2010). They are introduced to new possibilities of perceiving others, often starting with learning that not everything that feels bad is produced by malicious intent on the part of others. Mentalisation-based therapy (MBT) is a specific therapy with evidence of effectiveness in both individual and group form for personality disorder (Bateman *et al.*, 2016; Bateman and Fonagy, 2009). This is not the specific model of therapy usually delivered in TC small groups, but there are many elements in common.

Projection and projective identification

The group process can also help to illuminate the processes of projection and projective identification, or in other words, the ways that people in the group are pushed into roles within the group because of how they are perceived by others. For example, older members of the group may be on the receiving end of projections from younger members who experience them as paternal or fatherly, and may end up identifying with these projections, becoming authoritative or punitive figures who others rebel against and attack. Often these various projections and identifications can lead to offence-paralleling behaviour, which provides rich opportunities for learning, change and risk reduction (see Chapter 7).

> "It was helpful to look at the role I am playing in the group. This was a way of me coping socially while hiding myself (defence mechanism). A protection of me feeling low".
>
> – Former Millfields patient

Reflective capacity

The process of working through these dynamics can also help group members realise that there are unconscious or subconscious processes which can govern perceptions and behaviour. This encourages them to reflect on their internal experiences, to be curious about *why* they think, feel or react in certain ways and whether this is actually helpful to them or not. Related to mentalisation, it also helps them to be curious about the same process in others. Again, more senior group members can provide a model for this, and their relative maturity and capacity for self-reflection alongside their actual progression towards release from custody and a more meaningful life can be inspiring and motivating for others.

Social skills

Small groups also provide a more supportive and intensive environment for trying out new social skills. It can be easier to practise giving assertive, constructive feedback to others within a smaller environment where others may be less defensive, and meanings and conflicts can be supportively worked through. There is also more time for other members to let them know whether their communication was received as clear, constructive and assertive, or rather confusing, judgemental, aggressive or even passive. It is often in the small group environments where members will learn that shouting and aggression leads to others 'switching off' and indeed their communication style becomes the issue, and their original point is lost.

Exploring and connecting to life experiences

Whilst everyone in the community eventually presents the key aspects of their lives, offending and formulation to the whole community (see Chapter 14) and there are no 'secrets' in the TC (see Chapter 3), the respect, intimacy and connection in the small groups provide a safer and more trusting environment than a community meeting for the fuller exploration of painful life events, including experiences of abuse and neglect as well as offending. This is crucial, as it is these explorations which will help the group and individual members to identify the source of maladaptive ways of thinking and behaving which have led to offending behaviour and mental distress, and it is this understanding which helps to illuminate a path towards change.

Antigroup and the negative power of the group process

Whilst the group has a powerful positive potential, it also has an equally potent negative force, and this can be more prevalent and important to manage within a forensic TC environment, which essentially is just a larger group with often parallel dynamics at play.

As already highlighted, groups can be challenging and threatening. Few people seek out group therapy when they are struggling with mental health problems, despite the rich benefits and opportunities groups offer, because there is a natural aversion to sitting in a group of people who are largely unknown, and no two groups can be the same as each group is made up by its unique membership. There is a high level of uncertainty as the group collectively develops alongside the individuals within it, and as relationships between different members shift over time. The group process is always evolving; it is never completed.

> "It was insightful to be in a group with different offenders, and also victims of offences...it gave me the idea that I would have liked doing Restorative Justice ... [but it also raised the question]: 'Am I antisocial for choosing not to socialise with people who are antisocial?'"
>
> – Former Millfields patient

With all these characteristics at play, the group inevitably creates and mirrors the preexisting conflicts and challenges people have had in groups in their lives. This offers both the possibility for difference and change, but also the risk of repetition and destruction. Thus, much like the wider TC, the group is simultaneously the trigger for and treatment of participant's difficulties.

Nitsun (1991, 1996, 2015) highlights this all succinctly in his elucidation of the concept of the anti-group, which, simply put, is the rise of destructive forces within the group. This often shows up as marked and persistent mistrust and denigration of the group by its members. They may push for individual therapy instead of or in addition to group therapy (see Chapter 9 for how individual work is managed within the TC). They may fall silent, close their eyes and sleep or switch off from the group, or only engage in thinking around issues that are not personal to them. They may take frequent bathroom breaks or find any excuse to miss the group. At the more extreme end, members may refuse to attend or walk out of the group in protest.

> "Small groups were where the real work was done. It was distracting to have people walking out of the group and then be allowed to come back or arriving late – this diminished the value of the discussion by treating it with disrespect. It devalues the person talking. Staff needed the confidence to say no, e.g. to people going to the loo".
>
> – Former Millfields patient

As the small group is a more intensive group environment in which members are intended to explore sensitive and painful issues such as their offending and childhood experiences, there will also inevitably be resistance to this, both conscious and unconscious. For example, the group may become exclusively focussed on rehashing community meetings or wider TC issues or expressing their grievances. An atmosphere may be created where it feels that thinking is 'under attack', that the facilitators and/ or senior members are constantly questioned or made the focus of grievances so that they have little capacity to steer the group towards more vulnerable, personal topics and emotions. Alternatively, some members in the group may become locked into familiar interpersonal conflict or an overly logical, cognitive approach which allows them and the rest of the group to avoid important areas of exploration and feeling.

It is normal for anti-group dynamics or themes to develop in the small groups, particularly as new members join, or existing members encounter challenges in their progression. However, these destructive forces can quickly spiral out of control if not actively worked through. If the destructive anti-group process seems intractable in the small group, it is also likely to mirror similar dynamics in the wider TC, and this is a warning sign that the TC culture requires attending to (see Chapter 20 for more discussion of these challenges).

> "We couldn't talk about certain things with certain patients in our small group because of their manipulation. But it was good for what I learned and achieved. Small group was a learning process. Gave you a chance to be you without people attacking you. It was hard to do, but you could put yourself in a vulnerable position".
>
> – Former Millfields patient

Small group psychotherapy within a forensic TC – adaptations and practices

Small groups in a TC are similar, but not synonymous with a traditional psychodynamic psychotherapy group. They exist within a TC, and everything within a TC should be aligned with TC values and culture (see Chapter 3 for a fuller exploration of these values). For many experienced group therapists, this is likely to bring up dilemmas and conflicts with how they have run groups in other settings or how they think groups should be run, and it is important therefore to highlight these and how they can be thought through.

Risk management

Small groups in forensic TCs can be the most supportive spaces for residents, but they can also be the most intense, triggering strong projective, parallel and anti-group processes which can raise the risk of violence. Risk should be constantly assessed and monitored in the small group supervision spaces, and particular attention should be given when new members join or when conflict between members is heightened. Group members who are prone to losing control should be encouraged to leave the group before their emotions escalate beyond their capacity to self-regulate, and this can be either for a short time-out or for the remainder of the group if they are not able to calm down. Within a forensic TC, patients who leave the group will often have to be escorted back to the ward by a facilitator; but even if the group is held on the ward, staff on the floor of the ward need to be informed about the risk so that they can support the patient and also help determine whether they are ready to return to the group or not. Therefore, groups always require two facilitators so that whilst one is escorting and feeding back regarding risk, the other remains with the group and continues the work. Facilitators should take it in turns to escort patients out of the group, and they should return as quickly as possible to support each other. They can speak to the patient leaving the group to deescalate risk if needed (though this should be handed over to ward staff at the earliest opportunity), but they should not engage in prolonged one-to-one conversations which can undermine the group process or encourage splitting. If a group is going through a particularly volatile period, it may be necessary to have a member of staff sit outside the group room to offer further support.

Working with the inside and outside of the group

No therapy group exists within a vacuum; there is always an 'outside' that makes its way into the 'inside' of the group. For groups outside of institutions, this could be shared experiences of culture, society or events, or individual circumstances or problems that they bring to the group for support. These are legitimate areas of work for the group, but the focus remains on how the group functions in working through these issues or supporting individual members. Additionally, there is normally an expectation that group members do not form relationships outside of the group, so that the dynamics of the inside of the group are distinct from the outside.

For small groups within a residential TC, this distinction is blurred. So much of the outside is shared, as group members live together and the 'living learning' environment and culture of the TC encourages active involvement and participation between members as the fundamental mechanism of treatment. The small groups are a smaller and more contained space in which to explore individual and collective issues, but inevitably issues from outside the group will come into the group for working through, and issues and conflicts between people that come up predominantly within the small group will make their way outside the group.

For this reason, facilitators cannot be experts or therapists brought in from outside the TC. They must be active participants in the TC themselves so that they can be informed on how conflicts or problems have developed outside of the group and help to navigate these within the group. Essentially, the TC experience is one large, continuous psychotherapy group with a smaller, more intensive psychotherapy group within it (i.e. the small group) – an ecosystem within an ecosystem. Facilitators cannot effectively make sense of and help to negotiate these complexities if they are not involved in the wider TC process.

Confidentiality

As covered in Chapter 3, everything that happens within a TC is part of the treatment, and connected with this is the value of openness, meaning that there are no secrets in the TC. However, there can be a conflict between this value and the aim of the small group being a safer and more contained environment to do more intensive and deeper work. This is because members need to have some sense that they can open up and reflect in their small group in a way that will not be immediately broadcast in an uncontained manner to the wider community.

The way that this is managed is complex and depends on the specific issue at hand, but the general principle is that group members should be able to share details of their experience knowing that, whilst the fact of these experiences happening is not kept totally secret from the wider TC, the way they have disclosed and discussed them will be kept within the group unless they themselves choose to share them more widely. This is a more nuanced position than simply saying that everything within the group is confidential. Instead, it is a position where group members have respect for each other and do not talk about the issues raised in a way that will make members feel disrespected, vulnerable or exposed, particularly if there is a sense that this is intended to be hurtful or has the flavour of gossip. There is also a respect for group members in being able to share their experiences in more detail in their own time within the wider TC. Of course, there will be times when it is appropriate and constructive to bring up details of issues that have been discussed in small groups that relate to those at hand in a community meeting for example, but the key is that there should be consideration and constructive intentions behind this.

Group feedback

One way that this balance between respect/confidentiality and openness can be negotiated is through the process of reporting back to the community the themes of a small group after it has taken place. This is usually done in a regular 'feedback meeting' for the whole community where specific treatment groups and individual work are disclosed to the wider community. This does not mean every detail, but it does include the general themes of what was discussed. This formal feedback process can be led by more senior members initially, so that newer members can get a sense of the balance between respect for individuals to disclose details in their own time, and the need for the broader themes of group and individual work to be known by the wider community, in order for the TC to function.

Authority and membership

Just as there is a blurring of lines between what is inside and outside the group, there is also a blurring of the lines between therapist and group member. This is not an alien concept in group psychotherapy, as it is acknowledged that the facilitator is part of the group and will therefore be part of the group dynamic. However, within a TC, this line is further blurred by the culture of a flattened hierarchy and the encouragement for residents to take responsibility as well as authority within the TC. This means that, just as group facilitators cannot just focus on the internal dynamics of the group and ignore the broader TC group process, they also cannot just focus on being group leaders and ignore their dual role as TC members. As TC members, they can be questioned and held to account for their decisions or actions within the community, and they can be expected to hold a view on current events or decisions facing the community as well. Equally, as group facilitators, they should be thinking of the group dynamic and the defences or anti-group processes that could be in play if the group behaves only as a mini community meeting and not as a small group.

Supervision and support for facilitators

Facilitators of small groups in forensic TCs face many complexities and challenges. Not only are they working with a changing group of people with high levels of mental disturbance and trauma as well as offending and risk, but they are also navigating the dual roles of group leader and community member as well as the blurred boundaries of running a psychotherapy group within a TC. With all these challenges, even very experienced facilitators require regular support through training and supervision. Training should focus on TC practitioner competencies as well as group analysis, and at least one facilitator within the facilitator pair should have a clinical qualification in psychotherapy. Small group supervision at Millfields was held for an hour after each small group, and Millfields small groups took place twice per week. Other TCs may have a different frequency of groups, but it is important that they take place at least once per week and that supervision is delivered at the same frequency, by an experienced supervisor in both TCs and group analysis. This intensive support reflects the challenges of the work and should not be compromised. Equally as important, small group facilitators should also take part in the wider TC staff group supervision spaces, namely reflective practice sessions and staff support. This is so that the exploration of the themes and dynamics of the small groups can be integrated with the experience within the wider TC, as they often mirror and have an impact on each other.

References

Bateman, A. and Fonagy, P. (2009) 'Randomized controlled trial of outpatient mentalization-based treatment versus structured clinical management for borderline personality disorder', *American Journal of Psychiatry*, 166(12), pp. 1355–1364. doi:10.1176/appi.ajp.2009.09040539

Bateman, A. and Fonagy, P. (2010) 'Mentalization based treatment for borderline personality disorder', *World Psychiatry*, 9(1), pp. 11–15. doi:10.1002/j.2051-5545.2010.tb00255.x

Bateman, A., O'Connell, J., Lorenzini, N., Gardner, T. and Fonagy, P. (2016) 'A randomised controlled trial of mentalization-based treatment versus structured clinical management for patients with comorbid borderline personality disorder and antisocial personality disorder', *BMC Psychiatry*, 16(1), p. 304. doi:10.1186/s12888-016-1000-9

Fonagy, P., Luyten, P. and Allison, E. (2015) 'Epistemic petrification and the restoration of epistemic trust: A new conceptualization of borderline personality disorder and its psychosocial treatment', *Journal of Personality Disorders*, 29(5), pp. 575–609. doi:10.1521/pedi.2015.29.5.575

Kleinberg, J.L. (ed.) (2012) *The Wiley-Blackwell handbook of group psychotherapy*. Chichester: John Wiley & Sons Ltd.

Nitsun, M. (1991) 'The anti-group: Destructive forces in the group and their therapeutic potential', *Group Analysis*, 24(1), pp. 7–20. doi:10.1177/0533316491241003

Nitsun, M. (1996) *The anti-group. Destructive forces in the group and their creative potential*. London: Routledge.

Nitsun, M. (2015) *Beyond the anti- group: survival and transformation*. London: Routledge.

Tuckman, B.W. (1965) 'Developmental sequence in small groups', *Psychological Bulletin*, 63(6), pp. 384–399. doi:10.1037/h0022100

Yalom, I.D. and Leszcs, M. (2005) *The theory and practice of group therapy*. 5th edn. New York: Basic Books.

Chapter 6

How do you spell forgiveness? Finding a shared language of expression through art psychotherapy

Jessica Collier

Introduction

This chapter takes a retrospective look at some aspects of the creative work undertaken at Millfields. It will explore how art psychotherapy offered insights gleaned not only from the residents' own imaginations, but also how art making elucidated important relational dynamics and social structures that contributed to meaning making within the therapeutic community. This includes reflections on the importance of both residents and staff understanding their motivations and desires, so as to avoid unconscious enactments of destructive or distressing early experiences. At the foundation of art psychotherapy in forensic environments, is the aspiration to understand the purpose of violence, in order to reduce the risk of harm and enable the potential for a more meaningful life. For this to be effective, every member of the therapeutic community must endeavour to bring reflexivity and honesty to their work.

Beginnings

For many years, I have worked as an art psychotherapist in prison with incarcerated women. Almost without exception, the majority of these women have a history of violence done to them which far surpasses the offences for which they have been convicted. This violence, whether sexual, physical or psychological, has most often been done to them by the men in their lives; fathers, grandfathers, brothers, partners, friends, associates. Increasingly, I found myself appalled by the violence of men and the destruction caused, on a personal and a wider social level, through ubiquitous gendered offenses such as domestic violence and sexual assault, in addition to male-on-male violence, all amplified by pervasive codes of toxic masculinity. Through the narratives of domination I heard in the daily statistics reported in the media, it seemed to me that men were unceasingly brutal.

I was intrigued then, when I was invited to interview for the role of art psychotherapist at Millfields Modified Therapeutic Community. This was an unusual establishment, working in a deeply humane way, with some of the most complex and violent men in the criminal justice system, whose offences were

DOI: 10.4324/9781032717302-6

exactly of the nature committed by the men my female patients regularly spoke about, and often idealised. This was an opportunity for me to understand better from the male perpetrators' perspective, what lay behind the endemic violence and vengeance committed by men (Gilligan, 2000) and what might support them in escaping their appalling situation.

Once in role and emersed in the therapeutic community, what followed was an extraordinary seven years of professional and personal progress, during which I was witness to acts of compassion, kindness and humility, alongside behaviour that could be cruel and vicious. In short, the whole of the spectrum of human feeling and conduct was evident, from both the staff and the residents. Embracing this diversity of emotion and experience, Millfields offered every community member an opportunity to explore themselves, if they could tolerate the scrutiny this undeniably involved.

For the majority of staff who were not psychodynamically trained, the dropping of professional defences may have led to feelings of vulnerability and exposure which paralleled the residents; while for the psychological therapists, this open attitude and flattened hierarchy may have been at odds with the 'blank canvas' approach traditionally utilised by psychotherapists. Both these positions offered a useful opportunity to discover the inter-personal and intra-personal experiences of every community member. I have written elsewhere that working as an art psychotherapist is a transformative experience in which personal creativity can make change in the lives and outlook of both the therapist and the patient (Collier, 2015). Working at Millfields was an extraordinary learning experience, and I believe the embedding of creative expression as a fundamental element of the thinking in the therapeutic community changed many whose lives were made more meaningful by their time there.

Limitations of the work

While there was a sincere effort at Millfields to encourage open and transparent discussion by the community about any matter, there were difficulties in addressing some themes in the kind of depth that could have been useful for creating an even more responsive and enquiring culture. Conversations about gender, sexuality and ethnicity, areas that are increasingly central to contemporary therapeutic practice (Collier and Eastwood, 2022), were often excruciatingly hard to initiate and maintain. During my years as part of the community there were dramatic changes in staff which saw the community management team and reflective practice consultant change from a predominantly female leadership to a largely male one. Neither of these positions were generally remarked upon, despite such symbolic responses as one resident believing his genitals were shrinking following a medication review by the new male psychiatrist. Similarly, it was sometimes difficult to name the 'upstairs/downstairs' split in staff diversity (Aiyegbusi, 2012; Collier, 2016) as well as the anomaly of a largely white cohort of Millfields residents in a generally much more ethnically and culturally diverse wider hospital population and area of London.

Personality disorder, while currently undergoing transformation in thinking and nomenclature, has been seen as a principally white diagnosis (Hossain *et al.*, 2018). I was often conscious of the way in which the men's diagnosed personality disorder traits, particularly of Anti-Social Personality Disorder, seemed to mirror the traits of oppressive patriarchal societies and leaders; for example, features include feelings of entitlement, lack of remorse, difficulties seeing alternative perspectives and so on (Collier, 2022). Indeed, Millfields was often seen as more 'privileged' than the other wards by the hospital patients and staff. Nevertheless, despite the limitations in the inclusion of intersectional and feminist ways of thinking, the men and staff worked hard to understand themselves and each other; offensive language and behaviour was examined, compassion was encouraged and some extraordinary personal progress was made.

Community and practice

One conversation that *was* on-going in the community amongst the staff team was the split between different professions and the way these professional hierarchies were presented. Of course, there was an inherent dichotomy here in which the fundamentally hierarchical systems of the NHS and the criminal justice system were embedded in the structure, whilst simultaneously being in opposition to the ethos of the therapeutic community. This split of professional function was often along ethnic or racialised lines, as suggested earlier, but more readily discussed by the community was the way in which clinicians chose to primarily identify as either community members or in the capacity of their profession. Likewise, some staff preferred to be addressed by their professional title and surname, whilst others favoured the more egalitarian use of first names. These personal preferences inevitably influenced how time spent with some colleagues was valued differently to time spent with others by the men, and on occasion, this difference in professional standing could aggravate feelings of envy or neglect that reflected the dynamics of the men's families of origin.

Likewise, the provision of individual psychotherapy sessions, and in my early work at Millfields individual art psychotherapy sessions, often provoked rivalrous feelings between the men, and could elicit attitudes of superiority or persecution in those who were selected for one-to-one work or not. Quite quickly, I chose to offer group work only, as I witnessed the idealisation of individual therapy and wanted to avoid this. Of course, no system is perfect, and any difficulties playing out in the community dynamics could be taken up, reflected on and processed as a means of understanding the use of psychological attacks and projections. Indeed, the enactment of entrenched psychological defences and interpersonal conflict between community members often usefully illuminated the very same behaviours that led to the men's initial index offences.

My own position was that whilst I was contracted as an art psychotherapist, and this was my professional training, what I felt most important was to demonstrate my commitment to the values of the therapeutic community. This was not easy given I was employed for only two days a week, but early on I requested the opportunity to develop not only the art psychotherapy provision, but also to be a regular small group facilitator, and to create an informal clay group. In addition to this, along with everyone else, I attended community meetings, weekly reflective practice and ate lunch with the men. This unusual way of working often left me very far out of my comfort zone, a parallel process I thought might offer some insight into the therapeutic experience for the men.

Having been in analytic group psychotherapy myself for many years, I understood the importance of consistency, reliability and the transparent sharing of thoughts and ideas. Nevertheless, many of the men, and indeed many of the staff, found this revealing of their inner voice difficult in the group settings, engendering as it often did, feelings of shame and vulnerability which occasionally resulted in demonstrations of anger and aggression. Millfields was not an environment where the classic psychoanalytic stance of apparent neutrality worked very well. Indeed, the importance of the staff being able to reflect on their own feelings and responses with authenticity, including acknowledging their own discomforts and mistakes, was essential in gaining and maintaining the men's respect and trust.

With art psychotherapy available as part of the therapeutic milieu, those residents who found verbal expression particularly challenging could explore a different approach, trying out visual and embodied ways of encountering and expressing their emotions and experiences which could feel less risky – although sometimes highly emotive – than speaking out and potentially feeling humiliated.

Art psychotherapy at Millfields

It is important to note that art psychotherapy practice is extremely diverse, and that while clinicians are trained at post-graduate level and professionally registered by the Health and Care Professions Council, there is no specific praxis that is taught or approved. Art psychotherapists are as disparate as artists, and their work is most obviously influenced by their positionality or standpoint, aesthetics and life experience, alongside their preferred theoretical stance. Hence, the art psychotherapists at Millfields prior to myself, and the art psychotherapist at the time of Millfield's closure, will have had their own varying ways of thinking about and working in the community. My own ambition was to ensure that although optional, art psychotherapy was not seen as an adjunct to the main therapeutic endeavour, an additional extra, as can sometimes be the case in prison therapeutic communities (Player, 2022). Rather, I wanted art psychotherapy to offer an alternative language that could communicate feelings and thoughts that might be too painful or shaming to articulate verbally, but which aligned with the themes and conversations taking place in the small groups, which were mandatory.

Violence can be thought about as resulting from an inability to symbolise and thus a failure to develop the mature defence mechanism of sublimation (Klein, 1930; Segal, 1957). An art psychotherapy group might therefore offer an opportunity for men with entrenched defences who were prone to act out violently, a way of unconsciously sublimating the difficulties in their emotional world into their artwork. This expression of feeling could then be recognised, observed, noted, named and made conscious in discussion with his fellow art makers, and then further explored and made sense of in the other therapeutic forums. This communal aspect is fundamental to the task of a therapeutic community and informs the idea that the men are actively involved in their own and each other's understanding.

To assess which men might be best able to make use of art psychotherapy in the longer term, an open group was initially offered for several weeks at the beginning of my tenure at Millfields. During this group, one resident, charged with a sex offence and with a history of recidivism, demonstrated exactly this incapacity for symbol formation by drawing very competent, realistic and intricate images of penises which he pushed towards me. This seemed to be an explicit enactment of his index offence and designed to 'shock' me; a reaction which might offer the perpetrator confirmation of his potency (Collier, 2020). Importantly, it offered an opportunity for the group to think about the effect 'showing his penis' had on the audience he was showing it to.

Similarly, a man whose index offence had been presaged by years of shame and secrecy about his sexual preferences before finally murdering his lover and leaving his remains in a dramatic tableau, covered his vivid images under multiple layers of semi-transparent tissue, obscuring the content, hiding the details and making it secret and mysterious to others. Yet another resident, created a cardboard model that was an exact replica of the scene of his lethally violent index offence. While these visual enactments of the offences, a kind of pictorial offence paralleling (Shine, 2010), offered an extremely useful opportunity to safely note the on-going risk these particular men held, the aims of the art psychotherapy group in the long term were intended to use creativity and imagination to support the men in exploring the frightening patterns in their childhoods, adult lives and relationships that had caused so much disruption and distress to them and others.

Rather than facilitating a kind of parallel process and showing the group a visual reproduction of the offence, art could instead be used to interrogate the feelings and experiences that lay beneath the violent action. If verbal psychotherapy aims to understand unconscious feelings and actions and transform these into conscious thoughts and words, art psychotherapy can, conversely, take images, thoughts and words and transform them back into feelings that can be expressed and felt more safely.

Embodiment and expression

One of the foundational elements of art psychotherapy theory is the importance of embodiment. Schaverien's (1999) classic concept of diagrammatic and embodied imagery, whilst neglecting the importance of external systemic and cultural differences and influences, suggests that feelings which at first can only be demonstrated externally, can come to be felt and processed internally. Where violence is enacted, this theoretical idea is useful, as it offers the possibility of thinking and feeling replacing the desire to elicit action, so often expressed as violence. In art psychotherapy, this theory may manifest in diagrammatic images made by patients who want to tell their story and illustrate what has happened; for example, in the drawings of the penises mentioned earlier. These pictures may often include writing, instructions and labels, rather like scientific diagrams, and do not necessarily incite any feeling in the viewer.

These kind of images are very common in early work with forensic patients; I am frequently offered drawings of cut wrists, knives, razor blades and other weapons; gashes and puddles of blood; sad faces with tears. These images are rarely embodied or imbued with feeling, but seem to be signs describing deeds, actions and emotions. Especially if patients are alexithymic, and struggle to identify, name or share their feelings, this diagrammatic phase is an important part of the exploratory process. This process is not linear, and for anyone doing art psychotherapy, these diagrammatic images may come and go throughout the therapeutic journey; perhaps rather like the movement in and out of the paranoid schizoid and depressive positions during psychoanalysis (Klein, 1946). Diagrammatic images can be made, often images of words themselves (Collier, 2019), which offer a tentative foundation of the artist's experience before a more profound internal exploration can begin. Words can also be created to clarify a feeling or idea if the artist does not feel confident that their feelings can be understood by others.

The early days of the art psychotherapy group at Millfields seemed to be exploring exactly this landscape. For men who have very little epistemic trust, entering a shared space with the expectation that they should make art can be a frightening proposal. While image making may be considered safe by those who are not experienced in using art to express themselves, in reality the potential for humiliation or ridicule is high. In schools in the United Kingdom, art is taught and examined in a way that relies on skills and judgement of what is deemed 'good' or 'bad' by an external other, usually a person in authority, and this power imbalance and aesthetic assessment can be difficult to overcome, especially for those with limited ego strength. For the first year or so, it seemed to me that the group was checking out what aspects of their images could be verbally articulated through the questions they asked about spellings. The diagrammatic images they were creating seemed to require additional instructions to ensure they could be 'read'. As I noticed how many spellings were being asked about, I began to jot them down on a piece of paper, and found the words seemed to be both artworks in themselves, and an insight into the unconscious concerns of the men.

Words as art

Artists working in Western traditions have used words to express emotion for millennia. For example, the Book of Kells, created by Celtic monks sometime between the sixth and eighth century, used illuminated letters as the centrepiece of the work to communicate the wonder of their faith, and this form of decorated manuscript was created throughout the medieval period. More recently, conceptual artists have utilised the written word to explore meaning, imagination and radical thought. In the mid-twentieth century, the Scottish artist Ian Hamilton Finlay, created what he called 'concrete poems' through which he imbued words with visual layers; accentuating their meaning. Barbara Kruger, whose work spans over 50 years, has spent her entire career attempting to engage "the issue of what it means to live in a society that's seemingly shock-proof, yet still is compelled to exercise secrecy" (Public Delivery, 2024). Her text-based artworks offer a feminist cultural critique which explores stereotypes and structural violence and brings together the personal and political. Both these artists, and many others, have visually foregrounded the written word, making images that transform the ordinary into something clear and fundamental. Indeed, outside of Western culture, the written word, expressed through calligraphy, is considered the ultimate form of art, valued more highly than painting or sculpture as a form of self-expression.

In my own thinking, art psychotherapy embraces all historical art forms implicitly, expanding the potential meaning of images not only personal to the experience of the artists themselves, but across generations of human creativity; a kind of shared visual repository of artists images, perhaps akin to the concept of the collective unconscious (Jung and Hull, 1991).

Spelling out needs

Over the seven years I worked at Millfields, the art psychotherapy group went through many changes, depending on the men who were regular attendees, the colleagues who co-facilitated the group, as well as the atmosphere in the wider therapeutic community (TC). The words explored below, emerged during a year of the group's early life, but epitomise ideas that seemed consistent throughout the community. The group appeared to spell out the unconscious concerns of both the group itself, but also the themes significant to all the men in the unit, from shared experiences in their earliest years and families of origin, to their offences, and their current needs and preoccupations. Three pictures made by one group member demonstrate how his diagrammatic images, made while he worked out and named his emotions, transformed into embodied images, containing a multitude of different, ambiguous and contradictory feelings, and revealing a more layered and complex emotional landscape.

Attention

The first word the group needed help spelling was 'attention'. The giving and receiving of attention is essential for human connection from the earliest days of infancy. Indeed, attachment theory (Ainsworth and Bowlby, 1954), while situated firmly in Western middle-class values (Keller, 2012), remains a fundamental cornerstone of most psychodynamic psychotherapy, and incorporates the concept of shared attention. Art psychotherapy is equally concerned with shared attention; most notably the joint attention of patient and therapist looking together at an art object. It seemed to me then, that the earliest of interpersonal maturational processes was being evoked in the group, manifesting in the need for reassurance from the group and myself as facilitator, that we were indeed all paying attention, and that this attention would be demonstrated throughout the community.

Forgiveness

Another early word that required consideration was 'forgiveness'. The concept of forgiveness as it relates to violence is not simple. Gilligan (2000) suggests that we can only forgive violence if we have condemned it in the first place. While Millfields was not in the business of making moral judgements about the violence the men had committed, attempting rather to understand it, this was not always a stance that was easily held by the community. This enquiring attitude could be extremely difficult for some staff and men to accept. Often the residents minimised or denied their offences altogether, perhaps feeling highly ashamed and condemning of their own actions and unable to forgive themselves. The desire to spell out this word, and to share it with the group, appeared to suggest an internal dialogue and perception that they had done terrible and morally reprehensible things that needed forgiveness, suggesting an unconscious admission of the seriousness of their violence. To ask for forgiveness, is a completely different task to offering forgiveness.

Vulnerable

Showing vulnerability was an almost impossible undertaking for most of the men, and many of the staff at Millfields. While the residents made impressive attempts to take responsibility for their violence and acknowledge their mistakes, admitting fear or weakness was intolerable. The simple naming of this emotion in the art psychotherapy group seemed to demonstrate the importance of the triangulation art images offer in the therapeutic space. Writing the word vulnerable on an artwork, might feel considerably less risky than naming vulnerability as a state of being.

Scared and scarred

> When scarring is seen as the result of a violent encounter, it signifies strength or bravery in a guy, or it could be due to an accident, and so evidence of a risk-taking personality. Either way, it's another way of assessing a man's masculinity.
>
> (Burriss et al., 2009)

At Millfields, physical scars evidenced the 'war wounds' the men often spoke about competitively, distracting from their emotional scars and signifying power and dominance. However, in the art psychotherapy group, scarred was misspelt as scared, unconsciously providing a safe and objective starting point for discussion about the dread and terror of violence and the reality of the men's experience.

Angry

Almost without exception, the violent offences committed by the men resident at Millfields were perpetrated when they were angry, most likely as a reaction to feeling shame and humiliation (Gilligan, 2000). Understanding how feelings of anger could be safely felt, as a natural human emotion, was a large part of the work

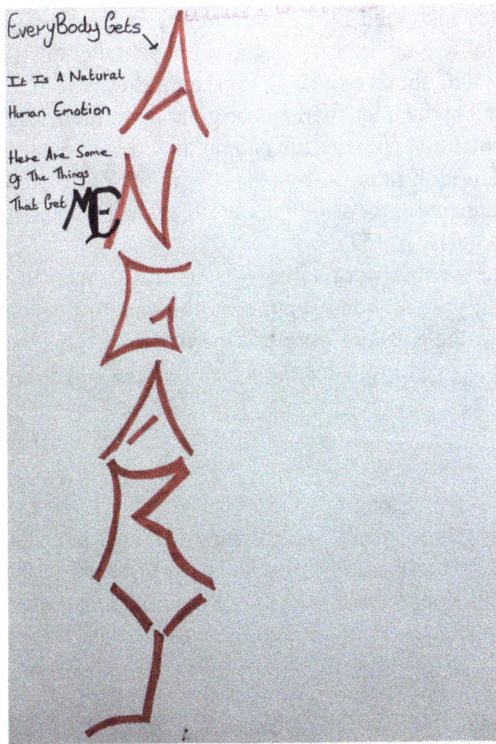

Figure 6.1 Artwork by Millfields art psychotherapy group member, *Angary*, pen and paper, 297 mm × 420 mm, shown with consent

within the community. In the art psychotherapy group, acceptance of these feelings could be explored as an emotion located individually, as well as one expected of men generally (Figure 6.1). The man who created this image had survived intra-familiar sexual abuse as a child, which had left him ashamed and questioning of his masculinity, resulting in the committing of a violent sex offence against a woman who rejected him. His relationships in the community were often full of tension and conflict stemming from this early experience, which resulted in his very poor self-esteem. Making images allowed him to express emotions without getting into conflict with others.

Envy

I slowly understood that one of the 'roles' I introjected from the community was that of the 'bad object' (Klein, 1946). I was frequently disparaged by some individuals in group meetings, who used various misogynistic and homophobic insults. Of course, this highlights the explicit hatred and fear of 'the other' that is intrinsic to much societal violence and male violence against women (Gilligan,

2000), and this was identified by the community in response to the comments. However, by explicitly naming envy in the art psychotherapy group, the purpose of this humiliating and abusive rhetoric took on a different meaning. The narcissistic injury endured by the men, perhaps originating in their incapacity to connect in an emotionally mature way with the people they loved, manifested as a need to disparage those who took interest in them. "Devaluation of an envied object is a typical defence manoeuvre, for as long as an object is devalued it does not need to be envied" (Bayne, 2011, p. 153).

I had to navigate between not retaliating when I was insulted, while simultaneously maintaining my dignity and supporting the men to understand the complex defence mechanism their insults were in the service of. This was able to happen in the art psychotherapy group, where images offered a way into this very difficult discussion.

Reflective

The aim of any psychotherapeutic endeavour is to think and reflect. Using image making to support this process, enabled the men to share their lives and experiences and then to consider them as a group. 'First I think and then I draw my think' (Stanisland, 1949). The layers of reflection are evident in this image (Figure 6.2),

Figure 6.2 Artwork by Millfields art psychotherapy group member, *a reflective past*, chalk pastel and pen, 297 mm × 420 mm

alongside the labelled perceptions of worthlessness. The creative journey this particular resident was on, seemed to be moving away from the purely diagrammatic communication of his anger (Figure 6.1) to a more embodied visual synthesis of feeling and thinking.

Conclusion

For some Millfields patients, art psychotherapy offered a different therapeutic approach, where they could express and explore their experiences and emotions visually and creatively. The flexibility in the group to work both verbally and with the art materials, helped the men to articulate their own concerns, as well as the unspoken fears of the community that lay beneath consciousness. The creative space allowed the men to explore and 'say the unsayable', and revealed the psychological defences that can keep individuals disconnected from the frightening and frightened aspects of their needs and vulnerabilities. As meaning was made explicit in the group, the men slowly began to depend less on words and verbal descriptions, and to make images that embodied emotion, encompassing multiple stories and layers of feeling simultaneously. A single image could evoke potential violence, tension, separation, isolation, safety, perspective, beauty, stillness and uncertainty, all within the same frame (Figure 6.3). As human beings,

Figure 6.3 Artwork by Millfields art psychotherapy group member, *untitled*, chalk pastel, 297 mm × 420 mm

recognising the layers of conflicting emotions we contain is essential to understanding ourselves. This process is challenging and takes time and courage. But
we can move from a one-dimensional concept of ourselves, rigid and immovable,
to an authentic, perhaps at times confusing, but more satisfying and substantial
self-awareness.

For the men at Millfields, this not only offered them the opportunity to tolerate
and know themselves better, but also to accept the contradictions and failings of
the people they loved and depended on. This insight could allow them to feel less
cruel and punishing of themselves, diminishing their self-hatred, and ultimately
reducing their risk of perpetrating violence against themselves and others in the
future. Equally, for staff members, the sometimes unconventional and imaginative
themes and conversations that emerged from the art psychotherapy group, presented new ideas and questions about their perspectives.

My own experience at Millfields challenged me in almost every aspect of my
professional, personal and intellectual life; the relationships with the men and
my colleagues elucidating the strengths and weaknesses of my practice, character
and moral principles. Working with men who commit violence against women
was itself an ethical dilemma, and a choice which left me with many questions
about the societal structures we operate within. Millfields also allowed me to
develop the confidence to share my own thoughts and speak them, even when I
understood they might just as likely be disregarded by the community as agreed.
There was always an invitation to bring yourself, and this has influenced all my
subsequent work.

Art psychotherapy, and many other forms of psychotherapy, increasingly strive
to be 'evidenced based'. This depends upon a multitude of evaluations, trials and
studies which aim to demonstrate the improved well-being of the participant over
the course of the therapy, sometimes with a follow-up later down the line. My own
extensive experience of personal psychotherapy is that often life does not necessarily seem to become 'better' during or immediately after the process, but that
the therapeutic relationship and experience can be internalised unconsciously and
drawn upon, perhaps years later, to navigate through life's challenges. Again, this
reflective understanding can bring huge benefits to the staff as well as the residents,
as their own internal struggles are illuminated in the light of those they hope to care
for and about. This kind of deep self-understanding may lead to less professional
burn out and mitigate the moral injury so many individuals who work in forensic
environments contend with.

Recently, many years after leaving Millfields, a colleague who had co-facilitated
the art psychotherapy group messaged to let me know she had bumped into a former group member we had both worked with. "He was saying how much he realised the art therapy with u helped him particularly afterwards" the message read,
"that he hadn't realised at the time but it was still something he saw as a major
element in his current progression, he was quite reflective about his past and positive about his future".

Acknowledgment

With thanks to the men who participated in the Millfield's weekly art psychotherapy group between 2012 and 2018.

References

Ainsworth, M.D. and Bowlby, J. (1954) 'Research strategy in the study of mother-child separation', *Courrier*, 4, pp. 105–131.

Bayne, E. (2011) 'Womb envy: the cause of misogyny and even male achievement?, *Women's Studies International Forum*, 34(2), pp. 151–160. https://doi.org/10.1016/j.wsif.2011.01.007

Burriss, R., Rowland, H. and Little, A. (2009) 'Facial scarring enhances men's attractiveness for short-term relationships', *Personality and Individual Differences*, 46(2), pp. 213–217. https://doi.org/10.1016/j.paid.2008.09.029

Collier, J. (2015) '3 man unlock: out of sight, out of mind: art psychotherapy with a woman with severe and dangerous personality disorder in prison', *Psychoanalytic Psychotherapy*, 29(3), pp. 243–261. https://doi.org/10.1080/02668734.2014.997835

Collier, J. (2016) 'Which road do you take? Art psychotherapy in a modified therapeutic community,' in Rothwell, K. (ed.) *Forensic arts therapies anthology of practice and research*. London: Free Association Books.

Collier, J. (2019) 'Cover stories: Art psychotherapy with mothers in prison who have killed or harmed their children', in Foster, A. (ed.) *Mothers Accused and Abused Addressing Complex Psychological Needs*. London: Routledge.

Collier, J. (2020) 'Mark making or making a mark? Perversion and sublimation in the work of Estela Welldon, Martin Frishman, and Aubrey Beardsley', *The International Journal of Forensic Psychotherapy*, 2(1), pp. 26–41.

Collier, J. (2022) 'Consent and the-rapist: positions of power in art psychotherapy with a sex offender', in Collier, J.; & Eastwood, C. (eds) *Intersectionality in the arts psychotherapies*. London: Jessica Kingsley Publishers.

Collier, J. and Eastwood, C. (2022) *Intersectionality in the arts psychotherapies*. London: Jessica Kingsley Publishers.

Gilligan, J. (2000) *Violence: reflections on our deadliest epidemic*. London: Jessica Kingsley Publishers.

Hossain, A., Malkov, M., Lee, T. and Bhui, K. (2018) 'Ethnic variation in personality disorder: evaluation of 6 years of hospital admissions', *BJPsychiatric Bulletin*, 42(4), pp. 157–161. https://doi.org/10.1192/bjb.2018.31

Jung, C. and Hull, R.F.C. (1991) *The archetypes and the collective unconscious*, 2nd ed. London: Routledge.

Keller, H. (2012) 'Attachment and culture', *Journal of Cross-Cultural Psychology*, 44(2), p. 175. https://doi.org/10.1177/00220221124722

Klein, M. (1930) 'The importance of symbol-formation in the development of the ego', *The International Journal of Psychoanalysis*, 11, pp. 24–39.

Klein, M. (1946) 'Notes on some schizoid mechanisms', *The International Journal of Psychoanalysis*, 27, pp. 99–110.

Player, E. (2022) *Questions of legitimacy in therapeutic programmes for women. Research seminar: critiquing enduring problems in the criminalisation and punishment of women prisoners serving long sentences*, Centre for the study of women and gender, Criminal Justice Centre, 11 May 2022. University of Warwick. Available at: https://warwick.ac.uk/fac/soc/sociology/research/gender/calendar/?calendarItem=8a17841b7d23c47e017d29701de04b8a (Accessed: 23 January 2025).

Public Delivery (2024) *Barbara Kruger – your body is a battleground*. Available at: https://publicdelivery.org/barbara-kruger-battleground/ (Accessed: 23 January 2025).

Schaverien, J. (1999) *The revealing image: analytical art psychotherapy in theory and practice*. London: Jessica Kingsley Publishers.

Schaverien, J. (2000) 'The triangular relationship and the aesthetic countertransference in analytical art psychotherapy', in McNeilly, A., & McNeilly, G (eds) *The changing shape of art therapy: new developments in theory and practice*. London: Jessica Kingsley Publishers.

Segal, H. (1957) 'Notes on symbol formation', *International Journal of Psychoanalysis*, 38, pp. 391–397.

Shine, J. (2010) 'Working with offence paralleling behaviour in a therapeutic community setting', in Daffern, M., Jones, L., & Shine, M. (eds) *Offence paralleling behaviour: a case formulation approach to offender assessment and intervention* Oxford: Wiley Blackwell.

Stanisland, L.N. (1949) *Let's understand art: A book on art appreciation for all*. London: Art and Educational Publishers. p. 59.

Chapter 7

Offence focussed work

Brittni Jones

Introduction

Everything that happens in a forensic therapeutic community (TC) links back to each resident's offending history and risk. He would not be in the TC or custody without this history, and the risk of future offending must be addressed for him to be released. As highlighted in Chapters 1, 2 and 13, risk and offending are linked with personality characteristics and happen in the context of a person's life, including experiences such as childhood trauma. In other words, risk and need are two sides of the same coin. This means that even when offences are not being specifically spoken about in a therapy group, factors linked with offending are often still being addressed. However, as also explored in Chapter 14 on formulation, serious offences are deeply uncomfortable, painful and frightening to think about for both residents and the staff. As a result, a dynamic of avoidance can develop, with a one-sided focus on vulnerabilities and experiences of victimisation, leaving risk factors unaddressed and failing the central task of the TC. TCs employ different methods to ensure specific and sufficient offence-focussed work takes place, and this chapter will explore these as well as the methods found to be most effective at Millfields.

Methods of offence-focussed work

TC practices and culture

A well-functioning forensic TC has a culture of constructively addressing a person's offending behaviour in everyday treatment. Firstly, the person's offending is fully understood through careful assessment (Chapters 12 and 13) and formulation (Chapter 14). These assessments are carried out by a multidisciplinary team, involve the residents and the formulation and treatment targets are working documents which are shared with the whole TC. This process embodies the culture of the TC which allows it to function as the method of treatment and change (Chapter 3).

DOI: 10.4324/9781032717302-7

Added to this is the specific practice of *offence disclosure*, in which residents disclose the primary serious offences which have led them to be in custody and treatment. This is usually done within a community meeting and is repeated whenever a new person (resident or staff) joins the TC, ensuring that all members are aware of the offences of residents. For new residents who have not yet completed the assessment and formulation process, this practice ensures that everyone is at least aware of the basic nature of the primary offences. This is crucial information in the assessment and formulation process, as it kickstarts the generation of ideas about the cause of a new resident's offending behaviour and maintenance factors of current risks.

For more senior residents, the offence disclosure process ensures that they and others are reminded of the central task of treatment and can help to identify and address any avoidance that has arisen. Residents are also expected to add more detail to their offence disclosure over time. Whereas a newer resident may only feel able to simply state the name of the offence, others who have been in treatment longer should provide a short narrative about what happened, including the main things they have learned about the reasons for their offending and what they are working on to prevent it happening again. This shows their progress in treatment and provides a model for newer members. If a senior resident is not capable of increased levels of mature disclosure over time, this should at least flag up the need for further development and review of their engagement. Alternatively, it could trigger a decision to end treatment if the avoidance cannot be overcome.

One of the TCs central tasks is to observe and work with *offence paralleling behaviour*. This is covered in more depth in Chapters 2 and 13, but it requires a mention in this chapter because it is the primary avenue by which offence-focussed work and risk assessment take place in a TC. As offending is often a method of communication, or a way of obtaining needs in relation to others, the relational, living-learning treatment of the TC naturally triggers dynamics that led to offending behaviour in the past, and therefore gives the opportunity to actively work with and change this behaviour in the here-and-now. This is the central method by which a TC completes offence-focussed work, and this must be the foundation for any further work completed in adjunct treatment groups.

Although research in forensic services is generally low quality, TC treatment (with or without specific adjunct offence-focussed treatment groups) is often assessed as having some of the most promising evidence of effectiveness for offenders with personality disorders (Richardson and Zinny, 2020; Shuker, 2010; Warren *et al.*, 2003). There is also specific evidence of effectiveness of hospital-based TCs such as Millfields (Wilson *et al.*, 2014) and prison-based TCs such as HMP Grendon in the United Kingdom in reducing risk and recidivism (Shuker, 2008).

Specific offence-focussed treatments

Outside of TCs, offence focussed work is often completed in individual or, more commonly, group treatments. In the United Kingdom, these treatments are often specific to types of offending such as Horizon for sexual offending, and Kaizen for violent offending, which are prison and probation accredited treatment groups delivered in custody (Ministry of Justice and HM Prison and Probation Service, 2018). Kaizen (previously known as the Self Change Programme or SCP), is the newest programme, which encompasses violent, sexual and intimate partner violence (though usually delivered to these offender groups separately). Kaizen was developed to have a 'strength-based' approach to addressing criminogenic needs and adapts elements of evidence-based therapies such as cognitive behavioural therapy (CBT), which has evidence of effectiveness in addressing offending behaviour (Lipsey, Landenberger and Wilson, 2007). Although research in violence reduction is limited, the programme out of which Kaizen was developed had some good evidence of effectiveness in reducing both instrumental and reactive violence (Henning and Frueh, 1996).

Delivery of an offence focussed group in a TC

Delivering a specific treatment group like Kaizen is not an absolute requirement for forensic TCs, as the offence focussed work can be done through the TC treatment alone. However, SCP and then Kaizen were chosen to be delivered at Millfields, because they were an additional evidence-based method of ensuring that all risk factors for offending were addressed. Completion of an HMPPS-accredited programme was also helpful evidence of risk reduction for residents when progressing towards release from custody (parole boards, rightly or wrongly, do seem to place more value on HMPPS-accredited programmes). When these programmes could be appropriately adapted to individual participants, they were found to add significant value to the TC treatment (Bull, Minoudis and Taylor, 2019).

Kaizen received overwhelmingly positive feedback from Millfields residents who completed it, and this was despite it being a challenging, mixed group (i.e. residents with general violent offending were mixed with those with intimate partner and sexual violence). As Kaizen is an accredited group which is owned by HMPPS and comes with a detailed delivery manual and facilitator training programme, this chapter cannot be a specific guide to delivering the group. However, we will draw on participant feedback and facilitator experience to highlight the aspects of the group which were most impactful.

"A really good thing [at Millfields] was the possibility of doing a prison accredited programme: Kaizen. Prison and probation officer said that I will have to go to prison to do Kaizen".

– Former Millfields patient

Building insight

> "Kaizen was fantastic. Learned about myself so much. The process really helped me to break things down, put together the jigsaw, see the patterns in my life with triggers, feelings. Going through those patterns cemented itself in my brain so it came naturally. I learned so much".
>
> – Former Millfields patient

Using a structured approach, Kaizen participants were supported to think through the triggers, thoughts, emotions and physical sensations that led up to either their historical offences or subsequent offence-paralleling behaviour. This insight building takes place in the wider TC groups as well, but the advantage of Kaizen was going through each element in detail using a methodical, structured approach which residents could learn to apply themselves.

For each of their serious offences, participants were supported to reflect on what was happening in their lives at the time, such as the stresses or unmet needs, or the influence of substance use. They then worked to identify the more immediate trigger for the offence, and the cascade of thoughts, emotions and physical sensations that this set off. Finally, residents identified the 'personal rules' (called 'rules for living', 'core beliefs' or 'schema' in CBT) that directed their behaviour in that moment (reference).

An example of this breakdown analysis could look like this:

1 Trigger: Someone said something negative to me
2 Emotions: I felt angry and humiliated
3 Physical Sensations: My body felt like it would explode with adrenaline and tension
4 Thoughts: I thought about what a horrible person they were and how unjust their behaviour was
5 Personal Rule: I believed that 'people who wrong you should be punished and taught a lesson'
6 Behaviour: I punched them

The resident with this understanding of his historical violent offence may then see this pattern arising in the TC when he is given challenging feedback in a community meeting. Of course, actual violence is prohibited in the TC, but offence-paralleling behaviour may be verbal aggression or threats, imagined violence or even self-harm (i.e. turning the violent impulse on oneself). These here-and-now examples are brought to the Kaizen group (as well as community meetings and small groups) so that all risk factors, patterns of behaviour, and common triggers and areas of vulnerability for violence are explored and understood.

Building skills

Developing insight and the ability to recognise unhelpful thoughts, emotions and personal rules as they arise, is an essential foundation for change. Once a person has gained the ability to slow down his internal experience after a trigger, he can start to see options beyond violence in dealing with it. Kaizen introduced many skills which residents in TCs are supported to develop outside of the group, but which they also seemed to find helpful to build on within the structured format of the Kaizen group. These included:

(1) Thinking before acting

For many residents, their behaviour feels 'automatic' or 'instinctual', impossible to change because it seems to happen quickly and without thought. However, the process of identifying the elements of what goes on internally after a trigger and before behaviour helps to challenge this notion and increase the possibility of control. Residents learn to pause and think before they act, sometimes visualising a stop sign or having a physical reminder to stop and think somewhere on them (for example, a mark or tattoo on their hand or a paper in their pocket). In this pause (and often after using other skills to calm down), they learn to observe their thoughts and emotions, as well as how the way they perceive a situation can impact on how they choose to react to it. Crucially, they also learn to think of the potential consequences for behaviour.

> "I learned that even if people upset you, you have no right to shout and scream at them. Don't mess yourself up by doing that. The older I get, the better I get at handling things like that".
>
> – Former Millfields patient

(2) Emotional regulation skills

After pausing to think, the next skill to develop is emotional regulation (it can be very difficult to think clearly when you are in a rage!). Broadly speaking, residents will fit in two categories: those who cope through suppression of emotions, and those who cope through expulsion.

For those who suppress emotions, it may appear that they are regulating their emotions because they may stay quite calm and unemotional, but they are actually burying emotions that will build up to an explosion. These residents must be supported to identify and communicate their emotions as they arise, and work through barriers such as fear of vulnerability or losing control. They will also need to learn self-soothing techniques, so that they can manage emotions through means other than suppression. This could be breathing techniques, grounding or mindfulness exercises, engaging in activities that they find calming such as music, gaming or art, spending time alone or with someone they can trust and talk to, physical activity or distraction.

> "One thing I can say to you for sure is that my crime came totally out of the blue and this rage from within was so hidden that I did not recognise it, nor did I understand this part of myself or where the hell it came from".
>
> – Former Millfields patient

For those who expel emotions, often through provocative or violent behaviour towards others, they should be supported to learn to identify and communicate their emotions in a prosocial manner, and to practice self-soothing techniques to reduce their intensity.

> "I started to understand why I was so angry, and in the process my anger dissipated. It was all about humiliation and anger about being hurt".
>
> – Former Millfields patient

(3) Challenging unhelpful thinking

After they can think more clearly when under stress or feeling strong emotions, residents need to be able to challenge unhelpful thinking, particularly when it can lead to violence. This is a complex task, and individuals will have different types of thinking that need to be prioritised. This can often include failure to accurately empathise or mentalise (perceive what another person may be thinking, feeling or intending), catastrophic thinking, hypervigilance to perceived threats, beliefs about how to deal with conflict or threat, or any of the other 'thinking errors' emphasised in traditional CBT (Gilbert, 1998).

For many residents, this process will start at the point of the trigger, where they have often misperceived or catastrophised a situation. This can be a tendency to view others as maliciously intending to cause harm (e.g. humiliation, rejection, exclusion), when it is more likely to be a miscommunication or constructive feedback. Residents may also overestimate the impact or consequences of another's behaviour towards them, such as believing that any perceived disrespect or threat, however small, must be severely punished to prevent future vulnerability or harm.

Often these are beliefs that were held or taught within their families, by those who promoted violence as a primary and effective way of protecting oneself or try to 'toughen up' their children through punishing perceived weakness. Unfortunately, these beliefs are often reinforced through antisocial peer groups and in prison settings, where perceived strength through intimidation and violence is often a survival strategy. As a result, significant work must be done on changing the environment (for example, ensuring the TC provides a sense of safety and encourages trust and openness) so that these beliefs can be effectively challenged. This work can also either be built on or undone, depending on where a resident goes after his treatment, and his future pathway is therefore a crucial element of treatment planning (see Chapter 17).

> "I learned that I have to accept responsibility – whether it was right or wrong what the other person did, I should have handled it better. You're going to meet people like that out there, and you have to know that you can't handle it like I used to. It was helpful for staff to relate to this and tell me how they would have handled it".
>
> – Former Millfields patient

(4) Social communication skills

To meet needs in prosocial ways, effective and assertive communication skills are key. Many residents, even if they can resist engaging in overt violence, will rely on aggressive verbal communication to get what they want or need. For example, they will demand something be done, often with no context or explanation given, and will expect immediate compliance out of fear or respect. However, in most situations this will appear unreasonable and entitled, and crucially the person on the receiving end of the demand will have little understanding of why it is being made or what is important about it. If he or she refuses to comply or asks questions, the resident may feel neglected, misunderstood, disrespected and vulnerable, and these emotions are likely to be subsumed and communicated as anger and rage.

On the other hand, a resident who suppresses emotions and relies on passive or passive-aggressive communication may just hint at things he needs rather than asking clearly, again resulting in the person on the receiving end not understanding and therefore not identifying and considering meeting the need. The resident often then stores up feelings of resentment and hurt from several instances of this occurring, before exploding in rage over a seemingly small issue, again resulting in confusion and resistance from others.

This pattern of behaviour and its consequences is often offence-paralleling and is therefore an exceedingly productive area of exploration in offence-focussed work. Participants in the group are supported to learn about assertive, aggressive, passive-aggressive and passive communication styles. They are then asked to reflect on the merits of each and learn about how to be a more effective, assertive communicator. These can include learning how to use 'I language' to communicate their feelings about or objections to another's behaviour in a manner which can be more easily understood and received. This strikes a balance between clearly communicating what feels negative, taking appropriate responsibility for their own destructive or unhelpful behaviour, and refraining from more extreme judgement, blame or condemnation. It also includes learning how to make themselves understood and how to negotiate and compromise to achieve the best outcome.

Helpfully, the TC environment provides constant opportunities to practise communication skills and receive feedback, as well as personally reflect on one's progress, all of which can be brought back to the offence-focussed group for both recognition and further development.

> " [It was helpful] being allowed to be in a social environment, which allowed me to observe my behaviour. I found staff feedback really helpful. I found some patients' feedback helpful. I found it very helpful [thinking about how I was] playing my role in a social environment. Installed in my ability to reflect".
> – Former Millfields patient

Identity, criminogenic needs and improving motivation

For many residents, violence and aggression is not just a survival mechanism; it is incorporated into their identity as people and feels impossible or even undesirable to change. There can be a sense of pride in their reputation as tough, respected or feared men in prison, whereas outside of prison they can feel small, lost or unimportant. There may also be a feeling of belonging amongst offenders that they struggle to find anywhere else. On the other hand, those who have committed sexual offences are often shunned and demonised both inside and outside prison. Being identified as a sex offender may be intolerable and literally denied, preventing them from doing the offence-focussed work that is needed. Both positions can mean that motivation for change, or even belief that change is possible is minimal.

Offence-focussed groups like Kaizen recognise this, and do not require that participants take responsibility for their crimes and commit to change. Instead, they are asked to commit to engaging with the reflective exercises and skills development that will make change possible if they choose it. By doing so, participants start to see the ways in which they could not only survive but gain more in life if they were to think and behave differently. For example, the more options they see for managing problems and getting their needs met in prosocial ways, the more likely it is that they can imagine living a healthy and meaningful life outside of prison. Most want to earn enough money for their basic needs, have a partner or healthy friendships, and gain a sense of purpose and value in society, and they only need to see that it is possible to meet these needs through pro-social means. This work is built on ideas from the Risk, Needs and Responsivity (RNR) framework and Good Lives Model (GLM), which are useful follow-up resources for this chapter (Andrews and Bonta, 2006, pp. 45–55; Ward and Laws, 2010).

Identity change and developing motivation are challenging endeavours, and nobody, let alone people with entrenched difficulties like the residents in TCs such as Millfields, can be expected to achieve linear or straightforward progress. Many will describe the process as an internal battle between their familiar ways of thinking and behaving and the new ways of perceiving themselves and the world and managing their difficulties. Groups like Kaizen conceptualise this process by highlighting a struggle between 'Old Me' and 'New Me'. Kaizen participants found it useful to develop a clear picture of their 'Old Me' and 'New Me' and to use this terminology to explore the internal battles that arise when they faced triggers. This was also useful in thinking through ways to strengthen their new identity and way of living if they chose to.

Crucial to this process is developing a new, opposing 'personal rule' or 'rule for living', as this is the thinking that governs behaviour. Again, it is important to highlight that participants are not expected to believe this new rule 100 percent, but instead it is a believable alternative that they develop and try out. For example, an 'old' or familiar rule for living may be that "people who disrespect me must be taught a lesson through violence", and a 'new' rule may be "people respect and listen to me more when I communicate assertively", or "I lose the argument when I am aggressive". To be meaningful and effective, the wording and development of these rules for living must come from the residents themselves, meeting them where they are in terms of their understanding and motivation at the time. They can then be developed further as he tries out this new way of being and experiences the merits of it.

Addressing specific risk factors

The risk factors and processes above are universal, but some risk factors only apply to specific individuals or offending behaviour. All residents should have a thorough risk assessment and formulation (see Chapter 13), and it is important that offence-focussed work, whether through the core TC treatment or through offence-focussed group or individual work, addresses all risk factors. For general violence, these could include substance misuse (see Chapter 8), use of weapons and the influence of culture or peer groups/gangs. For intimate partner violence, there may be a need to address experiences of intense jealousy or suspiciousness, beliefs or experiences which normalise violence towards partners and expectations around gender roles. And finally for sexual violence, there may be risk factors around beliefs about women, sexual preoccupation and entitlement and the influence of pornography or culture which normalises sexual violence.

Integrating specific offence-focussed individual or group work into the TC

Any work that takes place within a TC should be shared and integrated into the wider TC treatment, and this includes any offence-based work which takes place outside of core TC treatment groups. This can be challenging, particularly when there are difficult emotions such as shame around offences, a problem that often arises with sexual offending or intimate partner violence. Individual or small group-based offence-focussed work can help to create a safer environment in which to explore these aspects of offending which otherwise may feel impossible to approach within a large group setting like a community meeting. Likewise, insistence on disclosure of every detail of offence-based work to the wider TC would be counterproductive in this endeavour. However, it is also important that offence-based work does not get 'split off' from the wider TC to the extent that it can never be mentioned, and therefore the benefits of working with offence-paralleling behaviour in the TC are missed.

If participants in specific offence-based treatment groups feel uncomfortable disclosing certain details of what has been discussed, they can still disclose the broader themes of the work and what they have learned within the wider TC, and this should be done in community meetings after the group takes place. If it feels important for details to be shared to allow the TC to work fully with the resident, he can be supported to disclose these details over time, rather than all at once or straight away. Participants should be aware of the expectation of disclosure and the support available for them to do so from the start.

> "How I think I have benefitted from my therapy: firstly, I found a space to at last be able to disclose my index offence – which took me over 3 months to do. I recall the day I did in [small] group, I was so worried about what people would say or think of me and when I finally did it, I closed my eyes and I could feel the shame guilt and embarrassment all turning over in my stomach, making me feel sick, and when I opened my eyes to my surprise the world was still intact".
>
> – Former Millfields patient

Summary

This chapter highlights the importance of specific and direct offence-based work within a TC for offenders with personality disorder. This can and should be done through the core TC groups of community meetings and small groups, but the experience at Millfields indicated that a more structured offence-based group such as Kaizen was a highly valuable addition to the treatment programme.

References

Andrews, D.A. and Bonta, J. (2006) *The psychology of criminal conduct*. 4th edn. Newark, New Jersey: LexisNexis/Matthew Bender.

Bull, C., Minoudis, P. and Taylor, C. (2019) 'The use of an accredited violence reduction offending behaviour programme in a medium secure personality disorder service', *Personality and Mental Health*, 13(3), pp. 190–194. https://doi.org/10.1002/pmh.145

Gilbert, P. (1998) 'The evolved basis and adaptive functions of cognitive distortions', *British Journal of Medical Psychology*, 71(4), pp. 447–463. https://doi.org/10.1111/j.2044-8341.1998.tb01002.x

Henning, K.R. and Frueh, B.C. (1996) 'Cognitive-behavioral treatment of incarcerated offenders: an evaluation of the Vermont Department of Corrections' cognitive self-change program', *Criminal Justice and Behavior*, 23(4), pp. 523–541.

Lipsey, M.W., Landenberger, N.A. and Wilson, S.J. (2007) 'Effects of cognitive-behavioral programs for criminal offenders', *Campbell Systematic Reviews*, 3(1), pp. 1–27. https://doi.org/10.4073/csr.2007.6

Ministry of Justice and Her Majesty's (HM) Prison and Probation Service (2018) *Offending behaviour programmes and interventions: offending behaviour programmes and interventions currently available for offenders in England and Wales*. Available at: https://www.gov.uk/guidance/offending-behaviour-programmes-and-interventions (accessed 14 October 2024).

Richardson, J. and Zinni, V. (2020) 'Are prison-based therapeutic communities effective? Challenges and considerations', *International Journal of Prisoner Health*, 17(1), pp. 42–53. https://doi.org/10.1108/IJPH-07-2020-0048

Shuker, R. (2008) 'Treatment outcome following intervention in a prison-based therapeutic community: a study of the relationship between reduction in criminogenic risk and improved psychological wellbeing', *British Journal of Forensic Practice*, 10(3), pp. 33–44. https://doi.org/10.1108/14636646200800018

Shuker, R. (2010) 'Forensic therapeutic communities: a critique of treatment model and evidence base', *Howard Journal of Crime and Justice*, 49(5), pp. 463–477. https://doi.org/10.1111/j.1468-2311.2010.00637.x

Ward, T. and Laws, D.R. (2010) 'Desistance from sex offending: motivating change, enriching practice', *The International Journal of Forensic Mental Health*, 9(1), pp. 11–23. https://doi.org/10.1080/14999011003791598

Warren, F., Preedy-Fayers, K., McGauley, G., Pickering, A., Geddes, J.R., Kingsley, N. and Dolan, B. (2003) *Review of treatments for severe personality disorder*. Home Office Research. Available at: https://bulger.co.uk/prison/reviewtreatsseverePD.pdf (accessed 24 January 2025).

Wilson, K., Freestone, M., Hardman, F., Blazey, F. and Taylor, C. (2014) 'Effectiveness of modified therapeutic community treatment within a medium-secure service for personality-disordered offenders', *Journal of Forensic Psychiatry and Psychology*, 25(3), p. 243. https://doi.org/10.1080/14789949.2014.908317

Chapter 8

Substance use

Brittni Jones

Introduction

Substance use and addiction are common problems within prisons and forensic mental health hospitals and are particularly prevalent in patients with trauma and personality disorder who, lacking any other way of coping, seek relief from their difficulties through drugs and alcohol. Substance misuse is commonly a contributing factor in offending as well as offence-paralleling behaviour within therapy, often because offences are committed to acquire the resources to fund substance use, or because violence is more likely in a disinhibited or intoxicated state of mind. Addiction drives some patients to not only seek to use substances, but also to profit from supplying them to others (and, unfortunately, some staff members can be tempted by this possibility as well). This can become a powerful corrupting force within a treatment unit, wherein most are aware that prohibited substances are being supplied and misused, but addressing this seems impossible because people become tied up in unhelpful loyalties or fear the consequences of revealing what is going on. The denial of reality and splits between patients and staff that results from this corruption can make the environment untherapeutic if not overcome. This chapter will address both the treatment of substance misuse and addiction and the learning at Millfields about how to address the corrosiveness that accompanies it.

Need for substance use work in a TC

Secure establishments put enormous efforts into preventing and detecting the presence and use of illicit substances, whether this is illegal drugs, misused prescribed medications or legal substances that are nevertheless not permitted such as 'legal highs', alcohol or tobacco. Locked doors, background checks on staff, regular and random drug testing, use of technology like 'ion trackers' that can detect the presence of illicit substances on objects or a person's body or clothing, 'pat down' and more invasive body searches, CCTV and guidance for prescribing medication with the potential for misuse, are all methods that services use in this endeavour. However, despite these extensive security measures, illicit substances are rampant within most secure settings, even those with adequate resources and organisation to implement these strategies effectively. In the United Kingdom, prison and health data shows that over 50 percent of prisoners are in contact with drug and alcohol services, and many report finding it easy to access drugs in prison

DOI: 10.4324/9781032717302-8

(Her Majesty's Inspector for Prisons Annual Report, 2014; Public Health England and Department of Health and Social Care, 2018; UK Drug Policy Commission, 2008).

These facts highlight the clever methods drug dealers develop to subvert security and the strong motivations (including substantial financial gain) for this highly risky and effortful endeavour. This level of ingenuity and risk-taking is only worth employing because of the powerful hold that illicit substances have over substance users, whether through physiological addiction, psychological dependence or defences. The use and supply of drugs also becomes part of the identity of many and is used as a way of managing or manipulating the dynamics between themselves and others.

The primary task of a therapeutic community (TC) is to provide a therapeutic environment for patients, and clearly illicit substances produce the opposite. Just like any other forensic service, TCs therefore implement security strategies to try to eliminate the presence of illicit substances. However, questions remain about what TCs should do when, inevitably, some members of the community manage to supply and use drugs despite these best efforts. In addition to being a place of safety, the therapeutic environment is also a place where it is recognised that a patient's problems will not disappear on their own, that they will need time and support to work towards change. And in working with forensic populations, the use and supply of illicit substances is commonly a problem that contributes to physical and mental ill health and offending and therefore requires therapeutic work. However, the use and supply of substances is also one of the biggest contributors to an unsafe environment, and incidents related to illicit substances can bring a TC into disrepute and attract the scrutiny of wider systems. As such, there must be a limit to how much acting out in this area can be worked with. Thus, substance misuse is one of the most powerful corrupting factors that put TCs in the difficult position of balancing the needs of the community as a whole with the needs of individual members.

This was an issue repeatedly highlighted by former residents at Millfields:

> "The [substance misuse group] wasn't for me, but I was fighting against it. It was more helpful to me to do something wrong [such as take drugs] and then live with it in the moment, and the best thing was to feel safe to be open with it. Scary, but once you did it was the most important thing".
>
> – Former Millfields patient

> "The hardest thing was the wrong people there who are using or distributing drugs. But you can never stop that stuff happening in any unit".
>
> – Former Millfields patient

> "[On what he would have improved at Millfields] I would address the drug problems quicker. People have ways around [urine] drug tests, but they can't outsmart the hair tests. Some staff knew about drugs being brought in by other staff. You should punish the dealers and distributors more than the users".
>
> – Former Millfields patient

Substance use, mental health and personality disorder

Substance use is common in people with personality disorder and mental health difficulties as a way of coping and managing their difficulties (National Institutes on Drug Abuse, 2020; Trull *et al.*, 2018). It often starts from early adolescence, and, over time, becomes an addiction which is self-perpetuating. This ranges from misuse of legal substances such as alcohol or prescription drugs, to the use of illegal drugs, and the drug of choice can be helpful in understanding the person's difficulties.

For example, patients may prefer stimulants such as cocaine because of how they seem to intensify emotions which normally feel quite flattened or alleviate feelings of boredom (e.g. those with antisocial personality traits). Some patients enjoy how stimulants seem to boost their performance, mood and confidence (Miglin *et al.*, 2020), and this is applicable to many different personality profiles including those with narcissistic or borderline personality traits. The use of alcohol may have a similar effect for many (highlighted by the concept of 'Dutch courage'). On the other hand, patients who are very anxious may avoid these substances because they are fearful of losing control, or because their anxiety is made worse by effects such as racing heart or thoughts (e.g. obsessive compulsive traits).

Cannabis in low doses can produce a calming effect, making it attractive to patients who wish to reduce anxiety or other strong emotions (e.g. extremes of mood as often seen in those with borderline personality traits). However, particularly in higher doses or for those who are vulnerable, cannabis can have negative effects such as increased anxiety and paranoia, hallucinations and delusions (Hall and Degenhardt, 2008). Apart from alcohol and tobacco, Cannabis is the most used drug in the general public, and is legalised or partially legalised in many countries, which can make some patients reluctant to commit to stopping use and lead to debates about costs and benefits of use (Fischer, Lindner and Hall, 2022).

Opiates, both prescribed and illicit, are a commonly misused drug within the general public as well in forensic services (Katz *et al.*, 2013; Roberts and Richards, 2023). Many use opiates because of the feelings of warmth or euphoria they can give, as well as the sedation they cause. Not only does this provide temporary but powerful relief from the painful and distressing internal experiences associated with mental health difficulties and traumatic experiences, but it also helps to pass the time in custody. Unfortunately, prescribed opiates like Pregabalin and Subutex (Bupenorphrine), alongside prescribed anxiolytics such benzodiazepines, are on the rise in prisons, perhaps because of pressure from prisoners exhibiting challenging and distressing behaviour (Duke and Trebilcock, 2022). However, this exacerbates the problem long-term, as these drugs are regularly abused and traded (Advisory Council on the Misuse of Drugs, 2016).

With the cost and effort required to obtain illicit drugs, other drugs which were once classed as 'legal highs' in the United Kingdom (but are no longer legal) are also increasingly used. The most well-known of these in prisons is the synthetic cannabinoid commonly referred to as 'Spice', which is odourless and can be sprayed onto paper, easily avoiding detection. There are few positive symptoms of Spice and many dangerous ones, including convulsions, paralysis, aggression and psychosis. Those who use Spice are therefore willing to take great risks to alter their mental state in any way, even if the overall change is negative.

Not all drugs are covered in this section, but the general principle of assessment is to be curious about the drug preferences of the person and the psychological function of the drug for him personally.

Substance use and offending

Substance use is frequently a factor in offending and reoffending (Fridell *et al.*, 2008; UK Drug Policy Commission, 2008; Walter *et al.*, 2011). For some, addiction and the need to fund their substance use becomes the driving factor in their offending, often taking the form of thefts and robberies that become violent or involve the use of weapons. For others, substance use is a disinhibiting factor in violence, making them more impulsive or reactive, reducing their capacity to consider the consequences of their actions, and potentially causing them to use more extreme violence than they otherwise would. How substance use increases risk for a particular individual is important to understand so that these risks can be monitored and addressed through treatment.

Evidence base

The evidence base for addressing substance misuse is limited, and even more so in populations of offenders with personality disorders. Pharmacological interventions for detoxification and maintenance in people with addiction to opiates are often recommended, but it is well demonstrated that psychosocial interventions are necessary to address the factors that lead to relapse over the long-term, there are risks associated with using pharmacological interventions alone, and of course psychosocial interventions will be the mainstay of treatment for addictions to substances for which there is no pharmacological intervention (Amato *et al.*, 2011; Department of Health (England) and devolved administrations, 2007; Karen and Julie, 2022; National Institute for Clinical Excellence, 2007). There is some broad evidence for the effectiveness of psychosocial interventions such as motivational interviewing and CBT, and for 12-step programmes such as Alcoholics or Narcotics Anonymous (Perry *et al.*, 2019; Kelly *et al.*, 2020).

TCs specifically focussed on substance misuse have a different model to the one described in this book, although there is overlap, and they have a rich history and acknowledged evidence base, particularly within forensic populations (Perry *et al.*, 2019). However, one of the principal differences within these TCs is their greater emphasis on authority and consequences, which can have the result of excluding offenders with comorbid personality disorders who struggle to engage without the specialist support that the TC model described here can provide (see Chapter 3). However, simply providing the TC model without addressing the specific complexities of addiction or dependence on drugs would be ignoring the evidence base for treatment of addiction and setting many up to fail.

Treating substance use within a TC approach

Using an adapted approach, a group or individual intervention can and should be provided within the TC for those with substance misuse problems. To incorporate best practice and evidence-based guidelines (Department of Health (England) and devolved administrations, 2007; National Institute for Clinical Excellence, 2017), this should include:

1 Psychoeducation, including about symptoms, mechanisms of addiction and de-pendence, and issues around risks, tolerance and withdrawal
2 Addressing unhelpful beliefs and attitudes or false information about substance use
3 Learning about the links between substance use, violence and offending
4 Exploration of the links between mental health and substance use
5 Relapse prevention planning and strategies

The main purpose of the intervention is to provide the psychoeducation and the tools that are needed to specifically address the substance misuse.

At Millfields, substance use was addressed in a group, with individual sessions added when needed. The group was often plagued by challenges with non-attendance or other forms of disruption, and it was noted that these difficulties were strongest when drugs were suspected to be on the unit. When patients expressed problems with the group, it was rarely with the content or information provided (which they had often already received prior to coming to Millfields). Instead, problems arose when they believed that the information or strategies were ineffectual in preventing relapse, or that the real-world dynamics of substance use were unaddressed. This highlights that, whilst psychoeducation and practical strategies are very important, the dynamics and the deeper psychological processes at play must be addressed as well. It is therefore crucial that, as with all additional interventions in the TC, that what is learned in the substance use intervention, and the challenges that arise, are fed back into the wider TC so that they can be explored in the more psychodynamic therapy groups.

Dynamics of substance misuse between users and suppliers

It is rare that an individual within a custodial setting can attain and use illicit sub-stances without the involvement of others. Drugs can only make their way through tight security procedures usually with the involvement of a network of people. In a hospital setting, this could be an individual patient with community leave, who manages to bring drugs back onto the unit for himself and/or other patients who demand them. When security is more robust and well managed, or when demand is higher, the network often expands to include several different suppliers using drop points across the institution, to transport substances to different wards or wings. It is sadly not unusual for staff members or members of the public outside the institution to be involved, including visitors such as friends and relatives.

On the surface, this process and the motivations behind it seem straightforward: addiction fuels demand for substances and the motivation of financial gain drives suppliers to meet this demand. However, peeling back the layers and examining what is going on, there is often much more going on than initially meets the eye.

Some suppliers are pressured to bring in substances, and often these patients (or indeed members of staff) are in positions where they have achieved more freedom and responsibility, making them a source of authority to be tested. Many of those who end up supplying drugs in this way can end up following unhelpful examples from their own past. They may feel that they are 'helping' others by giving them what they feel they need, even if this is damaging. Alternatively, they may be gaining a sense of approval, admiration, power or acceptance through meeting the demands or wishes of their peers, or in some cases getting a thrill or some other psychological gain through being destructive towards others. In other words, they become the neglectful or abusive authority that they have experienced themselves. The psychoanalytic idea of 'identification with the aggressor' is useful in understanding this process, particularly for suppliers. In essence, the position of supplier/aggressor is preferable to what feels like the only other option: being a victim/user (i.e. 'identifying with the aggressor'; Frankel, 2002).

For those in the position of using the substances that they obtain from suppliers, they may really be searching for a person in authority who cannot be corrupted, who will look out for their best interest and not participate in their self-destruction. As a result, there may be a psychologically useful familiarity and a conflicting sense of triumph and disappointment if they succeed in convincing another to bring in substances for them. They are often suffering from symptoms of addiction such as cravings and withdrawals, or they may feel a psychological need for escape, punishment or self-destruction. What they are really seeking is for these difficulties to be truly understood and addressed so that they can live a more fulfilled life, but they are not able yet to trust and show the vulnerability needed to get genuine help. There is also a great deal of stigma attached to addiction and substance use, and the shame experienced by users can drive them repeatedly back to drugs as a short-term remedy for this shame, even if this makes it worse in the long run.

In this way, the issue of substance use for both users and suppliers is another avenue in which the dynamics of the original traumas and disasters in a person's life are replayed in the hope of a different outcome. Freud referred to this as 'repetition compulsion' (Freud, 1914).

Dynamics of substance misuse within the TC

One of the most corrupting elements of substance use within a forensic TC is that it is almost always shrouded in pseudo secrecy. This is because it is also almost always true that a majority of community members – whether patients or staff – 'know' about it. Some explicitly and clearly know, either participating in it themselves or as a bystander or observer. Many others know *something* is happening because of what they have noticed in others, and they can have a high degree of certainty that it is to do with illicit substances. Often this knowledge of the problem is present as a 'secret' in the community for some time, and when it is finally brought up publicly, even as a possibility, the reaction can be explosive. Denial of the problem, even for those who know with absolute certainty that it exists, can then be pervasive, leaving those who 'know' with less certainty filled with self-doubt, anger and frustration. If unaddressed, the issue can fester and repeat in this way for long periods of time. When the truth of the issue finally comes to the surface and is admitted or discovered in full, the anger on both sides is often amplified. Those with a greater sense of responsibility to care and look after patients can feel guilty, angry, impotent and tricked, whilst those who have been using or suffered because of substance use can feel neglected and let down.

> "Before prison I was isolated I used drink and use drugs, and I was a risk. I would target vulnerable people because I was so vulnerable, and I had a lot of shame around this".
>
> – Former Millfields patient

This process is made even more challenging by the culture against 'snitching' or 'grassing' that is pervasive in secure establishments and the social and cultural up-bringings of many patients (Pyrooz *et al.*, 2021). Offenders are expected to show loyalty towards their peers against the authorities, in what is often referred to as an 'us and them' culture. The TC culture is designed to combat this by providing a more humane, safe, helpful environment and authority, but the reality is that even a good service still sits within the wider criminal justice system where the environments and authority figures are too often lacking an orientation towards providing genuine help, trust or safety. Patients who are truthful and open about their concerns about substance use within the TC are at risk of being labelled as a 'snitch' or 'grass', and of having a disgruntled peer spread this information beyond the TC. If they then return to prison, this reputation could leave them vulnerable to social isolation and even violence. Users and suppliers of substances are also often accustomed to being removed from services and punished when their behaviour comes to light, making them fearful of the same result if they are honest about their actions. As a result, the TC needs to have enough of a sense of safety, cohesion and collective goodwill that members can trust that their honesty will not compromise their safety and future.

Winnicott's quote, "It is a joy to be hidden, and a disaster not to be found" (1971, p. 187) comes to mind when considering this dynamic. For those using or dealing substances, there is often a thrill and psychological gratification in the destruction of themselves, others and the TC. They are 'getting away with it', outsmarting the system, proving that they can meet their own needs and do not need others, relying on their familiar defences and ways of living that have felt crucial to their survival thus far. On the other hand, there is another part of them that is suffering, and they came to the TC to change and find a better way of living. Some have been so mistreated by their early caregivers and subsequent authorities that they learned to do things for themselves, but there is a wish for this to be different even if they find it difficult to trust that it could be. The trick is just as much a test - hoping that they will be caught and genuinely helped by a competent but compassionate authority.

Addressing the issue of substance use and supply in the TC

The best way for a TC to address and manage these dynamics is through its culture. Just as with offence-paralleling and other problematic behaviour, substance use must be a regular topic of exploration. Patients with substance use problems should be primed to understand that the TC has a culture of enquiry and reality testing (see Chapter 3) to help them, and that people will share their concerns about substance use when they have them. If they experience this as shaming, judgmental or frightening, and react negatively, this can be explored, but it will not (and should not) stop people from raising concerns when they have them.

It can be helpful to get patients with substance use issues to sign up to this process in advance, so that their initial intention to change, and their understanding that others will question them to help them achieve this goal, can be referenced and reinforced during times of relapse. This could take the form of a written contract stating their goals and their understanding of the culture of enquiry, as well as a commitment to more regular voluntary drug testing alongside mandatory testing. If these contracts are used, it is important for them to be shared with the whole TC so that everyone knows what has been signed up to and can participate in building up the culture and accountability that is needed.

It is also important that everyone is aware that relapse is common and expected in addictions; that relapse itself will not result in immediate expulsion. On the other hand, multiple, repeated relapses without efforts to change, and particularly repeated relapses with repeated denial and deception, will be more likely to result in removal from the TC. There should be an agreed process to follow after a relapse, which includes the individual going through a period of reflection and then presenting to the community his thoughts as to why the relapse occurred, what prevented him from being honest and making use of the support available in the TC, and what actions he will take to reduce the likelihood of relapse again in future.

Due to the pseudo secrecy and denial that often arise around substance use, even a TC with a strong culture can struggle to effectively address it. The denial, shame and outrage that can be expressed when concerns are raised about substance use can make it difficult for anyone in the community to face. For members of the TC (staff or patients) who act from a place of genuine concern and care for others, it can be very difficult to be accused of being unfairly judgmental or callous, and to manage the idea that they have unnecessarily caused conflict or distress. They must remain steadfast in their knowledge that the culture of enquiry is crucial to the effectiveness of the TC in helping its members; that ideas and concerns are not inherently dangerous or damaging.

Once a patient who has relapsed is honest about his substance use, he is still likely to struggle to be open about how he obtained the substances, particularly if this implicates others. Even if this barrier is never overcome, it is important that the TC addresses these dynamics, reflecting on the potential motivations of dealers and why many in the TC may be staying quiet or turning a blind eye. Unfortunately, in many scenarios, it will not be possible to learn the full circumstances of the substance use, and for many, it will be exceedingly uncomfortable to sit with this uncertainty and frustration.

This also means that those in positions of authority will sometimes need to make decisions based on incomplete or uncertain information, leading to complex dilemmas. At Millfields, this often came up with patients who repeatedly seeming intoxicated and appeared to subvert drug testing or other security measures, but consistently denied any substance use and became angry and offended when asked about it. In these cases, many staff felt that they 'knew' that substance use was happening, whilst others felt uncomfortable acting until they had hard proof. In some cases, this lack of action alongside continuous enquiry eventually created the right conditions for honesty and change. However, in other cases, it led to protracted substance use, the breakdown of the culture of enquiry and heightened destructive dynamics in the community that eventually put people at risk and compromised the sense of safety and containment in the community.

The only way to navigate these complexities and risks is to maintain the TC values and principles, whilst ensuring the needs of individuals are balanced with maintaining the therapeutic culture of the TC. Unfortunately, this means that some individuals will break boundaries and harm others beyond the point of recovery and will have to leave the TC. For users or suppliers of substances in this category, every effort should be made to help them understand what happened, what can be learned and done differently in future, and how they may continue the work either by returning to the TC in future or engaging in therapeutic work elsewhere. The message should not be one that reinforces the shame and stigma of substance use and reinforces hopelessness. Rather, the message should be that substance use and addiction (and, in the case of suppliers, offending behaviour) is a pervasive and challenging problem, that relapses are expected along the journey to change. However, there are consequences for relapses and sometimes behaviour is so damaging that time away for reflection is needed.

> "When I left Millfields I felt so let down and abandoned. When I was back in prison, I bought gear [drugs], and then again and then again. But then I said to myself that I promised myself I wouldn't let myself give up. And now here I am, I'm free [in the community]! It's not all easy. I don't have much money. But I have a job trying to help the homeless, many of them drug users, and I'm free!".
> – Former Millfields patient

Summary

This chapter explores the best practices and complexities in working with sub-stance use in Forensic TCs. To work effectively with entrenched difficulties, it is necessary to explore more deeply at the psychological factors and dynamics at play within and between substance users and suppliers, and to persistently work through silence and secrecy. To do this, the TC must have a strong culture of openness, trust and reality confrontation, and consideration must always be given to the balance between the needs of individuals and maintaining the therapeutic culture of the TC.

References

Advisory Council on the Misuse of Drugs (2016) *Diversion and illicit supply of medicines*. Available at: https://assets.publishing.service.gov.uk/media/5a81733ced915d74e33fe464/Meds_report-_final_report_15_December_LU__2_.pdf (accessed 27 January 2025).

Amato, L., Minozzi, S., Davoli, M. and Vecchi, S. (2011) 'Psychosocial and pharmacological treatments versus pharmacological treatments for opioid detoxification', *Cochrane Database of Systematic Reviews*, 9. doi:10.1002/14651858.CD005031.pub4

Department of Health (England) and the devolved administrations (2007) *Drug misuse and dependence: UK guidelines on clinical management*. Available at: https://webarchive.nationalarchives.gov.uk/ukgwa/20130123164248mp_/http://www.nta.nhs.uk/%2fuploads%2fclinical_guidelines_2007.pdf (accessed 27 January 2025).

Duke, K. and Trebilcock, J. (2022) "Keeping a lid on it': exploring 'problematisations' of prescribed medication in prisons in the UK', *International Journal of Drug Policy*, 100. doi:10.1016/j.drugpo.2021.103515

Fischer, B., Lindner, S.R. and Hall, W. (2022) 'Cannabis use and public health: time for a comprehensive harm-to-others framework', *The Lancet*, 7(10), pp. e808–e809.

Frankel, J. (2002) 'Exploring Ferenczi's concept of identification with the aggressor: its role in trauma, everyday life, and the therapeutic relationship', *Psychoanalytic Dialogues*, 12(1), pp. 101–139. doi:10.1080/10481881209348657

Freud, S. (1914) 'Remembering repeating and working through (further recommendations on the technique of psycho-analysis II)', *The Standard Edition of the Complete Psychological Works of Sigmund Freud*, 12, pp. 145–156.

Fridell, M., Hesse, M., Jaeger, M.M. and Kühlhorn, E. (2008) 'Antisocial personality disorder as a predictor of criminal behaviour in a longitudinal study of a cohort of abusers of several classes of drugs: relation to type of substance and type of crime', *Addictive Behaviors*, 33, pp. 799–811. doi:10.1016/j.addbeh.2008.01.001

Hall, W. and Degenhardt, L. (2008) 'Cannabis use and the risk of developing a psychotic disorder', *World Psychiatry*, 7(2), pp. 68–71. doi:10.1002/j.2051-5545.2008.tb00158.x

Her Majesty's Chief Inspector of Prisons for England and Wales (2014) *Annual Report 2013–14*. Available at: https://assets.publishing.service.gov.uk/media/5a7ed9eded915d74e33f2d10/hmiprisons-annual-report-2013-14.pdf (accessed 27 January 2025).

Katz, C., El-Gabalawy, R., Keyes, K.M., Martins, S.S. and Sareen, J. (2013) 'Risk factors for incident nonmedical prescription opioid use and abuse and dependence: results from a longitudinal nationally representative sample', *Drug Alcohol Dependence*, 132(1–2), pp. 107–113. doi:10.1016/j.drugalcdep.2013.01.010

Miglin, R., Bounoua, N., Spielberg, J.M. and Sadeh, N. (2020) 'A transdiagnostic examination of affective motivations for drug use', *Addictive Behaviors Report*, 29(12). doi:10.1016/j.abrep.2020.100279

National Institute for Clinical Excellence (2017) *Drug use in over 16s: psychosocial interventions*. Available at: https://www.nice.org.uk/guidance/cg51 (accessed 27 January 2025).

National Institute for Clinical Excellence (2017) *Drug misuse prevention: targeted interventions.* Available at: https://www.nice.org.uk/guidance/NG64/chapter/Recommendations#adults-assessed-as-vulnerable-to-drug-misuse (accessed 27 January 2025).

National Institutes on Drug Abuse (2020) *Common comorbidities with substance use disorders research report.* Available from: https://www.ncbi.nlm.nih.gov/books/NBK571451/ (accessed 27 January 2025).

Perry, A.E., Martyn-St James, M., Burns, L., Hewitt, C., Glanville, J.M., Aboaja, A., Thakkar, P., Santosh Kumar, K.M., Pearson, C., Wright, K. and Swami, S. (2019) 'Interventions for drug-using offender with co-occurring mental health problems.' *Cochrane Database of Systematic Reviews*, 10. doi:10.1002/14651858.CD010901.pub3

Public Health England and Department of Health and Social Care (2018) *Secure setting statistics from the National Drug Treatment Monitoring System (NDTMS): 1 April 2016 to 31 March 2017.* Available at: https://assets.publishing.service.gov.uk/media/5c3db2ee40f0b67c3973314b/Secure-setting-statistics-from-the-national-drug-treatment-monitoring-system-2017-18.pdf (accessed 27 January 2025).

Pyrooz, D., Mitchell, M., Moule, R. Jr. and Decker, S. (2021) 'Look who's talking: the snitching paradox in a representative sample of prisoners', *British Journal of Criminology*, 61(4). doi:10.1093/bjc/azaa103

Roberts, A.-O. and Richards, G.C. (2023) 'Is England facing an opioid epidemic?', *British Journal of Pain*, 17(3), pp. 320–324. doi:10.1177/20494637231160684

Trull, T.J., Freeman, L.K., Vebares, T.J., Choate, A.M., Helle, A.C. and Wycoff, A.M. (2018) 'Borderline personality disorder And substance use disorders: an updated review', *Borderline Personality Disorder and Emotion Dysregulation*, 5(15). doi:10.1186/s40479-018-0093-9

UK Drug Policy Commission (2008) *Reducing drug use, reducing reoffending: are programmes for problem drug-using offenders in the UK supported by the evidence?* Available at: https://www.ukdpc.org.uk/wp-content/uploads/Policy%20report%20-%20Reducing%20drug%20use,%20reducing%20reoffending%20(summary).pdf (accessed 27 January 2025).

Walter, M., Wiesbeck, G.A., Dittmann, V. and Graf, M. (2011) 'Criminal recidivism in offenders with personality disorders and substance use disorders over 8 years of time at risk', *Psychiatry Research*, 186(2–3), pp. 443–445. doi: 10.1016/j.psychres.2010.08.009

Winnicott, D.W. (1971) *Playing and reality.* London: Routledge.

Chapter 9

Individual work and how it is managed within a Therapeutic Community

Brittni Jones

Introduction

As explained in Chapter 3, the therapeutic community (TC) model is group-based and it is essential that there is a culture of openness: if the community is to function as 'doctor', as the agent of change, then it must have the privilege of information about residents and their internal and external experiences. However, there are times when this level of openness and trust is too difficult for some to achieve immediately, or when there are other mental health conditions or barriers to engagement that the TC cannot address alone. At these times, TCs for people with complex needs need to have the flexibility to offer some individual therapeutic work. There are also times when focussed, individual work is required to help patients progress or to meet institutional requirements. However, just as with small group psychotherapy (Chapter 5), it is essential that individual work is integrated into the TC, and this comes with complexities and challenges that require careful consideration and management.

Rationale for individual work in a TC

Specific mental health conditions comorbid with personality disorder

The most straightforward rationale for individual work in a TC is when a specific mental health problem requires an evidence-based treatment that cannot be reasonably provided by the TC core therapy groups. For example, a resident with marked obsessive compulsive disorder (OCD) or panic disorder may benefit from a course of cognitive behavioural therapy (CBT) to reduce his distress and symptoms. These types of treatment often consist of psychoeducation and skills or exercises to practise in a managed and graded manner, such as breathing techniques and exposure to triggers. Once the resident fully understands this process, the work can then be shared with the wider TC for further support.

This rationale becomes trickier to implement when addressing symptoms related to experiences of trauma such as hypervigilance to threat, negative perceptions of

DOI: 10.4324/9781032717302-9

self and others, mistrust, intense emotional experiences, difficulties mentalising or understanding others, dissociation, flashbacks and nightmares. There is a debate currently amongst clinicians about whether these types of symptoms indicate acute or complex post-traumatic stress disorder (PTSD or CPTSD), personality disorder or both (Cloitre *et al.*, 2014; Jowett *et al.*, 2020). The reality is that, regardless of diagnosis, trauma and the consequences of trauma will be part of the formulation of many, if not most, of the residents in a forensic TC for offenders with personality disorder. Often, the provision of a standalone treatment for trauma such as eye movement desensitisation and reprocessing (EMDR) or trauma-focussed cognitive behavioural therapy (TF-CBT) will not be sufficient to address resident's difficulties in this population, and the more intensive, trauma-informed (The Institute on Trauma and Trauma-Informed Care, 2022) TC treatment will provide the most promising way forward.

The TC model itself provides a relational, supportive and contained environment which should be ideal for stabilisation and treatment of residents with trauma. Through the introductory group for new members (see Chapters 3 and 16), residents are taught basic emotional regulation and coping skills, which they can then implement over time, supported by others. Residents then engage in the more intensive treatment and formulation process in which they build insight into their difficulties and the impact of their experiences, engage in supported exposure through talking through the events in therapy groups, and re-evaluate the beliefs and ways of living that have been borne from the trauma they experienced. Crucially, the TC living learning environment also provides constant opportunities for residents to try out new ways of relating and getting their needs met. Just as rewarding can be the discovery that they have many strengths and useful insights that have come from their experiences, and that they therefore have something to offer their fellow residents. With all these features, the TC treatment includes the basic elements of other discrete trauma therapies, but goes beyond them in terms of intensity, support, reciprocity and active learning.

Most residents in forensic TCs will have a complex presentation with personality factors that align more with personality disorder rather than PTSD or CPTSD diagnoses, and do not often suffer from dissociation or specific re-experiencing symptoms such as flashbacks or nightmares. However, when they are present, additional treatment for them may be warranted if the symptoms produce significant distress or are a barrier to engagement in core therapy groups. Depending on the training of therapy staff, they could include evidence-based therapies such as EMDR, TF-CBT, Narrative Exposure Therapy (NET; Bisson *et al.*, 2013; National Institute for Health and Care Excellence, 2018). It is again vital that these interventions are shared with the wider TC, in which further support can be provided.

Barriers to engagement in therapy

Another potential rationale for individual work within the TC is to address significant barriers to engagement in therapy. Many residents in forensic TCs will struggle with trust, shame, defensiveness, addiction and entrenched beliefs about the need for aggression or manipulation to get their needs met. The TC model is designed to work through barriers to engagement through intensive support in the form of modelling from senior residents and staff, gradual and supported progression over time and exploration of issues through intensive psychotherapy groups. Residents are also never forced to join or remain engaged in the TC; they choose to be there, and that choice should demonstrate some readiness to change.

However, there are cases where residents do wish to progress and change but find it impossible to do so within group treatments alone. For some, the intensity of shame around their index offence may be too great for full disclosure in the group environment from the start. This could be because of the nature of the offence or the victim (e.g. a family member or vulnerable person), or for some other reason (e.g. disclosure of sexuality or sexual deviance). Often the resident will feel able to disclose the offence category (e.g. murder, rape, assault), but unable to share particular details or the broader context. This is acceptable for new residents, but if it becomes an intractable problem, then individual work can be put in place to help the resident work towards full disclosure with the TC. This can include working on feelings of shame as well as their fears of being judged by others and can take the form that is the best fit between the clinician's qualifications in particular models and what works for the resident.

Another situation where individual work may be warranted is when residents experience such intense emotional reactions and defensiveness in groups that they are unable to stay in the room to receive constructive feedback from others; regularly become aggressive or engage in self-harm; relapse into drug-taking; or are persistently disruptive to the point where they are asked to leave (e.g. dominating the conversation, refusing to respond to the requests of the community meeting chair or staff members, interrupting or not following the rules of the group). If this behaviour is persistent and the resident shows little insight or interest in change, then this may mean that they are not ready for the TC treatment at that time. However, when they have insight and motivation to change but find it difficult to control their reactions, some targeted individual work to understand and work on the issue could be appropriate. This work may focus on emotional regulation (e.g. reducing reliance on aggression, anger, substance misuse or self-harm), changing entrenched beliefs about the need to defend themselves or control others, assertive communication skills or improving their capacity to mentalise or understand others so that they are able to recognise the constructive aspects of feedback in the moment it is given.

Specific training should have been done about how patients could vent out in one-to-ones but not in community groups, as it tends to wind up the people. Containment should be in one-to-ones. There is a limit on group work to hold patients, because it gets messy".

– Former Millfields patient

For these types of issues, there will often be frustration in the TC regarding the resident's behaviour or delayed progression in treatment. People may feel that too many exemptions or allowances are made for residents when they do not engage generally or, for example, disclose the details of their offences in the way that others are expected to. Many will feel impatient and frustrated with residents who are behaving in a way that is destructive, disrespectful or disruptive, and there will often be a perception that these patients take up all the time and energy in the group, leaving too little space for others. This is a real dilemma for the TC to address, and the professional team should regularly review the balance between individual needs and the functioning of the wider TC (see Chapter 20 for further exploration of these issues). It is helpful in these circumstances to ensure that the entire community is aware of the purpose and expectations of the individual work in overcoming and resolving these difficulties, and that the resident demonstrates a commitment to change and observable progress over time.

[I learned] self-control, how to manage my emotions in different circumstances. Everyone is different and you can't control how someone else will be. The small groups helped, and the one-to-one work, and the picture framing [activity group learning how to create picture frames]. Just learning how to manage from day to day".

– Former Millfields patient

Risk assessment and management

All residents will have some individual work around the development of their risk assessments (see Chapter 13) to ensure that the process is collaborative and thorough. Additionally, residents will need further support in assessing and managing risk if they are granted permission to spend time in the outside community (referred to as 'community leave' or 'section 17 leave' in UK hospitals), or if they are preparing for release. This work involves reviewing their risk formulation and thinking through the scenarios that could lead to challenges when they are outside the unit and how these can be addressed. Management strategies could include rules and monitoring that the resident needs to agree to follow (e.g. being escorted by staff, wearing an electronic tag, sticking to an agreed plan regarding where they will go and what they will do, being searched on exit and entry, being contactable on a mobile phone, complying with exclusion zones), and having a plan to follow if they feel distressed, triggered or at risk (e.g. calling the staff for support, returning to the unit immediately, practising coping skills, disclosing and working through difficulties in subsequent therapy groups). These assessments and plans can and should be spoken about in the groups, but individual work is often required to develop and document such a detailed and specific assessment and plan for one person.

A separate process will be needed to assess factors specifically related to sexual offending, particularly around issues such as frequency of masturbation and sexual preoccupation, interests or fantasies. These topics should not be automatically deemed inappropriate for group therapy spaces, but they must be considered carefully to achieve a balance between the utility of discussion, versus the potential distress caused by the resident to the other group members or the shame the resident themselves could feel on disclosure of such intimate details. Allowance should be made for maintaining the resident's basic privacy and dignity, particularly if such level of detail is not necessary for engagement in therapeutic work.

> Offence work can only be done one-to-one, otherwise I think people spend too much time defending themselves. People play the victim or try to turn staff to support them. You can have more honesty if people are confronted on a one-to-one, because they trust staff more and trust leads to respect and hope, especially if staff can see we're changing and give us hope that we are more likely to be released".
>
> – Former Millfields patient

Formulation

In addition to risk assessment, all residents will have individual work to collaboratively create their formulation and treatment targets at the end of their initial assessment period, and to share this formulation with the community. Further on in their treatment, they will also have individual support to write their own life story and formulation, incorporating what they have learned about themselves through treatment and their goals for the future (see Chapter 14 for a more thorough explanation of this process).

Treatment targets and goal setting

On a more regular basis (usually weekly or monthly, depending on the stage of treatment), residents will meet with staff individually to translate their treatment targets into specific short-term goals or steps. This process should draw on feedback and insights from the group forums, but often some individual work is necessary to come up with Specific, Measurable, Achievable, Relevant and Time-Limited (SMART) goals (Doran, 1981) and a process for monitoring progress, and to put these into a document. Once the document is completed, it should then be shared in group therapy forums for further support (see Chapter 14).

Care planning

In a hospital setting, there will be requirements for care planning to be completed individually for each resident by nursing staff, usually monthly. Care plans often cover in broad strokes the treatment targets and progress towards these, as well as any incidents that have occurred and how they have been managed. This offers the opportunity for residents and staff to collaborate on a plan for managing incidents when they occur. For example, what staff can say to help residents calm down and remember their goals or coping strategies, how staff can most helpfully respond if conflicts arise, and the steps for de-escalating and managing risk and aggression (e.g. staff will ask a resident to go to his room to calm down, pull their alarms if he refuses, take him to a safe de-escalation space, or – if all else fails and risk of harm remains high – restrain him and take him to seclusion). Care plans also often address physical health conditions and their treatment. Some of the information they contain will be relevant to share with the wider TC in therapy groups, but not all. For example, the wider TC probably does not need to know about medication changes for a resident's acid reflux, but it would be beneficial to hear a new plan for managing and reducing a pattern of evening conflicts with staff.

Challenges and risks

As highlighted throughout this chapter, it is important that the relevant and appropriate details of individual work are shared with the wider community, as this ensures the functioning of the primary method of treatment, the TC. However, particularly when working through issues that are barriers to engagement in the therapy groups, there is a need to first create a containing individual therapeutic relationship to address them. As a result, there will often be a genuine clinical need to preserve individual confidentiality for a period whilst this develops.

However, as the work progresses, many residents will understandably prefer the safety of a personal space and will resist it coming to an end. Therapists working individually may find themselves drawn into powerful dynamics which encourage them to collude with the desire to keep issues away from the wider TC. It may appear that the resident is always too vulnerable or fragile to cope with the group, or there may be fear about how the resident or other group members will react to them sharing details of their offence or risk factors. The TC membership may collude with this, allowing individual work to carry on for longer than planned, or unconsciously 'forgetting' to review or feedback the work.

On the other hand, people may be envious or suspicious of individual work that is granted to some and not others. As individual therapists will also be community members, attending community meetings and often also facilitating small groups, there can be complex dynamics that arise when there is an individual therapeutic relationship co-occurring within groups. There may be a sense that some residents are given special treatment, and ideas around favouritism or even inappropriate relationships. Staff are not immune to these dynamics and may also feel suspicious of what goes on between individual therapists and residents behind closed doors. This can have a destructive impact, both on that work and on the culture and functioning of the TC.

Whilst suspicions and even paranoia about individual work is usually unwarranted, there are justified concerns generated by the real risks inherent in working individually with serious offenders with personality disorders. Violence is a communication and a relational phenomenon, and the nature of therapeutic work is that it can often mirror earlier relationships and dynamics. This is what can make psychotherapy so powerful, as it provides the opportunity to experience those dynamics and triggers from the past, and to learn through here-and-now experience how to achieve a different way of relating. The group environment of the TC means that the dynamics, roles and patterns are held and contained by different individuals, and there are multiple people present to observe what is happening and offer perspectives and support. In contrast, the individual work environment can become intensely concentrated, with the individual practitioner bearing the full force of the resident's projections and transference.

If not properly supported and contained through supervision and use of the wider TC as much as possible, the risk of acting out between staff and patients can be heightened when working together one-to-one (Neumann and Gamble, 1995). Additionally, psychological injury such as vicarious trauma and burnout is a risk for mental health clinicians; this is increased when they are not working within a supportive system (McCann and Pearlman, 1990; Newman, Roche and Elliott, 2024; Vivolo, Owen and Fisher, 2024;). Burnout and work-related stress often lead to professional impairment which can not only be harmful to the member of staff, but also to those under their care and to the wider therapeutic environment (Everall and Paulson, 2004).

To manage these risks and complexities, it is essential that any decision regarding individual work is carefully thought through and monitored by the staff team as well as the wider TC. Apart from routine individual work (e.g. formulation, goal setting, care planning), no individual work should commence until all available methods of addressing the issues in group therapy spaces have been exhausted. Once it has been decided as a staff team that there is an appropriate rationale for individual work, both the decision and the rationale should be shared with the TC membership, and the ongoing work should be regularly fed back, with as much detail as possible about its salient aspects. This should be done in the same 'feedback meetings' where treatment groups (e.g. small groups, substance use group, offence-focussed groups) are shared with all TC members (see Chapter 5). This level of transparency helps to keep the whole TC membership included and informed about the work and reduces the sense of a 'special' or 'secretive' relationship being set up outside of groups.

It should also be made clear to any resident receiving individual work that they will be expected to increasingly share it with the TC, that it will come to an end at a specified time and that they will be expected to carry on the work they have done individually within their groups. They should also be aware that it is never kept secret from the staff team, and that it is regularly discussed in clinical supervision spaces. With all these caveats in mind, the group or 'outside' remains present in the individual therapy space, helping to reduce the intensity of dynamics and the inherent risks associated with them.

Individual therapists should be regularly supported in individual clinical supervision with an experienced supervisor, on at least a monthly basis, in addition to the mandatory weekly group supervision (see Chapter 18). Individual work should also be monitored and discussed regularly by the staff team to review progress and any complexities or difficulties that arise. This ensures that individual work remains a valuable adjunct to the TC treatment and that any destructive or counter-productive potential is managed appropriately.

References

Cloitre, M., Garvert, D.W., Weiss, B., Carlson, E.B. and Bryant, R.A. (2014) 'Distinguishing PTSD, complex PTSD, and borderline personality disorder: a latent class analysis', *European Journal of Psychotraumatology*, 5. doi:10.3402/ejpt.v5.25097

Doran, G.T. (1981) 'There's a S.M.A.R.T. way to write management's goals and objectives', *Management Review*, 70(11), pp. 35–36.

Everall, R.D. and Paulson, B.L. (2004) 'Burnout and secondary traumatic stress: impact on ethical behaviour', *Canadian Journal of Counselling*, 38(1), pp. 25–35.

The Institute on Trauma and Trauma-Informed Care (2022) *Trauma-informed organizational change manual*. Available at: http://socialwork.buffalo.edu/trauma-manual (accessed 22 January 2025).

Jowett, S., Karatzias, T., Shevlin, M. and Albert, I. (2020) 'Differentiating symptom profiles of ICD-11 PTSD, complex PTSD, and borderline personality disorder: a latent class analysis in a multiply traumatized sample', *Personality Disorder*, 11(1), pp. 36–45. doi:10.1037/per0000346

McCann, L.P. and Pearlman, L.A. (1990) 'Vicarious traumatization: a framework for understanding the psychological effects of working with victims', *Journal of Traumatic Stress*, 3(1), pp. 131–49. doi:10.1007/BF00975140

National Institute for Health and Care Excellence (2018) *Post-traumatic stress disorder*. Available at: https://www.nice.org.uk/guidance/ng116 (accessed 30 January 2025).

Neumann, D.A. and Gamble, S.J. (1995) 'Issues in the professional development of psychotherapists: countertransference and vicarious traumatization in the new trauma therapist', *Psychotherapy: Theory, Research, Practice, Training*, 32(2), pp. 341–347. doi:10.1037/0033-3204.32.2.341

Newman, C., Roche, M. and Elliott, D. (2024) 'Vicarious trauma and health outcomes in forensic mental health nurses', *Journal of Forensic Nursing*, 20(2), pp. 87–94. doi: 10.1097/JFN.0000000000000450

Vivolo, M., Owen, J. and Fisher, P. (2024) 'Psychological therapists' experiences of burnout: a qualitative systematic review and meta-synthesis', *Mental Health and Prevention*, 33. doi: 10.1016/j.mhp.2022.200253

Chapter 10

Pavilion, unstructured spaces, and the role of nurses and social therapists

Miguel Acha Gimenez, Jack Blake, Dean Bristow and Will Irvine

Introduction

Unstructured spaces serve as the backdrop for a unique therapeutic environment which facilitates spontaneous interactions and connections among community members. This chapter explores the theory supporting this approach, as well as what it can look like in practice. Embracing unstructured spaces and interactions involves inherent challenges, as the absence of predefined frameworks demands a fine balance between openness and maintaining therapeutic boundaries. However, when risks are managed, unstructured spaces and interactions offer vital opportunities for therapeutic growth and personal transformation.

Theory and value of therapeutic unstructured spaces

Within forensic settings, the staff who spend the most time with residents are usually those without formal therapy qualifications. In prison settings, this would be Prison Officers, and in UK-based forensic hospitals, it is 'Social Therapists' who are typically managed by qualified Mental Health Nurses (Bee *et al.*, 2006; Sharac *et al.*, 2010). This means that, in hospital-based therapeutic communities (TCs) like Millfields, the unstructured spaces are mainly the domain of the nursing team. These spaces, often taking place outside the working hours of the wider team, are used to build upon and incorporate what individuals have learned during formal therapeutic interventions.

This approach has considerable strengths, as it allows individuals with varying life experiences and a less formalised clinical style to support a patient's treatment. However, the TC model and the requirements of working therapeutically with severe personality disorders require staff members at all levels to take a more active role than might be expected in traditional settings; being intentional and thoughtful about their interactions with patients, as well as included in multidisciplinary team (MDT) discussions and taking part in clinical decisions. This is because the TCs recognise the therapeutic value of the everyday relational interactions and dynamics between staff and patients.

A key concept of group dynamics is that, over time, individuals within the group will automatically and inevitably resort to the relational patterns they have relied

DOI: 10.4324/9781032717302-10

upon in their everyday lives (Foulkes, 1971). Inpatient wards often develop into a microcosm of society (Hajek, 2007) whereby both staff and patients relate to one another based on their life experiences and belief systems. This provides an opportunity to be confronted with views, ideas and behavioural patterns that may be different from one's own and helps residents to consider how their own way of relating has served them or not in their life.

Offenders with personality disorders are often marginalised from society and thus have a skewed sense of the world and their place in it. The TC model offers an opportunity for patients to have this unhelpful perception challenged by giving them different experiences. The TC values of communalism, democracy, permissiveness and reality testing mirror the more helpful aspects of society and support the community to model prosocial ways of living (see Chapter 3), and it is within the unstructured spaces that these values and the culture of the TC have the biggest impact on everyday living. A main goal of the treatment is for this prosocial approach to be securely internalised by patients, reducing their sense of irrevocable exclusion and threat and thereby their risk (Wilson et al., 2014).

Unstructured spaces are a key element to the 'living learning' approach of the therapeutic community. For patients with severe personality disorders and a lifetime of disordered attachment, unstructured interactions with staff provide a unique testing ground for new ways of relating. Opportunities to experiment with trust, tolerating another's point of view, testing persecutory beliefs or repairing ruptures may feel easier over a game of basketball, for example, rather than in the high intensity therapy spaces.

These experiences can be referred to as 'corrective': in other words, patients' maladaptive ways of relating and insecure attachment styles can be altered where they are able to form more predictable and healthy relationships with other members of the community. Unstructured spaces inevitability produce conflict arising from confusion, miscommunication or transference related issues. But when these conflicts can be worked through, patients can experience reparation and change in a way they seldom have had the opportunity to do before.

It is often a challenge for those with severe personality disorder to relate to others as whole people, or what is referred to in psychodynamic theory as 'whole objects' rather than 'split objects' (Kernberg, 1966). It is therefore common that staff members become experienced as split off and an object for projected aspects of the patient's own inner world. A common split may be of the 'good self' into the psychiatrist, who is often seen as central to the patient's treatment. Alternatively, the 'bad self' may be projected into members of the nursing team who have to uphold boundaries on the ward and become experienced by the patient as incompetent or malicious. This is problem that mirrors what happens in patients' relationships at other times in their lives, with a tendency to see people as 'all good' or 'all bad', often misinterpreting behaviour of others as threatening or persecutory and responding with violence or other offending behaviour (see Chapters 1 and 2).

Unstructured spaces are an important arena to encourage patients to adopt a more integrated experience of professionals, other residents and themselves. For example, perhaps the opportunity to see one's psychiatrist getting the answer wrong in a trivia game (and seeing the humour in this!) can help patients seem them as human and relatable, rather than wholly idealised, powerful or threatening. Alternatively, having a nurse who enforced a boundary still choose to sit with you at dinner and be interested in having a conversation helps to humanise them and dispel the myth that they are completely evil or enjoy being mean.

It is common for patients to have longstanding suspicions of the motives of others, and they may find it impossible to believe that staff members have genuine, benign interest in them as people. Unstructured spaces in which people attend voluntarily are therefore essential in fostering a sense that staff and patients are indeed a community who have real positive relationships with each other. It is powerful for patients to see that staff behave in a way consistent with what is spoken about in therapy. This consistency is something that will have been lacking in their interpersonal relationships to date, and a sustained consistent experience of care can contribute significantly to a shift in relationship style (Adshead, 1998).

Winnicott (1971, pp. 71–86) also theorised that, through the addition of organic creativity and play, an individual can use their whole personality, thus allowing for the development and integration of the whole self. Unstructured spaces provide patients the opportunity to play in a healthy manner with each other, the nursing staff and the wider MDT. This can include appropriate humour and informal conversations, shared activities (e.g. games, watching films, sports, meals) and all the 'in-between' interactions that make up a normal day. These unstructured interactions allow for bolstering of the therapeutic alliance, ongoing assessment and review of progression in treatment, and live demonstration of (and opportunities to work through) the patient's continuing difficulties. Unstructured spaces are also a way of exploring the parts of themselves that have been heavily guarded or underdeveloped and can be hard to reach in formal therapy spaces. Concentrating on patients' healthier ego functions and aiding in developing skills also has an important impact on self-esteem and hope for change (Norris, 1983).

Unsurprisingly, patients will often find that positive play does not come easily or naturally. These men have had deep disturbances in their childhood and development, often with caregivers who lacked basic safety, let alone the ability to provide healthy opportunities for play. Many patients will have been subjected to play which appears harmless or fun, but then becomes unpredictably humiliating or dangerous. For example, a game of football between father and son begins enjoyably but ends with the father shouting and criticising his son for not playing well enough and then making fun of him when he cries. This type of repeated negative experience can lead to patients who have borderline character structures (Kernberg, 1967), unable to develop a full sense of self and splitting off the 'child' or vulnerable parts of themselves that they feel put them at risk of exploitation, humiliation or attack.

Thus, play can be not only difficult to engage with; it can powerfully activate a patient's defences. Suspicion, paranoia, subversion and other perversive means of relating to others, and ultimately how one plays, can contribute to either avoidance or corruption of play. Patients therefore often either engage in conversations or activities in a way which is dominating, competitive or passive-aggressive, or they may avoid being present in the spaces where play is encouraged by remaining in their bedroom on the ward and minimising their time in communal spaces.

Adaptations for individual differences and difficulties

A candid approach to the patients' pathology is crucial to making authentic progress within the treatment (Blake and Taylor, 2022). Patients tend to have highly distorted internalised objects, disturbed interpersonal relationships, and ineffective ability to mentalise or understand others (Livesley, 2001, pp. 572–574). In TCs, there is a heterogeneous group of people spending significant periods of time together, exposing patients to a diverse ethnic and cultural backgrounds, varied social classes and sexualities, and different attitudes and belief systems. This inevitably invokes strong anxieties and defences within patients, who often subscribe to the 'better the devil you know' mindset, preferring the familiar over the uncertain.

Men who have committed and been subjected to abuse and violence tend to see threat everywhere and consider others around them to have a higher potential for violence and harm than they are capable of (Blumenthal, Wood and Williams, 2018, pp. 44–61), leading to aggressive overreactions to perceived dangers and an unwillingness to trust that anyone can have good intentions. This volatility in the face of any perceived threat, a propensity to feelings of shame, humiliation and persecutory feelings, all further the interpersonal challenges within the TC. On the other hand, it also generates the bulk of therapeutic material.

> "Being in the Unit could feel constricting. Integrating with other people. Using other skills was rewarding, in tandem with therapy. I was very far down when I first started".
>
> – Former Millfields patient

Working with this group of patients requires understanding and respect for the individual and a holistic approach. The very nature of the patient's psychopathology means fragmented internal objects can be projected into others, and inattentive or inexperienced staff are at risk of identifying with these projections and becoming split in their own thinking, seeing the patient in a fragmented way as either 'all good' and vulnerable, or 'all bad' and powerful, therefore unknowingly playing out old patterns of relating which contribute to risk (see Chapters 2 and 18).

For example, a patient who experienced frequent childhood abandonment may behave in such a demanding and entitled manner that a staff member dreads and avoids them in unstructured spaces, provoking anger and aggression from the patient when their needs are not met. Through reflection and input from colleagues in supervision, the member of staff can identify that they have become the abandoning object to the patient's victimised part of themselves, an aspect of the relational dynamic which is often missed in traditional settings. Understanding of this dynamic provides opportunities to support patients to work towards greater insight and change, and more broadly reduces the risk of the therapeutic environment becoming retraumatising. A reflective approach to practice is thus essential and supported by the TC structures (see Chapter 18).

Unstructured spaces in practice

The TC is an environment which involves activities of everyday life as well as therapy. Like most residential spaces, there are communal spaces such as shared lounges and gaming spaces, laundry, dining and kitchen areas, outside spaces, and therapy rooms. Unlike more traditional settings however, TCs provide as open and accessible environment as possible, minimising locking of doors and requirement of constant staff supervision to what is absolutely required for safety. This helps to flatten the hierarchy at least within these spaces and allow for more authentic interaction. By necessity, some areas may only be accessed with direct staff supervision (e.g. spaces outside of the ward or using objects which could pose some risk like knives for cooking), making these spaces, by nature, more structured. The balance of free roaming and the need to interact with staff members within the TC allows for more variety of relational dynamics and opportunities for learning.

All members of staff should be encouraged to spend time in the communal areas to allow for unstructured interactions. This might be as simple as sitting on the sofa to be available for conversation, sharing tea or lunch, or playing table tennis. Not only does this provide more opportunities for learning, it also builds the therapeutic relationships and trust that are essential to successful treatment outcomes.

> "There was no favouritism, but rather egalitarianism. We could talk to who we wanted to. The social therapists took the time, which was a huge bonus that I had never had in my life before".
> – Former Millfields patient

In addition to these impromptu informal interactions, it is important to highlight the importance of the unstructured space by incorporating it into the weekly schedule in a more formal way. At Millfields this took the form of shared mealtimes and a regular Friday afternoon 'pavilion' time. Events would be held on a weekly basis in the pavilion area for the purpose of play and all staff and patients were encouraged to attend. Activities might be centred around food, sports, games or other activities such as karaoke or watching a film. Its position at the end of the week allowed time for people to wrap up the intensive therapeutic work of the past five days with more relaxed human connection and opportunities for reparation.

> "I think some of the other patients I grew to like, quite a lot in some cases. I had such a laugh at times, on a Friday ... we played Wii, pool, chatted and used the courtyard. I used to laugh so much with [psychologist]. I miss her a lot".
> – Former Millfields patient

It is also important for TCs to come together to celebrate holidays and significant events such as birthdays and significant milestones or achievements. Considering the often-ambivalent feelings towards their family members, friends and other significant relationships, many patients experience holidays and celebrations as painful and aversive. Whilst these types of events within the TC bring people together, they can also bring individuals back towards more uncomfortable aspects of themselves and narratives they may have rather remained repressed. As a result, patients may have to increase their engagement in communal holidays and celebrations over time, as their levels of trust and openness to new experiences and possibilities increase.

A major benefit of unstructured spaces is the lowering of the defence mechanisms that often impede engagement in more formal therapies. They allow patients to speak with members of staff they may not see as often in the ward environment or other unstructured spaces, to develop a deeper connection with them and ultimately foster a culture of curiosity. These 'unlikely encounters', where the patients meet reflective individuals they would likely never come across otherwise, further encourage patients to broaden their perspectives.

Considerations for staff from different professional backgrounds

Although unstructured spaces are a place to lower defences for the patients, it is important that this is not the same for staff. This is ultimately a therapeutic space and despite the nature of the space being very different from formal groups, the professional relationship between staff and patients must not be confused. For offenders with personality disorder, unstructured spaces are likely to become a target for subversion, corruption and undermining the therapeutic goals of the treatment. Additionally, the content of structured groups and other therapies within the programme can leak out into the unstructured spaces. It is crucial that these interactions are managed sensitively and safely and fed back into the formal therapy spaces to further the therapeutic work. This poses significant challenges for staff who must maintain consistent but appropriately flexible boundaries and keep in mind the overarching therapeutic tasks.

In an ideal world, all staff working in a TC will have rigorous training in personality disorders and attachment theory (Hinshelwood, 2002). Millfields provided all staff with tailored training, the 'Therapeutic Community Accredited Training', which provided the basic knowledge and skills required to understand personality disorder and work within a therapeutic community. In addition, all staff require clinical supervision and reflective practice and staff support groups to understand and manage the complex feelings evoked in their unstructured interactions with the patients (see Chapter 18).

Without this training and support, it is understandable that ward-based staff may retreat from unstructured spaces for fear of difficult interactions. For example, a nursing staff member who has had a verbal conflict with a patient may naturally wish to avoid interacting with them in unstructured spaces, and there may be times when, for reasons of risk or ward management, this might be necessary. However, it is essential to keep in mind that the patient is likely to experience this avoidance as a repetition of familiar acts of abandonment or rejection, and work to address this dynamic over time. With support for both staff and patient, they can be encouraged to continue to use the unstructured spaces instead of further embedding difficulties in the relationship.

> "Being in Millfields was like being escorted, reflecting about your life and other people's lives. A weird experience to have other people knowing about my experience. It helped me processing about my history and get more confident and positive".
>
> – Former Millfields patient

The nursing team often work with the occupational therapy (OT) team to facilitate patients accessing the library, gym and supervised use of the internet. Whilst there is usually a purpose for these activities, the time within the session can be negotiable and the goals of the session loosely defined. This means they often become forms of unstructured space with only one staff member and between one and three patients in a space away from others. One-to-one work is discouraged in TCs, but there are times where it is unavoidable, and unstructured time is the most susceptible to this. This requires staff to be thoughtful, not just about the interactions within those spaces, but how they impact on the wider group. For example, a patient who has three sessions in the library per week with an OT assistant might generate feelings of jealousy and suspicion among the rest of the group.

For non-ward staff whose interactions with the patients are more often through structured sessions, more proactive engagement in unstructured spaces is necessary. For example, psychologists, psychiatrists, psychotherapists and matrons all often have their offices based off the ward and have duties that require time spent away from patients. This limits their unstructured time and therefore increases the importance of prioritising opportunities to share the ward environment wherever possible. For this reason, the communal mealtimes are a crucial, daily unstructured space where all staff and patients can come together. Similarly, the weekly Pavilion and other social events such as leaving parties or holiday celebrations are strengthened by the broadest possible engagement from staff. The pillar of communalism is essential in mitigating against an 'off-ward', 'on-ward' staff split.

Boundary crossing and boundary violation – working safely in unstructured spaces

Whilst there are risks of overt violence and harm, the more common and often more challenging risks to staff are manipulation and corruption. This can be a slow process that happens largely in unstructured spaces and over time; and is the result of a series of small boundary crossings which can eventually result in irreversible boundary violations by either the staff or patient. Small requests to flex a boundary such as extending a library session by a few minutes can then lead to the expectation of extension. Where one crosses these boundaries without consequence, it can be easy to progress to other larger boundary crossings which could lead to security or personal risks or the inability of staff or patient to continue functioning in the TC. It is thus important that staff and patients alike remain accountable to the community and that relationship dynamics are always open to exploration.

Splitting poses multiple challenges to the community and is one of the central defences used by those with personality disorder. Within a TC, there are many factors at play that can put individuals at greater risk of becoming a split object. For example, witnessing conflicts between staff members can bring up memories and anxieties about conflict between caregivers in patient's early lives. This can elicit more primitive defences and powerful projections from patients, such as seeing one member of staff as an entirely vulnerable and good mother figure, and the other as a powerful and bad father figure. As the patient responds in kind to each staff member and, without exploration of what is really going on, staff members could start to identify with the content of the patients' projections, where the 'good' staff member confides in and advocates for the patient and indulges their wishes, and the 'bad' staff member becomes aloof and strictly upholds boundaries and denies requests.

When such splits and subsequent identifications with these arise, the dynamics within the unstructured spaces can become dangerous. It is therefore important to use the rest of the community and structured therapy and supervision groups to think about what is being played out. Where the unstructured spaces become detached from the community and are themselves split off and not spoken about, this paves the way to relationships between staff and patients which become untherapeutic and, at worst, significantly harmful.

In practice, this type of split might arise where a patient is viewed very differently by facilitators of his small psychotherapy group than the ward staff who are more exposed to challenging behaviours at night or weekends. The group facilitators will be in touch with a vulnerable and damaged side of the patient, whereas the ward staff will be in touch with the angry and damaging side. Unstructured spaces provide an important place for the patient to be experienced in a different way by all other members of the community, and work towards integrating these split-off parts of himself and his experience. It is a challenge to address such diverse views of patients, and it is important the community is thus setup in such a way that these can be heard, identified and worked through.

The way in which staff establish and maintain boundaries is increase or decrease the risk of serious splits developing. While some patients may actively test the limits of boundaries or try to break them (and this is part of the difficulties they are in treatment to address), others might not fully grasp the implications of their actions or enquiries and will just be exhibiting natural curiosity. It is therefore important for staff to clearly communicate important boundaries, but to do so in a way that does come across as shaming, belittling or rejecting. Humour or showing curiosity in turn about why a patient wants to know something and what different answers would mean to them can be useful strategies.

Boundary setting can be challenging to navigate in unstructured spaces where conversations are often freer flowing and without set tasks or aims. Staff should be supported through training and supervision to understand what topics can be discussed and what information about themselves can be revealed and what should not. For example, staff can reveal the music or hobbies they enjoy, the sports teams they support, and even experiences or ideas about life that are not high in levels of personal detail such as challenges faced, or lessons learned from their first experiences of work or education. Low level self-disclosure of this kind can help to build the therapeutic relationship and trust and is essential to the process of healthy exposure of patients to different life experiences and perspectives.

Self-disclosure which is more detailed in nature should be done rarely and only after careful consideration within supervision and staff support groups. Particularly at times of personal vulnerability with events in their own lives, members of staff can be at risk of identifying with the patients and treating them more like friends rather than maintaining the therapeutic relationship. At these times, staff members may be at risk of disclosing the things they are going through such as relationship, professional or financial difficulties, bereavements, or mental or physical health problems, and the purpose of this is to receive support or sympathy from the patients rather than to support them to reach their treatment goals. This type of boundary crossing damages the therapeutic relationship and makes staff at risk of increasing boundary crossing and violations over time.

> "For TCs to move forward, Millfields was a good example of how to approach therapy, however, at times the communication levels, for different reasons, meant there were issues on the ward".
>
> – Former Millfields patient

An essential aspect of maintaining safety in these spaces is to avoid 'lone working' – describing one member of staff in an unstructured space at one time with one or more patients. Operating within a TC where nursing staff are often working 12-hour shifts amplifies the frequency of opportunities for discussions, activities, humour and, ultimately, increases the risk of boundary crossings. It is the therefore the responsibility of any member of staff to be aware of their vulnerabilities and responsibilities, making use of supervision and staff support groups when needed, and to be consistently thoughtful and purposeful in their interactions with patients, particularly in unstructured spaces and when boundary testing occurs.

Whilst challenging, issues or conflicts around boundaries often present useful opportunities for patients to develop insights into themselves and their relational style. It can be helpful for members of staff to address issues as a collective, rather than relying on a single staff member's judgement. Avoiding solo-decision makers not only bolsters the treatment model, but it also helps to reduce and address splitting because all projections about authority or caregivers are not then channelled into just one person. It is also crucial that any issues like these that arise in unstructured spaces is fed back into the structured treatment groups for further exploration, holding both patients and staff accountable to the TC, and furthering the therapeutic progress of patients.

Summary

The utilisation of unstructured spaces within the therapeutic community framework at Millfields offers a unique and valuable opportunity for patients with severe personality disorders to engage in corrective experiences and develop healthier relational patterns. These spaces, facilitated primarily by the nursing team, provide an arena for patients to experiment with trust, challenge persecutory beliefs and repair ruptured relationships. Through unstructured interactions, patients can gradually internalise prosocial behaviours and reshape their attachment styles, fostering a sense of belonging and community. However, navigating these spaces demands a delicate balance between promoting therapeutic engagement and maintaining professional boundaries and safety. As the Millfields model demonstrated, purposeful use of unstructured spaces play a crucial role in the intricate tapestry of therapeutic interventions, contributing to the overall effectiveness of the treatment program and enhancing the potential for lasting change.

References

Adshead, G. (1998) 'Psychiatric staff as attachment figures: understanding management problems in psychiatric services in the light of attachment theory', *The British Journal of Psychiatry*, 172, pp. 64–69. https://doi.org/10.1192/bjp.172.1.64

Bee, P.E., Richards, D.A., Loftus, S.J., Baker, J.A., Bailey, L., Lovell, K., Woods, P. and Cox, D. (2006) 'Mapping nursing activity in acute inpatient mental healthcare settings', *Journal of Mental Health*, 15(2), pp. 217–226. https://doi.org/10.1080/09638230600608941

Blake, J.C. and Taylor, C. (2022) 'Examining influencers of treatment engagement by patients in an NHS medium-secure hospital treating high-risk offenders with personality disorder', *Therapeutic Communities: The International Journal of Therapeutic Communities*, 43(2), pp. 134–148. https://doi.org/10.1108/TC-07-2021-0017

Blumenthal, S., Wood, H. and Williams, A. (2018) *Assessing risk: a relational approach.* London: Routledge.

Foulkes, S.H. (1971) 'Access to unconscious processes in the group analytic group', *Group Analysis*, 4(1), pp. 4–14. https://doi.org/10.1177/053331647100400102

Hajek, K. (2007) 'Interpersonal group therapy on acute inpatient wards', *Groupwork: An Interdisciplinary Journal for Working With Groups*, 17(1), pp. 7–19. https://doi.org/10.1921/gpwk.v17i1.611

Hinshelwood, R.D. (2002) 'Abusive help–helping abuse: the psychodynamic impact of severe personality disorder on caring Institutions', *Criminal Behaviour & Mental Health*, 12(2 Suppl), pp. S20–30. https://doi.org/10.1002/cbm.2200120604

Kernberg, O. (1966) 'Structural derivatives of object relationships', *International Journal of Psycho-Analysis*, 47, pp. 236–253.

Kernberg, O. (1967) 'Borderline personality organization', *Journal of the American Psycho-analytic Association*, 15(3), pp. 641–685. https://doi.org/10.1177/000306516701500309

Livesley, W.J. (2001) *Handbook of personality disorders: Theory, research, and treatment.* New York: Guilford Press.

Norris, M.P. (1983) 'Changes in patients during treatment at the Henderson Hospital therapeutic community during 1977–81', *British Journal of Medical Psychology*, 56(Pt 2), pp. 135–143. https://doi.org/10.1111/j.2044-8341.1983.tb01541.x

Sharac, J., McCrone, P., Sabes-Figuera, R., Csipke, E., Wood, A. and Wykes, T. (2010) 'Nurse and patient activities and interaction on psychiatric inpatient wards: a literature review', *International Journal of Nursing Studies*, 47(7), pp. 909–917. https://doi.org/10.1016/j.ijnurstu.2010.03.012

Wilson, K., Freestone, M., Taylor, C., Blazey, F. and Hardman, F. (2014) 'Effectiveness of modified therapeutic community treatment within a medium-secure service for personality-disordered offenders', *The Journal of Forensic Psychiatry & Psychology*, 25(3), pp. 243–261. https://doi.org/10.1080/14789949.2014.908317

Winnicott, D.W. (1971) *Playing and reality.* 2nd edn. Oxon: Routledge.

Chapter 11

Occupational therapy, education, work and community leave

Helen Scott

Introduction

In the field of mental health, the concept of 'Recovery' has become well estab-lished. Within this model it is proposed that people can recover sufficiently from their mental disorder to return to living satisfying and meaningful lives (Jacob, 2015). However, for many of the men who arrived at Millfields, this model seemed to make an unfair assumption that they had a previously safe or satisfying life to return to. Working within Millfields Unit, it was often more appropriate to think about the process of 'discovery' for the men: offering them opportunities to dis-cover new ways of being, occupations to explore or roles they might consider for the future.

Role of occupational therapy

Occupational therapists (OTs) work with a wide range of conditions, through the use of meaningful and purposeful occupations for the development, improvement or maintenance of the essential skills people need to be successful (Townsend and Polatajko, 2007). Through occupational engagement, opportunities can be provided for developing identity, meaning and a sense of purpose, whilst also contributing to the community in ways that are socially valued (Christiansen, 1999; Kielhofner, 2002). The focus of the work includes all the activities considered important to the individual, and it aims at fulfilling fundamental needs such as autonomy, compe-tence and belonging. Many of the patients referred to Millfields had lived most of their lives in institutions, with their early years characterised by chaos, trauma and a lack of stability. As a result, by the time they arrived, they had either consciously or unconsciously sabotaged previous attempts at release. Other men, who had pre-viously been released, quickly returned to crime, resulting in them ending up back in custody.

Studies have shown that people with personality disorder, especially when in-volved in the criminal justice system, often find little meaning or satisfaction in their daily lives (Hill, Nathan and Shattock, 2013). For many of them, the pass-ing years have simply brought a perpetual cycle of lack of hope for a meaningful

DOI: 10.4324/9781032717302-11

future, combined with dangerous or reckless behaviour, which in turn cause more trauma and even more hopelessness. Further to this, acting in ways that are deemed unacceptable, illegal or immoral leaves them shunned both by those close to them and by society.

During the Millfields initial OT assessment, it was usually evident that some of the men lacked not just the domestic skills needed to take care of themselves, but also the social skills needed to relate to others. Due to chaotic experiences of family life and long periods of incarceration, some were unable to manage their finances, cook for themselves or look after their physical health. This, combined with their painful experiences of socioeconomic deprivation, discrimination or exclusion from peer groups, education and society had led to them feeling like failures, unable to live a fulfilling or prosocial life. Often the men's identities had crystalised around being an outsider, offender or prisoner, with little hope or self-belief for anything different.

> "I was usually locked up in a van overnight ... I wasn't even taught what toilet paper was for. From when I was seven, I used to run away all the time, sometimes for weeks. I'd steal food and sleep in alleys. I started at lots of school because we were always moving, but never for long ... I only learned to read and write in prison, when a mate taught me".
>
> – Former Millfields patient

Through this pattern of 'living on the margins' of society, many of the men never found a stable job or even productive ways of spending their time: life was about survival. This level of deprivation has been defined as "a state of preclusion from engagement in occupations of necessity and/or meaning, due to factors that stand outside the immediate control of the individual" (Whiteford, 2000). Occupational deprivation is the result of forces external to the person, such as families, criminal associates, or bureaucratic, cultural, political and economic systems (American Occupational Therapy Association, 2020; Whiteford, 2000).

Occupational deprivation can affect the person's whole life, through poor health (Miralles, Ramón and Valero, 2016), income loss, capacity atrophy and entrenched social exclusion. Unfortunately, despite the main aims of prison or secure hospital treatment being rehabilitation and risk reduction, the experience of occupational deprivation is often only increased by long periods spent in custody. Prisoners and patients are rarely given meaningful roles of responsibility, and the 'jobs' they are assigned are usually limited to menial tasks like cleaning the wing, which offer little mental stimulation or challenge. Even the increasingly common 'service user involvement' schemes in hospitals often involve patients in only a tokenistic manner, with important decisions being addressed elsewhere, or patient input being minimised or ignored. Not only is this lack of meaningful, inclusive involvement or work demoralising, but it also denies patients the opportunity to develop skills.

In fact, research suggests that living long-term in occupationally restricted environments like this can have an impact on moving on from institutions, including difficulty with acclimatising and reintegrating into community living, and difficulty structuring time in a meaningful way (Long et al., 2008).

This institutionalisation and lack of opportunity to develop life skills tends to reduce self-worth and the expectation that societal reintegration is possible (Farnworth, Nikitin and Fossey, 2004). Many of the men thus arrived at Millfields with a sense of 'learned helplessness'. This is the belief that through their repeated negative life experiences, lack of control and trauma they no longer have any power to achieve change (Carlson, 2010). This meant that many of the men had given up hope for a different future, and Millfields was often characterised by them as their 'last chance', the final time that they would try to change in the hopes of a different outcome.

A fundamental role of the Millfields OTs was to challenge this 'learned helplessness' and show how a different way of life could be possible. It was important that this was an individually tailored approach for each of the men, building on existing talents and interests and slowly developing self-belief. The OT assessments and interventions were guided by the Model of Human Occupation (MOHO; Kielhofner, 2002). The MOHO is a dynamic model where it is recognised that a person's occupational identity is impacted by their experiences, motivations and the environment surrounding them. Use of the model helps to explore the significant effect of these factors on their volition (motivation), habituation (habits, roles and patterns) and performance. For many of the men, experiences of failure and rejection throughout childhood resulted in an avoidance of trying new things, because they believed they would simply fail again. This pattern, established in childhood, often meant that as adults, the men would reject new opportunities or restrict their efforts to areas where they felt strong or capable (which, unfortunately, could often be violence and criminal acts). Trying new things, with the risk of failure, could result in crippling feelings of inadequacy and vulnerability. As such, they benefitted from OT assessments which identified their strengths and gave them confidence that they could succeed if they harnessed them.

One patient felt he had been a 'loner' all his life and was keen to stay that way – a stance he idealised as true, masculine independence. However, when elected to the role of Librarian, he took the job very seriously: another strong aspect of his character was his need for order, which he harnessed to catalogue all the books. Over time, he took a more and more active role in calling local libraries to ask for donations. He got another, nearly illiterate patient interested in reading by sourcing a book on his favourite topic: the ancient Egyptians. In this way, the Millfields OTs and Education Tutor aimed to offer patients the chance to develop the practical and social life skills needed for living successfully in the community. This was essential in order to achieve a fundamental aim of treatment: to develop a new, pro-social identity and the belief that a 'new' way of living was possible. Evidence suggests that occupational engagement can provide opportunities for developing a sense of identity, meaning and purpose, while exercising competencies and contributing to the community (Black *et al.*, 2019).

At the heart of the Millfields model was the goal of helping offenders to reduce their risk of harming both themselves and members of the public. Due to the evidence suggesting that offenders with personality disorder have higher rates of reoffending, and notably more serious violent offending (de Vries Robbé, de Vogel and de Spa, 2001), supporting this change is paramount. It has been observed that offenders who do not participate in prosocial activities, including employment, and positive relationships, but who instead participate in antisocial activities including gang affiliation and substance misuse are at higher risk of reoffending (Andrews and Bonta, 2014).

The role of OT fits very well within the Therapeutic community (TC) model, which encourages senior patients to take on increasing responsibility, and to provide hope and a role model for newer residents who might doubt whether change will ever be possible. A further way that the unit aimed to provide newcomers with hope and belief in the therapy was through encouraging ex-patients to return to the unit after their release to become 'experts by experience'; for example, as group facilitators in the 'Orientation to Therapy' group for those recently admitted. The inclusion of these former residents as group facilitators was a powerful and highly valued aspect of the treatment for residents. I t could be particularly helpful when the individual shared the same kind of index offence as the newcomer, for example a sexual offence. Not only did this help to break down the stigma around this type of crime for all residents, but one man in particular who was also convicted of a sexual offence, spoke about how seeing this man being accepted and valued for his experience, provided him with hope in a way that that no mental health professional could have done.

A strengths-based approach

With a focus on building skills and strengths, OT input at Millfields was based on The Good Lives Model (GLM; Ward and Fortune, 2013). This approach emphasises that, rather than only addressing criminogenic needs (i.e. offence related work), the focus of treatment should also be on the enhancement of offenders' abilities to obtain 'primary human goods'. They define these as a 'universal set of human needs' that comprises life, knowledge, excellence in play, excellence in work, excellence in agency, inner peace, friendship/relatedness, community, spirituality, pleasure and creativity. The GLM model is premised on the idea that we need to build capabilities and strengths in people, in order to reduce their risk of reoffending. Therefore, the intervention should be viewed as an activity that develops a person's ability to function, rather than an activity that simply removes a problem, or focuses on managing problems, as if a lifetime of restricting one's activity is the only way to avoid offending (Ward and Fortune, 2013). In line with this, the Millfields OTs tried to target some of these key areas, providing men with different opportunities to develop skills and enjoy rewarding activities, education and employment.

Protective factors

It is well-documented that offenders with personality disorders tend to experience worse mental and physical health, and a lower quality of life than other offenders (Black *et al.*, 2010). Through treatment at Millfields, the residents were supported to develop evidence-based protective factors, in order to reduce their risk of reoffending and improve their current and future physical and mental well-being. The aim was to assist them "to lead personally meaningful, purposeful lives, creating a positive sense of identity which reduces the risk of recidivism on discharge" (Cronin-Davis, 2017). In line with this, recent research has underscored the need for risk assessments to take protective factors into account. In the development of the GLM, Ward and Fortune (2013) defined protective factors as "strengths that can prevent individuals from committing violence by counterbalancing or weakening risk factors" (de Vries Robbé and Willis, 2017).

At Millfields, this work was supported by the use of the Structured Assessment of Protective Factors for Violence Risk (SAPROF; deVries *et al.*, 2014), which assesses protective factors for the risk of future violence and provides a holistic risk assessment when combined with the HCR-20 risk assessment tool (Douglas and Reeves, 2011). The SAPROF's seventeen protective factor items are divided into three scales: internal (e.g., intelligence, empathy, coping), motivational (e.g., work, structured leisure, financial management, attitudes to authority) and external (e.g., social network, intimate relationships, external control). Through the use of the SAPROF, goals are identified and included in treatment targets, to develop or bolster existing protective factors and therefore safer future living.

Many of the men in Millfields had very few protective factors apart from external controls, such as being in prison. Thus, therapy offered opportunities to explore life goals, work and leisure opportunities, as well as building skills such as budgeting. The therapeutic model of working alongside patients, or having ex-patients act as co-facilitators was very successful in combating negative attitudes to authority.

One service user spoke about how, for him, learning to trust in authority had been the turning point in terms of his rehabilitation:

> "In prison you couldn't trust people. Without trust I could not have done the treatment ... once I realised staff did support me, I started to open up about my problems ... I realised that people can still let you down, but I started to learn who I could trust".
>
> – Former Millfields patient

Treatment targets for residents often included exploring a new prosocial identity, incorporating protective factors such as developing new life goals, gaining experience of vocation and education and exploring structured faith and leisure time that was built into the day of the unit.

Structure

Through the therapeutic process, the men were offered opportunities gradually to earn more autonomy, gaining practical skills in organising their lives to assist in future community living. The Millfields week was structured to provide an experience of organised living, via planning and a structured routine. Mornings started at 9 am with a Planning Meeting, where all the patients gathered to plan their day together: no one stayed in bed, as one so often finds on wards for the mentally ill. The aim of this was to support sharing, taking turns and the facilitation of activities, building skills that would be needed in future to live in shared accommodation, run a household or participate successfully in a family or workplace. The Planning Meeting gave accountability to the patients to book with staff any sessions, appointments or off-ward activities they might have. This encouraged working together to think about staffing capacity and the needs of others. After the Planning Meeting, the mornings were focused on Community Meetings and Small Groups. The afternoons were structured around offence-focussed treatment, art psychotherapy, education, cooking, vocational work, sports, gym or community leave.

Cooking and cooking groups

An essential life skill outside of institutions is learning how to cook one's own meals, rather than relying on others, or having the money always to buy ready meals or eat out. As result, many of the men at Millfields joined a weekly cooking group, especially in their first year. Before starting the group, careful consideration would be taken of their risk profiles, including whether knives had featured in the offending history. When deemed appropriate, an OT would complete a cooking assessment to appraise skill and safety levels in the kitchen. This could also include some graded work focusing on use of a knife, especially if the person had a history of offending or trauma associated with knives. Working with the men in the kitchen could be emotive at times; for example, even the smells associated with cooking familiar foods could bring up memories of childhood, both positive and intensely negative.

One man did a series of graded exposure sessions (gradually increasing his participation in the group over time) in the kitchen, as he had no experience of cooking and associated knives only with using them against others, resulting in intense anxiety in the kitchen. Another man who had been in high secure prisons for many years told his OT that, after his cooking assessment, he broke down in his room: cooking a meal with another person and then sharing that meal has been the most 'normal' thing he had done in over two decades.

Following the initial kitchen assessment, the men would be added to a cooking group, graded for their functional level. Within the group, the men would be expected jointly to plan and cook lunch, which would then be eaten together with the group facilitators. This meant that the groups not only provided the opportunity for men to develop skills in cooking healthy meals, but also in the social element of sharing them with others. Many of the men who came to the unit had experienced significant neglect and abuse throughout their childhood and had rarely if ever experienced shared meals or home cooking. As a result, food was seen purely as necessary for survival, and not something to be enjoyed in a companionable way.

As the cooking group progressed, the men would begin to take pride in the meals they prepared, and able to respect social norms such as waiting until all members sat down before starting, or until all had finished before clearing the table. One young man had been fed like an animal as a child, and, at the beginning, could not even sit down for a meal with the others. He said of the cooking group that it was 'therapy he could understand'. Initially, he would eat in the room but standing at the counter rather than at the table with the others. He reported that his goal was to be able to eat with them, and one day have a family of his own who would eat together every night – something he had never in his life experienced. Eventually, he was able to take part in cooking the Christmas meal for the entire unit, perhaps 35 people, and to feel a real sense of belonging amid the festivities.

Vocation

Within Midfields, all the men were encouraged to take up at least one vocational role or job, separate to their core therapy. The unit worked on a semester system, with each semester lasting four months. Every semester the different roles were advertised, and the men would be encouraged to write an application for the one they were interested in. The OTs held drop-in sessions focusing on how to write a job application, including exploring previous experience and transferable skills. The men would then be invited to an interview where they would gain some interview practice, being asked a series of questions by a couple of the OTs or the wider therapy team. Following the interview, the men were given feedback as to how they had done in the application process and interview. This process gave the men multiple opportunities to develop and practice job application skills, including communication, and confidence in responding to questions in a formal situation. Many found this very beneficial.

> "it was pretty good ... it gets you prepared for the outside world. The interviews were not as in-depth, but the experience helped when I went for jobs".
> – Former Millfields patient

Examples of some of the vocational roles within Millfields included a picture framing project, librarian, social events organiser, kitchen worker (serving meals), magazine editor and a range of cleaning jobs. Later in treatment, the men could also apply for paid work in the cafes within the wider hospital, or even in service-user run cafes in the

TC. All the different vocational roles within the unit contributed to the running of the community – a parallel of what happens in the outside world. Being able to contribute to society has been shown to be integral to the desistance and recovery process, which involves a transition from the old identity of 'criminal' to the new one of working person or 'breadwinner' (Connell *et al.*, 2019). Thus, there was a focus on exploring different roles in order to develop a new concept of self, or 'who I am'.

The OT team supported men in holding different roles based on both merit in the selection process, and quality and consistency in their execution: anyone neglecting his duties would be encouraged and supported but ultimately could be fired. Finding a meaningful and rewarding occupation, paid or voluntary, was an explicit treatment target for most. After leaving Millfields, one man reflected on his experience of being the activities co-ordinator, which required both persistence and social skills – for example, when garnering support for his suggested programme of activities over the Christmas period:

> "I didn't really want to do it at the start as I didn't have any confidence. But the job challenged me and did help me build confidence over time".
>
> – Former Millfields patient

A further example of this path towards a new identity included encouraging one man to apply for the role of magazine editor, after he had been working hard in education for the previous year, focusing mainly on his literacy and computer skills. This man, who was then in his sixties, had spent most of his adult life in prison and had never used a computer. Over time, he began to take real pride in designing illustrations and editing articles for the Millfields Chronicle, and in sharing the finished edition with all the members of the TC.

For another man, working in the picture framing project was about much more than just vocational skills:

> "The bonding helped you build relationships and trust others to help. When there were issues you would work with others to think of different solutions. It helped me think in different ways ... for me, relying on others and trust was a problem. We worked together to get things done ... we could use the space to talk about other things too".
>
> – Former Millfields patient

Education

Education was recognised as intrinsic to the rehabilitation process for the men. There was a designated Education Tutor who was an integral part of the TC structure, balancing attending community meetings with running a range of individual and group classes. For most of the men who came to the unit, early experiences of education were shrouded in shame and a sense of failure. Many had been let down by the school system, being expelled or just dropping out, often almost unnoticed, with minimal or no qualifications. They were reluctant to join group classes, as they did not want to reveal to their peers how much they struggled, for example, with reading simple texts. A surprising number had only learned to read in prison, either by themselves or being taught by a fellow inmate. A very small and informal 'Reading Aloud' group helped some to graduate from individual sessions to a group setting. The tutor also worked with those men who were granted community leave, to help them become sufficiently proficient to survive in modern society, and not to be ashamed to ask for help when it was needed.

One man spoke about how important education had been in his treatment at Millfields. Like the patient in the previous example, he also first started working with the tutor to learn how to use the computer. Over time, he progressed all the way to attending a local college, with the Education Tutor accompanying him for the first few classes. He was eventually proud to pass two courses in Information and Communication Technology (ICT) skills. He reflected that having the structure of going to college on a weekly basis provided much support for his routine, as he gradually found his feet and grew in confidence in the outside world. Another man spoke about how working with the Education Tutor helped him when they completed a dyslexia assessment. He reflected that having the cause of his difficulties officially confirmed removed a great deal of the shame he was carrying around with him. He went on to learn strategies to overcome them, which helped him to see his dyslexia 'not as a label but as a strength' because it led to greater self-awareness.

Community reintegration

For some of the men in the unit, the route to living in the community was through being discharged directly from Millfields, rather than being remitted to prison (usually to a Psychologically Informed Planned Environment or PIPE; Turley, Payne and Webster, 2013). These men undertook carefully graded community leave that was focussed on achieving reintegration – or simply integration for the first time for those who had never felt they were a legitimate or worthwhile part of society. The transition from hospital to the community is notoriously difficult and carries a high risk of self-harm and suicide (Owen-Smith *et al.*, 2014), or of reoffending. Another common pattern is that of suddenly starting to break the rules again, just prior to discharge, to avoid the terror of having to leave the institution. As a result, these men required intensive support as they approached potential discharge. Before starting community leave, the men would be encouraged to explore their hopes and fears about reconnecting with society, and to contribute to a robust risk management plan. The latter included scenarios considering what could go wrong, for example, getting lost or dealing with a rude member of the public. A Community Living Skills checklist was developed, so that possible challenges could be thought about systematically. The first few leaves were always facilitated by one of the OTs, who would conduct a robust assessment of strengths and gaps in knowledge or skills. This included areas such as road safety awareness, travel skills and social interactions. I also considered how safe or confident the men would feel when they were eventually granted unescorted leave and might, for example, be offered drugs or have their wallet stolen.

For many of the men, community leave meant there were new skills to be learnt. These included familiarisation with the local area and using new (to them) technology such as self-service check out tills, touch screens and card payments rather than cash for bus fares. These early leaves progressed at a slow and graded pace, with a focus on learning and gaining confidence. Many of the men reported considerable anxiety about being outside the unit, especially after very long periods of incarceration: the volume of traffic and sheer numbers of people on crowded tube trains (in London) or buses could feel daunting.

> "My first leave was very overwhelming; I went with the OT. He knew to check-in with me, but I was really nervous after not being out for twenty-five years ... I was worried about all the cars and crossing the road. As I got more leave, I realised that so much has changed, like Oyster cards (for paying fares) and smart phones. Over the next year I slowly set up things like a bank account and got a phone. The Education Tutor helped me download all the apps and learn how to use FaceTime with my family".
>
> – Former Millfields patient

Many of the men reflected on the sensations they experienced: the noise and hustle and bustle of being on a busy East London high street could be intimidating at first. The smells of cannabis or alcohol could bring back strong memories or cravings, depending on the person's history. For some of the men, the challenge of identity came up: one individual who had been locked up for over thirty years spoke about how scared he was about being outside as a changed person and trying out new ways of living. He was anxious to cope with situations without resorting to any of his old patterns of behaviour. This man had a reputation for extreme violence in the past and now found situations such as being bumped into by a group of teenagers unnerving, as he could no longer use aggression to resolve conflict or maintain his status. During therapy groups following his leaves, he would reflect on how he used to command respect on the streets through fear, which now sat in conflict with his desire to live a 'different, straight life'. Another difficult part of exploring his identity in the community included the fact he was now a much older man. He was no longer physically capable of using his body to intimidate through conveying strength, as he had previously.

For those who had grown up locally, returning to the area and seeing the changes that had taken place over the last twenty or thirty years could be an emotional shock. Some of the men had lost parents or loved ones whilst incarcerated, so visiting specific neighbourhoods, including graveyards, could bring up difficult emotions including loss, shame and regret. For some, returning to the location of their index offence, if allowed, could evoke both profound guilt and traumatic memories. As part of the process, these more challenging leaves would be planned and prepared for by the whole clinical team, as well as supported on return through the exploration of the whole experience in the community meetings and small groups.

As the men moved through the process of reintegration, they would be encouraged to consider how they might develop a new role in the community, shifting the focus of their rehabilitation from inside the hospital to the outside world. Some worked on repairing relationships with family members – with the help of formal family therapy if warranted – while others took on voluntary jobs helping the disadvantaged. For example, for several Christmases in a row, a few of the patients worked at Crisis, a UK charity for the homeless. There is a growing body of evidence, both personal and from research studies, that helping others improves mental health, happiness and wellbeing (e.g. Post, 2014).

One man reflected that the process of his community reintegration was 'hard work'. He spoke about how he wanted to move much faster than his treating team thought wise:

> "I'd been away for such a long time, and I was in a rush ... it took me over a year to get unescorted leave. It was hard work, but the therapy helped me to heal".
> – Former Millfields patient

He slowly developed a routine: going to college, visiting the local Sikh temple several times a week, volunteering and shopping with a few of his peers. After leaving hospital, he reflected on how important building this structure was:

> "Without college and the temple, I could see how I might get bored and restless like when I was younger".

This boredom and restlessness had led to high levels of drinking and ultimately to repeated, escalating sexual offending.

Men with leave were invited to join the weekly community gym group. For many of them, going to the gym had been one of the few reliable and consistent activities available to them as they moved through different prisons or hospitals. Supporting them to continue this habit, with an emphasis on health rather than building intimidating strength, was often crucial for maintaining their sense of self-worth, for managing stress and for building friendships. One area of particular challenge for the unit was whether to apply (to the Ministry of Justice) for community leave for men who would be returning to prison after their treatment at Millfields. Due to the length of their sentences, some who came to the unit would have to return to custody to progress through the lower category prisons and gain release from there.

Ultimately, we felt it would be beneficial for some to initiate this community reintegration and skills acquisition work at Millfields, even though they would lose their leave as soon as they were back in prison. One man, for example, had extreme social anxiety and a long history of substance misuse: he had used drugs since he was a child to manage difficult feelings, especially fear and distress. An application for community leave was successfully submitted for him, so he could complete some graded work alongside his substance misuse programme, to build his confidence and self-belief in being able to manage without drugs. Another man was granted community leave to help him further develop an identity distinct from being an 'offender'. However, when it was granted, he began to struggle with the rules and limits of the leave. He pushed boundaries, including by walking away from his escort, or wanting to change the agreed plan whilst he was out. After a while, he was able to talk about how difficult and tantalising it was to have a 'taste of freedom', knowing that ultimately, he would have to return to prison.

For a few of the men, it was possible to stay in hospital to complete treatment and have their parole hearing there, rather than return to prison.

> "It was important for me that I didn't go back – in prison I could never trust people. You can't open up. If I had gone back, it would have affected me, I would have put my guard back up and become paranoid".

The process of trying to explore and develop new, prosocial roles within Millfields was always a challenge. Having the hope that they might leave through the hospital route and be supported with mental health accommodation on discharge allowed men with that pathway to engage more fully with the treatment. For others, starting to develop new ways of coping through talking openly, or trying new roles, seemed an impossible task when faced with returning to the prison estate. These men would talk about the risk of lowering their defences or allowing any vulnerability to show, which they felt would be impossible to maintain if they were to return to the harshness of a custodial environment. For the OTs working with the men, the aim was that they would leave with some improved skills, and with the confidence that they had been able to try something new and succeed. This experience of accomplishment encouraged many to take chances and set ambitious goals for the future.

References

American Occupational Therapy Association (2020). *Occupational therapy practice framework: domain et process* (Vol. 74, No. 7412410010). Bethesda, MD, USA: American Occupational Therapy Association. https://doi.org/10.5014/ajot.2020.74S2001

Andrews, D.A. and Bonta, J. (2014) *The psychology of criminal conduct*. London: Routledge.

Black, D.W., Gunter, T., Loveless, P., Allen, J. and Sieleni, B. (2010) 'Antisocial personality disorder in incarcerated offenders: psychiatric comorbidity and quality of life', *Annals of Clinical Psychiatry*, 22, pp. 113–120.

Black, M.H., Milbourn, B., Desjardins, K., Sylvester, V., Parrant, K. and Buchanan, A. (2019) 'Understanding the meaning and use of occupational engagement: findings from a scoping review', *British Journal of Occupational Therapy*, 82(5), pp. 272–287. https://doi.org/10.1177/0308022618821580

Carlson, N.R. (2010) *Psychology: the science of behavior*. Pearson Canada. p. 409.

Christiansen, C.H. (1999) 'Defining lives: occupation as identity: an essay on competence, coherence, and the creation of meaning', *The American Journal of Occupational Therapy*, 53(6), pp. 547–558. http://dx.doi.org/10.5014/ajot.53.6.547

Connell, C., McKay, E.A., Furtado, V. and Singh, S.P. (2019) 'People with severe problematic personality traits and offending histories: what influences occupational participation?, *European Psychiatry*, 60, pp. 14–19. http://dx.doi.org/10.1016/j.eurpsy.2019.05.002

Cronin-Davis, J. (2017) 'Forensic mental health: creating occupational opportunities', *Occupational Therapy Evidence in Practice for Mental Health*, pp. 139–163. http://dx.doi.org/10.1002/9781119378785.ch7

de Vries Robbé, M., de Vogel, V. and de Spa, E. (2011) 'Protective factors for violence risk in forensic psychiatric patients: a retrospective validation study of the SAPROF', *International Journal of Forensic Mental Health*, 10(3), pp. 178–186. http://dx.doi.org/10.1080/14999013.2011.600232

de Vries Robbé, M. and Willis, G.M. (2017) 'Assessment of protective factors in clinical practice', *Aggression and Violent Behavior*, 32, pp. 55–63.

Douglas, K.S. and Reeves, K.A. (2011) 'Historical-Clinical-Risk Management-20 (HCR-20) Violence Risk Assessment Scheme: rationale, application, and empirical overview', in Otto, R.K. and Douglas, K.S. (eds.) *Handbook of violence risk assessment*. Routledge, pp. 157–196.

Farnworth, L., Nikitin, L. and Fossey, E. (2004) 'Being in a secure forensic psychiatric unit: every day is the same, killing time or making the most of it', *British Journal of Occupational Therapy*, 67(10), pp. 430–438. http://dx.doi.org/10.1177/030802260406701003

Hill, J., Nathan, R. and Shattock, L. (2013) *Report of a pilot randomized controlled trial of an intensive psychosocial intervention for high risk personality disordered offenders (the Resettle programme)*, Unpublished manuscript, University of Manchester.

Jacob, K.S. (2015) 'Recovery model of mental illness: a complementary approach to psychiatric care', *Indian Journal of Psychological Medicine*, 37(2), pp. 117–119. http://dx.doi.org/10.4103/0253-7176.155605

Kielhofner, G. (2002) *A model of human occupation: Theory and application*. Lippincott Williams & Wilkins.

Long, C., McLean, A., Boothby, A. and Hollin, C. (2008) 'Factors associated with quality of life in a cohort of forensic psychiatric in-patients', *The British Journal of Forensic Practice*, 10(1), pp. 4–11. http://dx.doi.org/10.1108/14636646200800002

Miralles, P.M., Ramón, N.C. and Valero, S.A. (2016) 'Adolescents with cancer and occupational deprivation in hospital settings: a qualitative study', *Hong Kong Journal of Occupational Therapy*, 27(1), pp. 26–34. http://dx.doi.org/10.1016/j.hkjot.2016.05.001

Owen-Smith, A., Bennewith, O., Donovan, J., Evans, J., Hawton, K., Kapur, N., O'Connor, S. and Gunnell, D. (2014) 'When you're in the hospital, you're in a sort of bubble', *Crisis*. http://dx.doi.org/10.1027/0227-5910/a000246

Post, S.G. (2014) 'Altruism, happiness, and health: it's good to be good', in *An exploration of the health benefits of factors that help us to thrive*, pp. 66–76. http://dx.doi.org/10.1207/s15327558ijbm1202_4

Townsend, E.A. and Polatajko, H.J. (2007) *Advancing an occupational therapy vision for health, well-being, and justice through occupation*. Ottawa, ON: Canadian Association of Occupational Therapists Publications.

Turley, C., Payne, C. and Webster, S. (2013) *Enabling features of psychologically informed planned environments*. London: National Offender Management Service.

Ward, T. and Fortune, C.A. (2013) 'The good lives model: aligning risk reduction with promoting offenders' personal goals', *European Journal of Probation*, 5(2), pp. 29–46. http://dx.doi.org/10.1177/206622031300500203

Whiteford, G. (2000) 'Occupational deprivation: global challenge in the new millennium', *British Journal of Occupational Therapy*, 63(5), pp. 200–204. http://dx.doi.org/10.1177/030802260006300503

Chapter 12

Assessment and selection for treatment

Jack Blake and Celia Taylor

The assessment process can never result in perfect patient selection, so it is important to bear in mind that the person's time in therapy might indeed not go smoothly, and if things do go wrong, what the consequences might be for him and those around him. Not managing to complete treatment is a deeply disappointing and demoralising experience for people who have had a lifetime of being regarded as serial failures. So-called 'drop-outs' have worse clinical outcomes, including ongoing distressing symptoms and having to spend much longer in treatment in future (Hansen, Lambert and Forman, 2002) – or, indeed prison, if personality disorder treatment is part of the sentence plan and thus obligatory in order to secure freedom. The breakdown of treatment can lead to severe acting out behaviour, including aggression towards the self, and/or to others. Those who do not complete treatment have higher rates of reoffending compared to those who do not start treatment at all, even if the initial risk of reoffending is similar (McMurran and Theodosi, 2007). As this last finding implies, there is a considerable financial and societal cost associated with incomplete treatment, because of longer subsequent periods of incarceration (Sampson *et al.*, 2013).

The referral process

From the earliest days, we welcomed referrals from all relevant organisations, such as prisons, probation officers, secure mental health services and occasionally commissioners. The vagaries of the UK Mental Health Act influenced our decision-making, as patients detained under a Hospital Order (Section 37/41 or Section 37 of the UK Mental Health Act) cannot be returned to prison even if they drop out of treatment entirely, and it is often extremely problematic to find an alternative health-based service willing to accept them. Over time, the commissioners decided that the focus of NHS Offender Personality Disorder (OPD) services needed to be on supporting the criminal justice system and from then on, we accepted only transfers from prison of individuals serving a sentence sufficiently long that it would not expire until after treatment had ended.

Referrals are the life blood of a unit, so it is important to send out a thoughtful summary of the purpose and aspirations of the service, which can be read – and understood – by professionals and prospective admissions alike. Ideally, it will be

DOI: 10.4324/9781032717302-12

written in collaboration with the current patients. More than one person we accepted said, with a sense of shock, that he recognised himself in our description of the difficulties our patients face in their lives. In other words, he felt that we understood something about him before we had even met. The information pack should also give clear criteria for acceptance, a description of the treatment model and expectations of engagement, the approximate length of stay and up-to-date contact details so that referrers can call and discuss cases they might be uncertain about.

Millfields referrals process

- Once a written referral is received, obtain background reports
- Complete a screening checklist to identify any obvious exclusion criteria
- Send an information pack to the referrer and prisoner
- Arrange assessment interview by senior psychiatrist or psychologist
- Discussion in multidisciplinary referrals meeting
- Proceed to nursing assessment
- Final discussion in referrals meeting: a consensus must be reached before accepting the individual
- Discussion in hospital's directorate admissions panel
- Formal letter of acceptance, including copies of the assessment reports sent to referrer and prisoner. Consider including condition of return if treatment is unsuccessful
- Mental Health Act detention papers completed by prison
- Admission agreed by Ministry of Justice Mental Health Casework Section

---

Examples of individual complexities that will need to be thought through include prisoners appealing their conviction or sentence, and those denying their index offence altogether. The former might not accept aspects of his offending, while the latter have rejected responsibility altogether, both of which could significantly undermine the clinical work. On the other hand, one purpose of Millfields was to offer help to people with problematic presentations, and we had examples of success with both groups. One transferred prisoner gained his release by a parole board after spending 40 years in prison denying his index offence. Sometimes, the decision to admit will depend on the patient mix and levels of stress experienced by staff: severe, repeated self-harm might not be manageable if a current patient has the same difficulty, while the presence of more than a small proportion of patients with psychopathic traits could engulf the service in corruption and scandal. There is a balance to be struck between admitting the most disturbed patients with greater needs, or those most likely to work well, and a reasonably high proportion of established and engaged residents is essential for preserving the culture of the unit.

Our inclusion and exclusion criteria are shown in the box below. Most of the latter relate to whether or not the person is able to work within a complex and intensive, integrated psychological therapy programme: we fully recognise that those who cannot also need help, but would recommend referral to a highly specialised service, such as the therapeutic community Plus at HMP Grendon for prisoners with learning disabilities. We took the decision early on not to accept individuals with paedophilic psychopathology, because so many of our patients had been sexually abused as children. It was already extremely challenging for them to be required to attend groups with peers who had committed sex offenders against adults, let alone with offenders against children. We were also acutely aware of the risk of serious violence towards child sex offenders that can be extremely difficult to predict.

Millfields inclusion and exclusion criteria

Inclusion criteria

- Adult males
- Primary diagnosis of personality disorder
- Serving a prison sentence
- History of serious offending/posing a high risk to others
- Able and willing to engage in treatment
- Treatment needs can only be met in hospital

Exclusion criteria

- A co-morbid mental illness that is too severe to engage in intensive psychological therapy.
- Severe Autistic Spectrum Disorders
- Organic brain damage
- IQ below 70
- Sexual offenders with paedophilic psychopathology
- Those who refuse to engage in treatment
- Referrals for emergency assessment or admission

Unusually perhaps, we welcomed 'self-referrals' – prisoners who wrote in asking to be considered for admission. Such letters could come from a place of hope after hearing about the unit by word of mouth, or from a place of near despair of ever receiving help. Most had been labelled as 'untreatable'.

"I committed a murder and am doing a life sentence for that crime. It was a terrible thing that I did and the sentence was correct. Looking back on that fearful night, I realise it was only a matter of time before I snapped".

Each letter was responded to individually, in recognition of its importance to the writer, and sometimes several letters were exchanged, in order to foster the beginnings of trust and of confidence in our reliability.

All who were referred, or who themselves asked for an assessment, were sent a psycho- dynamically-informed questionnaire about their early experiences and the trajectory of their lives: what kinds of people were their parents; what was the home atmosphere like while they were growing up; and was there even one benevolent figure that they could turn to? How do they see themselves, their difficulties and their offending, now? Do they consider themselves to have any positive attributes at all?

Poem sent in by a prisoner

"It's back, this anger that is inside me, trying to break free
I can't let it, it will kill, I will kill
If it gets out – no, it has to stay inside
It must stay locked away,
For the sake of all human life".

Again, a personalised reply was sent, acknowledging the thought and effort put in to respond to our questions – which was in itself a promising sign of future commitment. We let them know, from the outset, that their probation officer would be contacted for his or her agreement to carry out an assessment, and for background reports.

The assessment interview

The assessment interview is the first face-to-face meeting between the clinician conducting it and the prospective patient, and is an opportunity for each to gain an impression of the other: the professional is being assessed, just as much as the individual prisoner. At Millfields, the first interview was conducted by a senior psychiatrist or psychologist, and if it went well, it was followed by a nursing interview. The environment in which the assessment was conducted could be a bit chaotic and required flexibility, depending on the prison's circumstances at the time. Occasionally a second visit was needed, if the initial interview was interrupted by an emergency elsewhere, or an especially prolonged 'bang-up' period for lunch. Privacy is of the utmost importance, unless of course the individual invites a member of staff to join the interview. Holding the interview off the Wing is preferable: if the topics covered evoke tears in the prisoner, he will not want his fellow inmates to see his vulnerability. It is, of course, valuable to speak with a member of staff before or afterwards.

Interview style

Individual clinicians will have their own approach to carrying out the assessment interview. However, a key task is to build rapport: achieving this will greatly enhance the quality of the information elicited, while finding rapport difficult to establish can say a lot about the prisoner and his readiness for treatment. Sitting nearby, rather than across the room or behind a desk, will signify genuine interest and minimise a likely negative transference reaction to an authority figure. Many prisoners are not told who is coming to see them, when, or why, so it is worth introducing everyone in the room, and explaining the purpose of the meeting. Even better, the prisoner should be written to directly to ensure he is informed about the date of the interview and whom he will meet, as this allows him to prepare himself for the day. The interviewer should adopt a respectful approach, aiming to put the person at ease by adapting to his level of knowledge and vocabulary. Asking some less personal questions to begin with can help this process. One approach is to start with his parents and family, and from there to build up a chronological picture of his life story in his own words, rather than from all the reports. This leads naturally into questions of how and why he reached the point of committing his index offence, and to his current circumstances. Rigidity of structure is generally unhelpful, however, and the interviewer should respond flexibly to what the person wishes to convey in the moment, while not forgetting to circle back to any omissions. It is far preferable to allow for some silence rather than push for a quick, but ill-thought-out response to a question.

There are ways of conveying that no topic is too condemning to raise. For example, "Some men I've talked to say they masturbate ten times a day – how about you?" Or, "Are you afraid that you might kill someone one day?". Such questions are designed to give the individual 'permission' to talk about what is likely to cause him most shame. The purpose is to elicit thoughts and attitudes that he will simply not confide if he anticipates being judged. If the person's cultural background is unfamiliar but relevant, invite his thoughts and comments on the topic.

Hervé *et al.* (2011) have written very helpfully about the importance of the interviewer being self-aware, in order not to allow aspects of him- or herself to intrude. For example, ego or a need for control should take a back seat in favour of allowing the prisoner to express himself. It is important not to ask leading questions or put words into the person's mouth – although rephrasing what he has just said in a way that conveys a real understanding can be beneficial. The interviewer should ensure that his or her own experiences of, for example, violent crime or childhood sexual abuse, do not 'telegraph' an underlying negativity or counter-transference that, even if it is unspoken, the prisoner will be acutely sensitive to. If these experiences are unacknowledged or unprocessed by the clinician, unconscious distaste, fear or anger will influence the outcome of the assessment and hence decision-making. Hervé et al. (2011) also explore facets of the interviewee's memory during the assessment process, and the judgements we tend to make about make about forgetfulness. For example, a prisoner who cannot remember every detail of his index offence is often assumed to be 'minimising' his crime, or even lying about it. In fact, many serious offences are committed in overwhelming emotional states, such as to cause dissociative amnesia for all or part of what happened (Gray *et al.*, 2003).

It is also helpful, in terms of building a sense of connection, to show real curiosity about the person's interests and how he spends his free time. What kinds of music does he listen to, in order to manage stress? What does he read, or watch on television? Does he have any special skills such as art, writing or peer mentoring? Does he have a trusted job, go to education or to the gym? Does he have any contact with the outside world, either through visitors or phone calls? Who still cares about his life? Whom does he most care about? Be prepared to read anything the person might have prepared for you with attention and interest, and to call a relative later if you say you will, for independent or additional information.

Interview content

Family, childhood, relationships and work

The contribution of family background and parental characteristics to the development of personality disorder is discussed in some detail in Chapter 1. It is important to spend time exploring what the individual can recall of his early years, how he feels about his parents now, and how his life progressed into adolescence and adulthood, rather than relying solely on reports. For most of these patients, the trajectory will have been from appalling early abuse and/or neglect, to involvement in drugs and a criminal peer group, to adolescent offending. The nature of the abuse does not necessarily determine what kinds of personality disorder will result later in life (Koolen and Keulen-de Vos, 2022), but does set the scene for pervasive mistrust, difficulties with tolerating frustration (Chakhssi, Bernstein and De Ruiter, 2014), emotional dysregulation and poor or distorted mentalisation (Wagner-Skacel *et al.*, 2022). The behaviour of the parents will often have cemented a deeply ingrained resentment and sense of betrayal, which has strong links to later offending. Idealisation of one parent is also a possibility. There is frequently a history of multiple broken attachments, from being placed in care to being moved between children's homes and specialist boarding schools, where abuse is repeated. Some individuals will have been able to hold down a job, but usually not for long, and problems with employment are ubiquitous. Likewise, intimate relationships are often fraught with difficulties such as jealousy and violence. Sometimes experiences of childhood sexual abuse by an adult male (the most common kind) can lead to confusion about one's sexuality (Tremblay and Turcotte, 2005), and there can be a history of homophobia, experiments in cross-dressing or experiences of gender dysphoria.

Each individual story is different, however, and some patients have managed better in life, especially when it has been lived within structures imposed by, for example, their work circumstances. A military career provides boundaries, routine and hierarchy, with clear consequences for rule-breaking. Some of these men only decompensate once they have returned to civilian life and the containment provided has been removed. It is also our clinical experience that a subgroup of offenders exists who have no criminal or drug history, and who have to all appearances led reasonably successful lives. Then one day, seemingly out of the blue, they commit what has been termed an explosive or 'rage type murder' (Bezuidenhout and Wharren, 2013). The victim is almost always often a near relative – especially a mother or father – or a spouse, with whom he has had an intense but ambivalent emotional relationship. These offenders tend to have narcissistic features in the context of a highly over-controlled personality (Megargee, 1966), and the violence is felt as self-preservative at an existential level. Such men are often haunted by the fear of reoffending, especially if asked to explore their anger in therapy, since their explosive violence was perceived to be outside of their understanding and control.

History of offending

As mentioned above, these men will often have become involved in low level crime from a very young age. Typical behaviour includes shop-lifting, criminal damage, breaking into cars, setting fire to bins and the like. These early signs of delinquency were described by Bowlby in his classic 1944 paper, *Forty-Four Juvenile Thieves: Their Characters and Home-Life*. Of the children he studied, 86% had experienced early and prolonged separation from their primary caregivers, as well as multiple placements in care. He concluded that this was the principal reason for the development of what he termed the 'affectionless character' so often seen in the persistent offender. He explained the psychopathology of these children thus:

> Through stealing, the child hopes for emotional satisfaction, though in reality it proves ineffective because the symbol of love has been mistaken for the real thing … A child separated from its mother comes to crave both for her love and for its accompanying symbols. If this craving is unsatisfied then it later presents itself as stealing.
>
> (Bowlby, 1944, p. 40)

Dixon (2003) has noted that, "the development of an indifferent or dismissive pattern of attachment protected these children from forming close, personal relationships, hence eliminating 'any risk of allowing {their} hearts to be broken again'". More recent studies show that the experience of childhood maltreatment *per se* has a similar effect (Follan and Minnis, 2010).

A pattern of early offending introduces these individuals to the police, whom they experience as authoritarian, punitive and inherently unjust: most will cite an example, with great indignation, of an occasion when they were falsely arrested or convicted. Over time, their criminality becomes increasingly serious, leading to longer and longer prison sentences. It is always worth asking about serious crimes for which the person has not been caught. A few of these individuals have lived in custodial settings for most of their lives, so much so that they come to experience the prison walls as safer than the outside world, and will reoffend to make sure that they are sent back 'inside'. The institution thus has a parental function: it provides food and shelter, acts as a container for out of control behaviour and dangerous emotions, and removes the individual from any entanglement in problematic relationships or responsibilities.

It is difficult for us to imagine deriving almost the whole of our life experience from a prison setting. Haney (2003, 2012) has written extensively about the psychological changes that many long-term prisoners are forced to undergo in order to survive, and has coined the term 'prisonization' to describe what he sees as normal adaptations to such an environment – without the person necessarily being fully aware of them. They include dependence on a structured regime, with little opportunity for making decisions or using one's initiative; hypervigilance for signs of threat, and a willingness to attack first; emotional over-control and psychological distancing to avoid showing any sign of vulnerability; and conforming to a prison culture that includes bullying and exploitation. People with childhood histories of maltreatment often experience prison as retraumatising. All these factors will impact on the presentation of the prisoner being assessed.

Substance misuse

Drug-taking also starts very early in these patients' lives. It can be related to thrill-seeking, but also serves to block out unbearably painful emotions and memories. It might have led to previous episodes of psychosis, and significantly increases the risk of violence (Zhong, Yu and Fazel, 2020), as does alcohol. As Graham and Livingston (2011) point out, the link between alcohol and violence has been recognised as far back as the fourth century BC. Substance misuse can be very entrenched in some of these individuals, and continues even in prison or, on a lesser scale, in health-based secure units.

Previous contact with mental health services

By the time these patients have reached the stage of being considered for a diagnosis of severe personality disorder, it is likely that their difficulties will have been attributed to a number of other kinds of mental illnesses. These alternative diagnoses will often be erroneous, but not always, and it is important to take seriously historical descriptions of psychosis, for example, rather than only lend weight to the current presentation. For admission to Millfields Unit, any co-morbid mental illness needed to have been stabilised with medication before admission. Co-morbid anxiety and depression are often found in patients with borderline personality disorder, and if identified after admission might need to be treated with medication alongside the therapy programme. Severe obsessive-compulsive disorders often came to light after the patient's arrival in the unit, and were addressed with individual psychological work.

Prescribed medication

Unlike some prison-based therapeutic communities, patients were accepted for Millfields even if they were taking antipsychotic or antidepressant medication: any necessary adjustment or withdrawal could be undertaken after admission. We learned over time to require abstinence from prescribed addictive medication, such as Benzodiazepines, Methadone or Pregabalin, before the patient arrived.

Many patients find the kind of wide-ranging, exploratory interview described above to be revealing, in terms of what they learn through being asked to think about themselves together with an interested 'other'. In a way, it is their first taste of therapy, and the very beginnings of a potential attachment to the service. As such, it is important to explain what will happen next at each stage of the assessment process, and roughly how long it will take. The individual also needs to be told more about the therapy programme, the expectations for attendance, and about working in groups with sex offenders. It is important to be clear and realistic about the duration of the therapy, and where the person will go afterwards if he makes good progress; this will often depend on practical factors such as the length of his sentence and his security category. Likewise, be open about what will happen if the therapy does not go well, including what kinds of rule-breaking will lead to removal from the unit. However promising the interview, never raise hopes that you cannot fulfil: this initial assessment will always need to be discussed further with colleagues and external agencies. In Millfields, it was always followed by a nursing assessment. We viewed it as essential to reach a consensus about admission, in order to avoid later recriminations when a patient's behaviour might have become challenging.

Current difficulties

A fuller discussion of the nature of personality disorder, and the difficulties it leads to, is to be found in Chapter 1. Suffice it to say here, an important part of the assessment interview is to get a picture of what the person views as problematic in his life, and how he understands his predicament. It can be helpful to ask about three domains: the interpersonal (e.g. repeated alienation of those close to him), the intrapersonal (e.g. subjective distress, volatility, confusion or hopelessness) and the social (e.g. an inability to hold down a job, co-exist with neighbours, or use health and other services appropriately). Bear in mind the diagnostic criteria for the most common subtypes of personality disorder in this group, which are antisocial, borderline, narcissistic and paranoid, and make sure your questions cover these. Many individuals will have a combination of traits from different categories of personality disorder.

Motivation for treatment

No one was admitted to Millfields who did not express a willingness to engage in treatment. However, not only can motivation vary over time, but ambivalence is to be expected and must be worked with. These patients will need encouragement and validation for their efforts. Many will not have sufficient understanding of themselves, or of what treatment really entails, to give an informed view. Nevertheless, in the assessment interview it is important to explore what he says about his wish for treatment and what he hopes to get out of it. There is some evidence that higher levels of emotional distress are predictive of greater motivation (e.g. Martínez-González *et al.*, 2020; Van Beek and Verheul, 2008). Antisocial or psychopathic individuals might express a superficial motivation because their sentence plan directs them to complete treatment, but have little intention of pursuing change in their lives. A useful set of questions can be asked around what the person thinks he might have to give up, and what he feels about losing this aspect of his identity.

The assessment report

This should be as comprehensive as possible without being book length, since an accurate view of risk and treatability can only be formed when all the relevant details are known. It should be written with the awareness that it will be sent to the patient as well as the referrer, and so must be factual but not overly critical or judgemental: most have already ruthlessly condemned themselves. At the same time, it should not gloss over the harms the individual has committed or his responsibility for them. The OPD pathway specifies simply that eligible individuals are 'likely' to have a diagnosis of personality disorder, but in a health-based service it is important to establish a formal diagnosis. When communicated sensitively, many of our patients were grateful to be told what they were suffering from, as this information helped them to make sense at last of longstanding confusion, and conferred the right to treatment. One accessible approach to writing up the report is to include a summary of how the person meets diagnostic criteria for the applicable types of personality disorder, giving examples from his life (see Box 3 for some examples). Thus the assessment report itself becomes an opportunity to teach the patient what his diagnosis actually means for him. In due course, it was also used to help the patient to write his own formulation of his difficulties.

Examples of how a patient does/does not meet diagnostic criteria for personality disorder (using DSM)

- **Lack of remorse, as indicated by being indifferent to or rationalising having hurt, mistreated or stolen from another:** X himself says he has no concern for the prison officers he has abused or hurt.
- **Frantic efforts to avoid real or imagined abandonment:** Towards the end of each important relationship, Y reacted with fury and with desperate measures to force his partner to stay with him.
- **Identity disturbance: markedly and persistently unstable self-image or sense of self:** Z admits that he has a tendency to 'walk away', even from good jobs and relationships, because of a strong sense of being trapped.
- **Deceitfulness, as indicated by repeated lying, use of aliases, or conning others for personal profit or pleasure:** There is no evidence that this criterion is fulfilled.

Who is likely to do well in treatment?

It can be very difficult to predict, before admission, who is likely to use the therapy well: surprises are not uncommon, and sometimes the best test is to accept the individual for a probationary period. Unsurprisingly, the very nature of personality difficulties in themselves, and their impact on these patients' lives, is associated with non-engagement. By definition, these people have problems with interpersonal relationships, especially when it comes to coping with perceived slights without responding impulsively or resorting to aggression and hostility. Since the entire process of therapy is about challenging the person's view of himself and others, every session is rife with the possibility of causing deep offence.

Nevertheless, there is some evidence from the research literature to guide us. A systematic review carried out by McMurran, Huband and Overton (2010) found the average drop-out rate to be 37%. This might seem shockingly high, but in fact the drop-out rate from psychotherapy generally is 47% (Wierzbicki and Pekarik, 1993), so the authors suggest we should not be unduly pessimistic. They found that demographic factors, such as lack of education and employment are important, as is making an early start to a criminal career (Copas *et al.*, 1984). Meeting criteria for several personality disorders (a reflection of severity) also reduces the chances of effective participation (Webb and McMurran, 2009). Those who drop out early tend to lack the skills needed for therapy (McMurran, Huband and Overton, 2010). For example, they are less good at social problem solving, or at managing the ordinary daily misunderstandings and potential conflicts that arise. They are more likely to use avoidance as a coping mechanism, and tend to walk away from situations that feel too confusing or painful to address. In our experience, these potential obstacles to successful engagement could be addressed through a specifically tailored 'Orientation to Therapy' group, which taught newcomers not just about the nature of personality disorder, but also skills for managing in treatment and the likely impact of early trauma on their present-day relationships with others.

A small but important study by Horner and Diamond (1996) comes, in our view, close to identifying a core difficulty that poses the greatest threat to treatment. The authors looked at the patterns of those object relations which could distinguish the patients at risk of premature termination of therapy. In those who dropped out early, they found a preponderance of 'narcissistic themes' relative to 'rapprochement themes' (the capacity to reconcile with others). People with a preponderance of 'narcissistic themes" showed a pattern of interaction with the therapist in which perceived slights were responded to as deliberate and wounding narcissistic injuries. These perceived slights tended to precipitate rage, and a 'relentless devaluation' of the therapist that all but erased any positive aspects to the therapy. This pattern will be familiar to anyone who has worked with severe personality disorder, and there is often no link to the person's apparent level of functioning. Kernberg (1975) has observed that pathological narcissism is often an integral feature of borderline psychopathology especially, and poses a serious risk to treatment (p. 267). This kind of patient is showing aspects of both 'grandiose narcissism' (such as self-absorption and the wish to dominate) and 'vulnerable narcissism' (such as distress, hypersensitivity to criticism and distrust). This finding is echoed by a more recent study of offenders with personality disorder in a specialist high secure prison (Bennet, 2015), where those with narcissistic features were more likely to become treatment 'dropouts'.

It is possible to test out a patient's object relations style within the assessment interview. One might try out a challenge to the person's story or interpretation of something that happened to him, to see how he manages being disagreed with. It is worth bearing in mind, however, that he might be on his best behaviour during the assessment. An alternative is to ask him to recount a recent disagreement he had with someone else. Caligor, Levy and Yeomans (2015) provide some useful advice for eliciting narcissistic traits: they tend to describe important people in their lives in either idealistic or denigrating ways, which are markedly vague and superficial, and couched in terms of how like or unlike the other person is to them. Common counter-transference reactions to narcissistic patients include

feeling idealized and pressured to provide a magic cure; feeling belittled and devalued; feeling treated like someone who is incompetent and has nothing to offer; or feeling like a sounding board, ignored, without recognition of the clinician as an individual or any interest in what he or she might have to say.

In our experience, narcissism reveals itself when the prisoner being assessed is much more interested in the facilities and being geographically closer to potential visitors, than in the treatment.

As Jinks, McMurran and Huband (2012) point out, there are factors external to the patient, *which we are responsible for*, that also influence treatment success. Are the staff well trained and supported, for example, and does the treatment programme prepare patients adequately? Does the overarching organisation in which the service sits have a positive, welcoming attitude to this patient group?

Suitability for admission

As outlined above, the final decision as to whether or not to admit a patient will be based on a combination of complex, dynamic factors, but should always be a consensus. It is not only a question of whether a particular individual is a good choice for treatment, but also is he a good choice right now and is the service a good choice for him? His potential 'fit' with the current patient group will also need to be taken into account. It is important to think ahead to his probable pathway once treatment is completed, whether this will be discharge directly into the community or a return to a specialist prison unit. The individual patient will need to be aware of what is possible and what is not, and to agree to the planned route onwards.

References

Bennett, A.L. (2015) 'Personality factors related to treatment discontinuation in a high secure personality disorder treatment service', *Journal of Criminological Research, Policy and Practice*, 1(1), pp. 29–36. http://dx.doi.org/10.1108/JCRPP-09-2014-0001

Bezuidenhout, C. and Wharren, M. (2013) 'The role of narcissistic personality disorder in rage-type murder (Part 2)', *Pakistan Journal of Criminology*, 5(2), p. 275.

Bowlby, J. (1944) 'Forty-four juvenile thieves: their characters and home-life', *The International Journal of Psychoanalysis*, 25, pp. 19–52.

Caligor, E., Levy, K.N. and Yeomans, F.E. (2015) 'Narcissistic personality disorder: diagnostic and clinical challenges', *American Journal of Psychiatry*, 172(5), pp. 415–422. http://dx.doi.org/10.1176/appi.ajp.2014.14060723

Chakhssi, F., Bernstein, D. and De Ruiter, C. (2014) 'Early maladaptive schemas in relation to facets of psychopathy and institutional violence in offenders with personality disorders', *Legal and Criminological Psychology*, 19(2), pp. 356–372. http://dx.doi.org/10.1111/lcrp.12002

Copas, J.B., O'Brien, M., Roberts, J. and Whiteley, J.S. (1984) 'Treatment outcome in personality disorder: the effect of social, psychological and behavioural variables', *Personality and Individual Differences*, 5(5), pp. 565–573. http://dx.doi.org/10.1016/0191-8869(84)90031-X

Dixon, A. (2003) 'At all costs let us avoid any risk of allowing our hearts to be broken Again': a review of john Bowlby's forty-four juvenile thieves', *Clinical Child Psychology and Psychiatry*, 8(2), pp. 278–289.

Follan, M. and Minnis, H. (2010) 'Forty-four juvenile thieves revisited: from Bowlby to reactive attachment disorder', *Child: Care, Health and Development*, 36(5), pp. 639–645. http://dx.doi.org/10.1111/j.1365-2214.2009.01048.x

Graham, K. and Livingston, M. (2011) 'The relationship between alcohol and violence–population, contextual and individual research approaches', *Drug and Alcohol Review*, 30(5), p. 453. http://dx.doi.org/10.1111/j.1465-3362.2011.00340.x

Gray, N.S., Carman, N.G., Rogers, P., MacCulloch, M.J., Hayward, P. and Snowden, R.J. (2003) 'Post-traumatic stress disorder caused in mentally disordered offenders by the committing of a serious violent or sexual offence', *The Journal of Forensic Psychiatry & Psychology*, 14(1), pp. 27–43. http://dx.doi.org/10.1080/1478994031000074289

Haney, C. (2003) 'The psychological impact of incarceration: implications for post-prison adjustment', in Travis, J. and Waul, M. (eds.), Prisoners once removed: The impact of incarceration and reentry on children, families, *and communities*, Volume 33. The Urban Institute, p. 66.

Haney, C. (2012) Prison effects in the era of mass incarceration. *The Prison Journal*, pp. 1–24. http://dx.doi.org/10.1177/0032885512448604

Hansen, N.B., Lambert, M.J. and Forman, E.M. (2002) 'The psychotherapy dose-response effect and its implications for treatment delivery services', *Clinical Psychology: Science and Practice*, 9, pp. 329–343. http://dx.doi.org/10.1093/clipsy.9.3.329

Hervé, H., Psych, R., Cooper, B., Schweighofer, A. and Santarcangelo, M. (2011) 'Assessing and treating sexual offenders: the importance of effective interviewing and evaluating truthfulness', in Schwartz, B. (ed.), *The sex offender*, Volume 8. New York, NY: Civic Research Institute, pp. 7-2 to 7–42.

Horner, M.S. and Diamond, D. (1996) 'Object relations development and psychotherapy dropout in borderline outpatients', *Psychoanalytic Psychology*, 13(2), p. 205. http://dx.doi.org/10.1037/h0079648

Jinks, M., McMurran, M. and Huband, N. (2012) 'Engaging clients with personality disorder in treatment', *Mental Health Review Journal*, 17(3), pp. 139–144. http://dx.doi.org/10.1108/13619321211287229

Kernberg, O. (1975) *Borderline conditions and pathological narcissism*. New York: Aronson.

Koolen, R. and Keulen-de Vos, M. (2022) 'The relationship between adverse childhood experiences, emotional states and personality disorders in offenders', *Journal of Forensic Psychology Research and Practice*, 22(1), pp. 18–37. http://dx.doi.org/10.1080/24732850.2021.1945834

Lewis, G. and Appleby, L. (1988) 'Personality disorder: the patients psychiatrists dislike', *The British Journal of Psychiatry*, 153(1), pp. 44–49. http://dx.doi.org/10.1192/bjp.153.1.44

Martínez-González, J.M., Caracuel, A., Vilar-López, R., Becoña, E. and Verdejo-García, A. (2020) 'Evaluation of motivation for the treatment of drug addicts with personality disorders', *The Spanish Journal of Psychology*, 23, p. e15. http://dx.doi.org/10.1017/SJP.2020.13

McMurran, M., Huband, N. and Overton, E. (2010) 'Non-completion of personality disorder treatments: a systematic review of correlates, consequences, and interventions', *Clinical Psychology Review*, 30(3), pp. 277–287. http://dx.doi.org/10.1016/j.cpr.2009.12.002

McMurran, M. and Theodosi, E. (2007) 'Is treatment non-completion associated with increased reconviction over no treatment?', *Psychology, Crime & Law*, 13, pp. 333–343. http://dx.doi.org/10.1080/10683160601060374

Megargee, E.I. (1966) 'Undercontrolled and overcontrolled personality types in extreme antisocial aggression', *Psychological Monographs: General and Applied*, 80(3), p. 1. http://dx.doi.org/10.1037/h0093894

Sampson, C.J., James, M., Huband, N., Geelan, S. and McMurran, M. (2013) 'Cost implications of treatment non-completion in a forensic personality disorder service', *Criminal Behaviour and Mental Health*, 23(5), pp. 321–335. http://dx.doi.org/10.1002/cbm.1866

Tremblay, G. and Turcotte, P. (2005) 'Gender identity construction and sexual orientation in sexually abused males', *International Journal of Men's Health*, 4(2). http://dx.doi.org/10.3149/jmh.0402.131

Van Beek, N. and Verheul, R. (2008) 'Motivation for treatment in patients with personality disorders', *Journal of Personality Disorders*, 22(1), pp. 89–100. http://dx.doi.org/10.1521/pedi.2008.22.1.89

Wagner-Skacel, J., Riedl, D., Kampling, H. and Lampe, A. (2022) 'Mentalization and dissociation after adverse childhood experiences', *Scientific Reports*, 12(1), p. 6809. http://dx.doi.org/10.1038/s41598-022-10787-8

Webb, D.J. and McMurran, M. (2009) 'A comparison of women who continue and discontinue treatment for borderline personality disorder', *Personality and Mental Health*, 3, pp. 142–149. http://dx.doi.org/10.1002/pmh.69

Wierzbicki, M. and Pekarik, G. (1993) 'A meta-analysis of psychotherapy dropout', *Professional Psychology: Research and Practice*, 24(2), p. 190. http://dx.doi.org/10.1037/0735-7028.24.2.190

Zhong, S., Yu, R. and Fazel, S. (2020) 'Drug use disorders and violence: associations with individual drug categories', *Epidemiologic Reviews*, 42(1), pp. 103–116. http://dx.doi.org/10.1093/epirev/mxaa006

Chapter 13

Assessing personality and risk

Phil Minoudis

Introduction

Risk can be a controversial subject in the field of mental health when it relates to the risk of harm our service users pose to others. It tends to jar with the clinician's intrinsic motivation to support their clients, as if attendance to risk were contraindicated in the pursuit of promoting engagement and therapeutic alliance. On the one hand, there may be an idealistic notion that treating the underlying trauma or personality difficulties will by extension reduce risk of harm. But this entrusts risk reduction to chance and happy coincidence rather than an intentional and important focus of the work. Another view sees the clinician holding a dual role of care and support alongside risk management, akin to the parental role of limit setting occurring as a necessary extension of love and attention. The two are so closely intertwined, that you cannot provide genuine support and care without considering containment and management of risk. To do so would be neglectful, as to protect the individual from causing harm is as central an aspect of promoting wellbeing as reducing the symptoms causing distress. In practice, they are often one and the same.

Take for example a person whose impulsive aggression as a means of coping with fears of abandonment, has led to repeated intimate partner violence. The risk behaviour can be seen as a coping strategy to control the partner, employed to protect against the underlying 'clinical' problem of abandonment fear. It is this linking of risk to personality that is the essential business of working with people with personality difficulties in the criminal justice system who present a high risk of harm to others (National Health Service England, 2023). Risk may be a difficult subject to raise with a service user and one which is initially resisted; and consequently, it may challenge the therapeutic alliance. But it is an essential part of an intervention which sees the individual as a whole person. In our experience, the quality of the engagement is superior when the individual is able to speak about their entire self with their team and trusts them to view and hold the most dangerous and unappealing aspects, without fear of rejection or judgment. It is this dual focus in the treatment which is most likely to promote psychosocial wellbeing and at the same time reduce risk of harm; and in this way is more likely to promote lasting and meaningful change.

DOI: 10.4324/9781032717302-13

This said, the historical application of risk assessment in the forerunner to what is now called the 'Offender Personality Disorder' (OPD) programme in the United Kingdom, the 'Dangerous and Severe Personality Disorder' (DPSD) programme, lent too far towards a dependence on formal assessment tools. The approach, driven by a research agenda and government's anxiety to be seen to address the dangerousness of high-profile offenders, led to clinicians, often psychologists, completing an extensive battery of assessments, including multiple risk assessments, and sometimes more than one tool to measure the same underlying construct of violence potential. Many hours were, and are, spent on the over-inclusive completion of structured professional judgement tools (Douglas et al., 2013), perhaps in the hope that the very act of assessing risk will itself manage it. This is the other extreme which reifies tools as outcomes in themselves, rather than an instrument to guide professional opinion towards strategies to reduce harm to others.

The aim at Millfields, as the service transitioned from DSPD to OPD, was to review the use of risk assessment to ensure it acted in the service of the treatment, by linking personality to risk, both to reduce harm to the public and to improve the psychosocial wellbeing of the residents passing through the service. The adapted therapeutic community at Millfields offered opportunities for multi-disciplinary risk assessment, supported by flattened professional hierarchies and a culture of joint responsibility for duties with a blurring of professional roles. The living-learning environment offered a potential for testing risk management strategies and giving ownership of the process to the service user, who would be encouraged to incorporate their risk into a formulation, presented to the whole community (see Chapters 3 and 14). Reality confrontation in community meetings offered peer-led challenge to service users who struggled to acknowledge their risk, as presented to them by professionals (see Chapter 4).

An unforeseen advantage of setting up OPD medium secure services as a health provision, was the breadth of clinical presentations referred to the service from prisons. Custodial settings do not discriminate by personality style and house all types of personality presentation (Roberts and Coid, 2009), and contrary to traditional community 'personality disorder' settings, Millfields was not designed around a specific vogue diagnosis appearing in the latest international diagnostic manual. There was no restriction to the eligibility criteria which narrowed admissions to one diagnosis or another. Most research evidence about the effectiveness of treatment for personality problems is focused on Borderline or Emotionally Unstable Personality Disorder (Leichsenring et al., 2024), after BPD/EUPD services proliferated in the wake of the third edition of the Diagnostic and Statistical Manual's (DSM III) move to separating personality into a separate axis or cluster of problems from mental illness (Widiger and Frances, 1985). Guidelines recommending best practice for working with personality difficulties are similarly restricted to antisocial or borderline presentations (e.g. NICE ASPD/BPD guidelines). Millfields admitted residents who met the diagnostic criteria for antisocial, narcissistic, borderline, paranoid, schizoid personality styles, amongst others (Freestone et al., 2012). There was a breadth to the clinical presentations, which more closely mirrored general offending populations. This provided an abundant training potential for the clinicians working in the service and developed a group of professionals who gained a breadth and depth to their skills and experience, rarely repeated in mainstream mental health personality services. The downside was that there was little in the way of evidence to guide individualised risk assessments, which were specific to offence types and personality presentations. There is a reasonable literature on offence types (e.g. Gannon *et al.*, 2012; Holtzworth-Munroe, 2000; Mullen *et al.*, 1999); however, there was little on the integration of individual personality types and offence patterns.

In the absence of an established evidence base, some authors have turned to a 'theory-knitting' approach (e.g. Ward and Siegert, 2002), in which established theories are integrated to provide an explanatory framework or model for thinking about highly specific presentations. In the literature on sexually harmful behaviour, Yates, Prescott and Ward (2010) bring together desistance theory with the self-regulation model to develop a widely used strengths-based approach to preventing future offending with the Good Lives Model. In a similar way at Millfields, we developed an approach drawing on accepted theories of offending and theories about personality patterns to help our understanding of personality as it pertained to risk, making the link in our formulations of our residents (see Chapter 14). The following chapter outlines the more common patterns of personality and offending which we encountered, illustrating the main features with case examples, drawn from multiple cases and combined into one example to preserve anonymity.

Inhibited personalities and overcontrolled violence

Offence typology

A perplexing and yet not uncommon pattern of offending presents itself in the form of extreme violence which occurs in the absence of a significant previous history of offending. These cases stand in stark contrast to the larger proportion of people in the criminal justice system, whose high-harm violence emerges from a background of a long history of violent and assaultive behaviour which increases gradually in severity over time. As a result, they present a challenge to the most reliably accepted doctrine of risk assessment, that previous violence is the best predictor of future violence. Common characteristics of such perpetrators include a predominantly quiet and mild-mannered persona, without overt expression of emotions such as anxiety or anger, and often a rigid cognitive style and associated behaviour which is largely compliant and rulebound. Sometimes their offending may be accompanied by seemingly callous displays, such as a dismissive attitude to remorse, a matter-of-fact description of harrowing detail or gratuitous aspects to the violence, including grossly inhumane yet dryly pragmatic approaches to the disposal of evidence, sometimes including the bodies of victims.

This is not a new phenomenon. In 1966, Megargee established a typology separating overcontrolled and undercontrolled aggressors. This included a description of the respective personalities, with undercontrolled violence characterised by a weak capacity for inhibition and restraint of their violent impulses, and resulting in regular incidents of aggression. Contrariwise, overcontrolled violence was characterised by a strong capacity for inhibitory control, with aggression occurring only on rare occasions when anger arousal was sufficiently raised to overwhelm an otherwise controlled disposition. Attacks by this group were infrequent, but when they did occur it was with extreme intensity and was associated with more severe forms of violence, such as homicide and serious violent assaults. The overcontrolled group were described as having a rigid defensive style which suppressed the expression of negative emotions and aggressive impulses, regardless of provocation. This overcontrol could be maintained only until excessive provocation exceeded the limits of their inhibitory control, resulting in a total loss of control and explosion of violence of great intensity.

Megargee (1966) found that boys with a history of extreme assault, were rated as being more controlled and generally less aggressive and self-reported a conventional personality style on testing. These findings were replicated by Blackburn (1968), who found those with a record of extreme violence to be more controlled, inhibited and defensive in psychological measures; they were also less likely to have previous convictions. In a later study of 56 people who had committed murder, nearly half showed these characteristics (Blackburn, 1971). Lang et al. (1987) showed those with a conviction of murder had less offending history and scored lower on hostility, recklessness and aggression, but higher on defensiveness, measured using a lie scale and associated with conforming behaviour. Lane and Kling (1979) developed an overcontrolled hostility scale to identify the group, which was distinguished by infrequent and intense violence, rigidity, excessive control, repression of conflicts and a reluctance to admit psychological vulnerabilities. Others repeated the findings, including a proneness to chronic suppressed anger and hostility, a lack of assertiveness and less anger expression (e.g. Quinsey, Maguire and Varney, 1983).

Personality traits

Inhibited personality styles, such as Millon's description of schizoid, avoidant and obsessive-compulsive (Millon, 1997), are closely aligned to characteristics associated with overcontrolled aggression; all three defined by social inhibition, detachment and a rigidly defensive cognitive style. Millon's (1997) description of the compulsive personality bears a remarkable resemblance to the common features of overcontrolled aggression:

...[they are] intimidated into accepting demands of others...[experiencing] conflict between hostility towards others and fear of disapproval...[which is] resolved by suppressing their resentment and over-conforming...[and] behind this front of propriety and restraint, however, are intense anger and oppositional feelings that occasionally break through controls.

Table 13.1 shows the similarities between traits of schizoid, avoidant and compulsive personalities and features of overcontrolled aggression. These three personality styles are closely related to one another, according to Millon (1997), and are consistent with the main characteristics of overcontrolled aggression. The task of explaining the link between personality and risk (Dowsett and Craissati, 2008) is made easier by combining the features of an offence-based typology of overcontrolled aggression with personality trait descriptions. This helps to explain the underlying process leading to the aggression, and contributes to an

Table 13.1 Similarities between trait descriptions of schizoid, avoidant and compulsive personalities and features of overcontrolled aggression

Megargee's description of overcontrolled aggression	Millon MCMI-III trait descriptions		
	Schizoid	Avoidant	Compulsive
Rigid	Mechanical/formal		Cognitively constricted
Do not display anxiety	Intellectualisation		
Quiet, mild mannered	Apathetic mood	Timorous, hesitant	Solemn mood
Conforming		Seeks acceptance	adherence to social conventions/ approval
Social avoidance/ withdrawal	Interpersonally unengaged	Interpersonally aversive	
Social skills deficits	Cognitively impoverished	Socially inept	
Inhibition		Fearful and inhibited	
Poor self-esteem		Alienated self-image/ inferior	
Lack of assertiveness		Social anxiety	
May deny/avoid anger			Reaction formation
Defensive/reluctant to admit flaws			Repeated displays of socially commendable behaviour
Suppression/strong emotional control	Emotionally unexcitable	Avoidance and escape	Expressively disciplined

understanding of the maintaining factors, whilst isolating targets for intervention which are most closely linked to the risk. This is explained further in the case example below.

Process

The overcontrolled aggression theory rests on the hydraulic model of aggression (e.g. Bushman and Huesmann, 2010), that anger arousal accumulates over time with repeated provocations. Anger is maintained by rumination or cognitive rehearsal of grievances, leading to a selective bias to be triggered more readily by further provocations. The process is explained by two subgroups of overcontrolled aggression. The first denies their tendency for anger and hostility and presents overtly as conforming, compliant and pro-social. The second describes a strong tendency for anger and avoids social situations and confrontation likely to trigger anger, with an underlying low self-esteem and social skills deficits. Both subtypes are thought to have an avoidant coping style when faced with interpersonal conflict, and respond generally in non-aggressive ways, whether this is to deny anger and hostility altogether, or to have a problem with expressing their anger and underlying difficulties. Hostility and anger are maintained if there are barriers to interpersonal communication, including social withdrawal and a lack of assertiveness, which would otherwise alleviate their emotional state. Anecdotally, clinicians explain the apparently callous post-offence behaviour, such as gratuitous methods of disposing of evidence, as a pragmatic approach to problem-solving, which is unencumbered by empathic concern.

Case example

A patient was admitted to Millfields with little previous history of offending, except for a current offence of murder, for which he was serving a life sentence. His early life was marked by witnessing domestic violence between his parents, with his father leaving the home in his early childhood and his mother described as cutoff and unavailable, though occasionally explosive and controlling. He grew up caring for his mother and learnt to project an image of the 'good boy', who was rule abiding, thoughtful and self-sacrificing. After an 18-year marriage, in which he was reportedly deferent and persistently belittled, he became overwhelmed with rage after an instance of being criticised for incompetence and beat his wife to death with a household utensil.

On the unit, he was seen to be compliant and often referred to as the 'good patient'. However, on confrontation, he was reluctant to admit to negative experiences, such as his difficulty expressing hostile feelings towards others who had clearly slighted him. He revealed little of his emotions and came across as lacking in range and intensity of feelings. He found it hard to negotiate around rules and could become rigid and unyielding. When questioned about his emotional experience, he would tend to intellectualise and dismiss any impact.

He worked well in the treatment model and took up positions of responsibility, conforming to and modelling the principles of the therapeutic community and presenting few management problems. However, the issue for his treatment focused on reaching the emotional experience underlying his overt presentation and getting behind his intellectual explanations of events.

Narcissism and rage

The so-called narcissistic rage reaction (e.g. Kohut, 1972; Kernberg, 1985) is an additional distinct personality pattern of violent offending, which may not feature a significant history of previous offending. Typical characteristics include a frenzied attack using violence beyond that which is necessary to overpower the victim, for example a prolonged knife attack with multiple stabbings. Offences driven by rage are often uncontrolled and show features of poor or rudimentary planning, such as taking place close to public view or during daylight hours. There are sometimes astonishing interactions with the victim, with the perpetrator communicating in a manner which seems oblivious to the harm caused. In one such example, after a rape during the day just off a busy thoroughfare, the perpetrator asked to borrow money from the victim to buy fast food and requested exchanging telephone numbers. Other features might include coming from a high-functioning family, with siblings or parents with professional jobs, indicative of the family striving for high standards and instilling high expectations as well as being critical or intolerant of failure. The offence itself may be triggered by a personal collapse or event which meaningfully challenges a highly regarded and positive self-image, internalised from family values of high achievement.

Process

The interpersonal dynamics of narcissistic personality are most richly described in psychodynamic literature. Meloy (1998) summarises the work of Kernberg (e.g. 1985) and Kohut (e.g. 1972) and applies the theories to explain stalking behaviour. However, this process can equally be applied to other forms of violent behaviour. Narcissism is described in essence as a 'felt quality of perfection', with other people viewed as insentient objects whose primary purpose is to gratify the self. There is an extreme sensitivity to shame and humiliation, especially when triggered by rejection. It is the response to these intolerable emotions, which underpins the risk. The authors describe a 'rage reaction', distinct from anger, with an intention to significantly diminish or devalue the object which triggers these emotions. Rage is driven to dominate, devalue and sometimes destroy the object which threatens the idealised self-image. Narcissistic equilibrium is restored when the object which threatens the view of the self is removed and the idealised self or grandiose self-image is retained. Shame plays an important role, being both likely to occur, given the unsustainable pressure of living up to an idealised view of oneself, and experienced as intolerable as the sense of perfection does not permit any blemish or shortcoming. These are sometimes described as 'narcissistic injuries' which are strongly defended against with rage.

Development

There are intuitively sensible clinical descriptions of the development of narcissism, albeit lacking an empirical basis. The literature describes over-indulgent parenting which overlooks transgressions and does not help the child to tolerate frustration of needs. This may be interspersed with a harshly disciplinarian approach, critical of flaws and failures, leading to a sensitivity to humiliation. Psychodynamic theory describes the 'illusion of exclusivity' which in normal development is gradually eroded as the primary carer does not instantly meet the needs of the infant. Slowly and manageably, the infant realises that the primary carer is an autonomous being not exclusively devoted to the infant. This breaks the illusion of exclusivity, with the realisation that the object does not exist solely to serve one's needs. In narcissism, it is thought that this normal process of child development has not occurred satisfactorily, and the illusion of exclusivity is preserved.

Relationship to offending

This underlying theory explains some of the relationship to risk, and the literature would suggest that narcissism is related more to offending when it co-exists with aspects of antisocial features. Typical types of offending may include sexual coercion, incest offending, some paedophilia, stalking and occasionally murder. The literature identifies a link between sexual coercion and narcissistic tendencies and 'reactance' (Meloy, 1998). For example, if someone with strong narcissistic tendencies has his sexual advances rejected, he may experience 'reactance', which is described as an increase in sexual desire and a subsequent attempt to take what has been denied, coupled with a willingness to use aggression to overcome the person who has denied them. There are additional features associated with narcissism which make offending more likely. These include a tendency for self-serving interpretations, low empathy towards others which would otherwise inhibit harmful behaviour, and an inflated sense of entitlement which permits coercive means to meet personal goals. In this way, rape is understood as a felt entitlement to satisfy sexual urges and refusal is viewed as a secondary consideration next to the primary goal of attainment of personal need.

Case example

One illustrative case was an Asian male from a high functioning family, whose siblings were successful in high status professional roles. He had a history of child sexual abuse, which was not recognised by the family or permitted to be discussed openly. He described a 'special' relationship with his mother, but a father who he experienced as intimidating and demanding of respect. He described a conflict in his desire to be a 'good Muslim son' and his homosexuality. There was little history of offending, except for two low level cautions. The index offence was preceded by a lover ending their relationship and subsequently failing at university and dropping out. He visited his ex-lover and stabbed him multiple times over the body, including the face and neck.

Complexity and paranoia

There are complexities associated with paranoid personality, which bring challenges to management and progress. Common characteristics include management difficulties in secure settings which impede progression through the sentence to the community. The prison environment particularly exacerbates this problem. Frequent arguments and conflict challenge relationships with professionals, damage the therapeutic alliance and may escalate to institutional violence. There can be a tendency for hostility and complaints which drive professionals away and hampers collaborative working. In extreme cases, paranoia may escalate to psychosis, with this risk heightened when under significant stress. A characteristic rigidity or inflexibility can prevent adapting their style of relating, which can perpetuate a stuck position. Some such cases on indeterminate sentences can find themselves significantly over tariff in repeating cycles of confrontation with the system.

Paranoid personality; triggers and maintaining factors

Trait descriptions of paranoid personality are helpful in formulating an understanding of the factors which precipitate problems. Millon (1997) described how a paranoid personality can generate their triggers internally. They may be guarded and vigilant for malice, with a suspicion of other people's motives, leading to misinterpretation of innocuous events, perceiving attacks which may not be apparent to others. Their rigidity can make them highly strung and uncompromising when faced with changing circumstances, such that unexpected changes or stressors can ignite explosive responses. The interpersonal style can come across as provocative and inviting of conflict; for example, bearing grudges and a hostile interpersonal approach which precipitates anger in others by intrusively searching for hidden motives. The resting mood state may be hot-headed or ill-natured, which can appear edgy and quick to anger and exacerbate tense or fragile situations. There can be an accompanying self-righteousness which is a hallmark of paranoid personality. This can leave the individual feeling justified in their aggressive responses and serves to maintain the cycle. The primary defence mechanism is one of 'projection', where undesirable personal traits go unrecognised and are instead attributed to others, with an accompanying tendency to be critical of these perceived aspects others and a determination to correct them. There may also be jealousy and preoccupation about perceived infidelity or untrustworthiness, such as with intimate partners or work associates. These factors in combination provide ample opportunity for triggers to interpersonal conflict.

In addition to triggering conflict, paranoid traits can maintain problematic situations. A blindness to flaws and a tendency to project undesirable traits into others provides little motivation for self-reflection or change. The prototypical paranoid stance is one of righteousness, proudly standing up independently for values believed to be for the greater good. By intention, this stance is impervious to challenge by others, whose views may be cast aside to prevent them being distracted from what is perceived as an honourable crusade. The paranoid position is to mistrust others, keep internal struggles to themselves and resistance to listening to feedback, which could help adapt behaviour. Fixed ideas can be unrelenting and deeply held, and this can be reflected in unchanging feelings and inflexible thinking; features which serve to maintain a damaging and self-defeating stance.

Case example

For some time at Millfields, there had been very few incidents of interpersonal violence and looking back over that period, the majority exemplified paranoid patterns. The following example crystallises these experiences into one persona. He would actively take up issues with other residents he viewed as being in the wrong, sometimes perceiving an attack on his character, but also capable of confronting others about issues which did not directly affect him. He would harbour grievances against historical wrongs and, when irritated, would resurrect these as live issues. The way issues were raised in the community was often provocative, inviting conflict as a means of promoting his righteous position. In a heightened state, he would be particularly hard to reach and would not respond to invitations to slow down or remove himself from situations, appearing implacably locked in hostile interactions. As described by Millon (1997), the need for projection and projective identification was paramount. This was seen in difficulties self-regulating emotion without locating the flaw in another and not relenting until he could see a reaction in the other person, confirming his position as righteous and the other as flawed. After incidents, his perspective would reinforce his stance – showing pride in a war wound as concrete evidence of having stood up for what he was certain was right.

Antisocial personality and violence

Antisocial personality is highly prevalent in offending populations, making the more committed and persistent antisocial presentations harder to differentiate. Models of violence have attempted to separate different types of violence to distinguish a more callous and calculated instrumental violence, personally justified as a means of achieving goals, from reactive violence, described as a temporary failure of the capacity for self-control and therefore considered less intentional. Reactive violence is thought to be caused by poor inhibition and controls – the antithesis of overcontrolled violence described earlier in this chapter. Instrumental violence is thought to be caused by a lack of concern for others, which sees less need to inhibit the use of violence to meet one's needs. In the literature, instrumental violence is associated with psychopathy and considered more concerning and harder to work with therapeutically. As recently as 2008, prominent authors recommended not to use mentalisation-based therapy for instrumental aggression (Bateman and Fonagy, 2008). In our experience, this binary distinction is rarely seen, and we would question the ethics of denying access to services based on a professional's categorical judgement about an unobservable process such as the internal motivation for behaviour.

Typology of violence

Howard *et al.* (2011) put forward a quadripartite typology of violence, which allowed a dimensional understanding of violence motivation which was less restrictive than the binary models which preceded it. In his model, violence is assessed across two dimensions with opposing poles; impulsive or controlled violence and appetitive or aversively motivated violence. This generated four subtypes which were further characterised by the motivation or goal, positive/negative affect, typical type of emotion and a specific description of the type of anger motivating the violence (see Table 13.2).

This model allows for a more nuanced understanding of multiple interacting motivations for violence. Even in so-called prototypical instrumental violence, it

Table 13.2 Quadripartite model of violence (Howard et al., 2011)

Appetitive		*aversive*	
Impulsive	Goal Affect Emotion Anger type	Enhancement of positive affect by infliction of harm and suffering Positive Exhilaration/ Excitement; desire to maximise excitement Thrill-seeking anger	Reduction of negative affect through removal of interpersonal threat Negative Fear, distress, desire to eradicate threat Explosive/reactive anger
Controlled	Goal Affect Emotion Anger type	Achievement of positive outcome/reinforcement Positive Pleasant anticipation; desire for positive outcome 'Coercive anger'	Removal of interpersonal threat/ grievance by considered, premeditated action Negative Vengefulness; desire to 'get even' with source of grievance Vengeful/ruminative anger

allows for inclusion of aversive experience preceding the behaviour in addition to the more callous 'appetitive' motivations. To note, a binary model is also limited in explaining more severe violence beyond which is necessary for instrumental gain.

Process

Fonagy and Target (1995) offer a model for how childhood physical and emotional abuse can result in aggression. In normal development, the child typically looks into the mother's face to have his own mental state reflected back, "giving back to the baby the baby's own self" (Winnicott, 1991). This provides emotional containment, supports the development of self-regulation and helps the child develop a self-structure – a sense of self and a consistent identity. The child is actively searching for himself in the caregiver. In cases of emotional or physical abuse, the primary carer reflects their own disturbed mental states and not those of the child, and the child is being offered experiences he cannot integrate. As the child struggles to assimilate this unrecognisable experience, it becomes a persecutory object lodged in the self but split off; this is referred to as 'the alien self'; something dreadful and unbearable which must be held at bay. For psychological containment and equilibrium, this alien self needs to be located outside the self so it is not threatening. This is described a need for another as a receptacle for the alien self (Bateman and Fonagy, 2008). This equilibrium is maintained by controlling people around them through fear, which locates the alien self in others and at the same time inflated their own status and esteem by demanding respect from others. Violence occurs when an individual is forced to view the alien self as part of his own self-structure; he uses violence to relocate the alien self in another and restore his self-image. As Fonagy and Target (1995) put it, "if I kill you, I won't have to think about what you think [about me]".

Case example

A resident had a background of emotional and physical abuse by a parent, including sustained experiences of cruelty. He was initially bullied at school, latterly learning to become the aggressor and using violence to demand respect and develop relationships with likeminded peers. He developed a criminal lifestyle to support himself; with a pattern of dominating his antisocial peer group to instil some semblance of order and organised acquisitive crime to sustain them. The index offence involved feeling cheated in a deal over illegal goods. After some rumination, he returned with co-defendants to stab the associate and steal money. Despite being recognised, and at great risk to his personal freedom, he returned a week later to repeat the humiliation of further violence and theft. A binary model of violence would most likely have assessed the motivation as instrumental and ignored the role of shame and humiliation in driving the repeated visitations and necessity to demonstrate power and superiority over the victim.

Summary

Through the experience gained in a medium secure hospital specialising in working with high-harm personality difficulties, the shortcomings of the literature on risk assessment and personality disorder became evident. This led to approaches to integrate theories of offence types with personality patterns to develop a nuanced and individualised understanding of violence and offending, which helped to explain the link between personality and risk and develop specific and individualised targets for intervention and risk management.

The theories linking personality to predictable patterns of violent behaviour share an underlying notion that personality seeks equilibrium (e.g. Bateman and Fonagy, 2008; Millon, 1997) and achieves this by exerting a limited repertoire of behaviours on the environment to restore stability. This challenges the theory that personality 'disorder' is genetically predisposed; and introduces the idea that individual difference or personality types have evolved to be genetically primed to offer a selective advantage in early environments of violence and trauma. Violence emerges as a response to trauma or unmet needs, with specific patterns of behaviour expressed through individual difference or personality.

A repertoire of behaviours typical of specific personality types is supported by anecdotal clinical experience. Larger scale empirical research would determine the generalisability of these as reliable explanatory frameworks. This emphasises the importance of investing in units such as Millfields to further understanding of violence and personality, to improve risk management and treatment approaches to reduce future violence. It is a privilege to work in specialist units, such as the Millfields adapted therapeutic community, and it remains important to share the experiences and preserve the learning to inform future practice for working with personality and risk.

References

Bateman, A. and Fonagy, P. (2008) 'Comorbid antisocial and borderline personality disorders: mentalization-based treatment', *Journal of Clinical Psychology*, 64(2), pp. 181–194. https://doi.org/10.1002/jclp.20451

Blackburn, R. (1968) 'Personality in relation to extreme aggression in psychiatric offenders', *The British Journal of Psychiatry*, 114(512), pp. 821–828. https://doi.org/10.1192/bjp.114.512.821

Blackburn, R. (1971) 'Personality types among abnormal homicides', *The British Journal of Criminology*, 11(1), pp. 14–31. https://doi.org/10.1093/oxfordjournals.bjc.a046276

Bushman, B.J. and Huesmann, L.R. (2010) 'Aggression', in Fiske, S.T., Gilbert, D.T. and Lindzey, G., (eds.) *Handbook of social psychology*. 5th edn. New York: John Wiley & Sons.

Douglas, K.S., Hart, S.D., Webster, C.D. and Belfrage, H. (2013) *HCR-20V3: assessing risk of violence – user guide*. Burnaby, Canada: Mental Health, Law and Policy Institute, Simon Fraser University.

Dowsett, J. and Craissati, J. (2008) *Managing personality disordered offenders in the community: a psychological approach*. London: Routledge.

Fonagy, P. and Target, M. (1995) 'Understanding the violent patient: the use of the body and the role of the father', *The International Journal of Psychoanalysis*, 76(3), pp. 487–501.

Freestone, M., Taylor, C., Milsom, S., Mikton, C., Ullrich, S., Phillips, O. and Coid, J. (2012) 'Assessments and admissions during the first 6 years of a UK medium secure

DSPD service', *Criminal Behaviour and Mental Health*, 22(2), pp. 91–107. https://doi.org/10.1002/cbm.1823.

Gannon, T.A., Ciardha, C.O., Doley, R.M. and Alleyne, E. (2012) 'The multi-trajectory theory of adult fire-setting (M-TTAF)', *Aggression and Violent Behavior*, 17(2), pp. 107–121. https://doi.org/10.1016/j.avb.2011.08.001

Holtzworth-Munroe, A. (2000) 'A typology of men who are violent toward their female partners: making sense of the heterogeneity in husband violence', *Current Directions in Psychological Science*, 9(4), pp. 140–143. https://doi.org/10.1111/1467-8721.00079

Howard, R.C. (2011) 'The quest for excitement: a missing link between personality disorder and violence?, *Journal of Forensic Psychiatry & Psychology*, 22(5), pp. 692–670. https://doi.org/10.1080/14789949.2011.617540

Kernberg, O.F. (1985) *Borderline conditions and pathological narcissism*. Oxford: Rowman & Littlefield Publishers.

Kohut, H. (1972) 'Thoughts on narcissism and narcissistic rage', *The Psychoanalytic Study of the Child*, 27(1), pp. 360–400. https://doi.org/10.1080/00797308.1972.11822721

Lane, P.J. and Kling, J.S. (1979) 'Construct validation of the overcontrolled hostility scale of the MMPI', *Journal of Consulting and Clinical Psychology*, 47(4), pp. 781–782. https://doi.org/10.1037/0022-006X.47.4.781

Lang, R.A., Holden, R., Langevin, R., Pugh, G.M. and Wu, R. (1987) 'Personality and criminality in violent offenders', *Journal of Interpersonal Violence*, 2(2), pp. 179–195. https://doi.org/10.1177/088626087002002004

Leichsenring, F., Fonagy, P., Heim, N., Kernberg, O.F., Leweke, F., Luyten, P., Salzer, S., Spitzer, C. and Steinert, C. (2024) 'Borderline personality disorder: a comprehensive review of diagnosis and clinical presentation, etiology, treatment, and current controversies', *World Psychiatry*, 23(1), pp. 4–25. https://doi.org/10.1002/wps.21156

Megargee, E.I. (1966) 'Undercontrolled and overcontrolled personality types in extreme antisocial aggression', *Psychological Monographs: General and Applied*, 80(3), pp. 1–29. https://doi.org/10.1037/h0093894

Meloy, J.R. (1998) 'The psychology of stalking: clinical and forensic perspectives', *Security Journal*, 13(2), pp. 71–72. https://doi.org/10.1057/palgrave.sj.8340053

Millon, T. (1997) *Millon clinical multiaxial inventory-III*. 2nd edn. Bloomington, MN: Pearson Assessments.

Mullen, P.E., Pathé, M., Purcell, R. and Stuart, G.W. (1999) 'A study of stalkers', *American Journal of Psychiatry*, 156(8), pp. 1244–1249. https://doi.org/10.1176/ajp.156.8.1244

National Health Service England (2023) *The offender personality disorder (OPD) pathway: a joint strategy for 2023 to 2028*. Available at: www.england.nhs.uk/long-read/the-offender-personality-disorder-pathway/ (accessed 23 January 2025).

Quinsey, V.L., Maguire, A. and Varney, G.W. (1983) 'Assertion and overcontrolled hostility among mentally disordered murderers', *Journal of Consulting and Clinical Psychology*, 51(4), pp. 550–556. https://doi.org/10.1037/0022-006X.51.4.550

Roberts, A.D.L. and Coid, J.W. (2009) 'Personality disorder and offending behaviour: findings from the national survey of male prisoners in England and Wales', *The Journal of Forensic Psychiatry & Psychology*, 21(2), pp. 221–237. https://doi.org/10.1080/14789940903303811

Ward, T. and Siegert, R.J. (2002) 'Toward a comprehensive theory of child sexual abuse: a theory knitting perspective', *Psychology, Crime and Law*, 8(4), pp. 319–351. https://doi.org/10.1080/10683160208401823

Widiger, T.A. and Frances, A. (1985) 'Axis II personality disorders: Diagnostic and treatment issues', *Psychiatric Services*, 36(6), pp. 619–627.

Winnicott, D.W. (1991) *Playing and reality*. London: Routledge.

Yates, P.M., Prescott, D. and Ward, T. (2010) *Applying the good lives and self-regulation models to sex offender treatment*. Vermont: Safer Society Press.

Chapter 14

Formulation

Brittni Jones

Introduction

The extreme acts of violence from patients are often so disturbing and frightening that people do not want to think about them, let alone understand them. This response of turning the mind away from thinking about the patients and their offences can lead to an assumption that they are senseless, and the risk therefore unquantifiable and untreatable. However, psychoanalytic ideas such as 'identifying with the aggressor' (Berger, 2014) or 'core complex' (Glasser, 1979), alongside a thorough understanding of the patients' personality and way of thinking at the time of the offence, can help to make sense of what happened and how to prevent it from happening again in future. This is the 'formulation' of a patient's personality traits, difficulties and offending, and is the foundation for treatment. Millfields developed a multidisciplinary method of formulating which uses psychoanalytic ideas in a structured manner to consider all aspects of a patient's psyche that contribute to difficulties and risk. Drawing on the therapeutic community (TC) principles of responsibility taking, openness and shared authority, this method involved the patient inputting their own ideas and reflections on themselves as well as setting their own goals for therapy, which were then merged with the team's views and shared with the TC membership.

What is formulation?

A formulation is, at its core, a psychological theory-based explanation or hypothesis about the nature of a person's difficulties and their origins in early experiences, relationships, social circumstances and life events, as well as their responses to their difficulties and the further impact this has had. The formulation can sit alongside diagnosis (which is often a requirement for decision-making regarding service/treatment provision) but also goes beyond broad categorisation of symptoms or behaviours, delving into the individual presentation of these symptoms and what has caused and continues to drive them. It also puts the person in context, understanding the external factors such as family, culture and society which have contributed to the internal processes that lead to mental distress and maladaptive

DOI: 10.4324/9781032717302-14

functioning or offending (Division of Clinical Psychology, British Psychological Society, 2011).

Why is a formulation needed?

To deliver an effective psychotherapeutic treatment, a thorough understanding of the person and their difficulties is needed. When done well, this understanding, or formulation, becomes the guide for treatment, the map showing the most promising directions of travel to support that person towards a more fulfilled and safe life. A simple description or categorisation of symptoms though a diagnosis (or, indeed, a poor formulation), does not serve this function. It may lead to a one-size-fits-all approach that can work for some (for example, provision of a psychoeducational book or course for mild anxiety symptoms). However, particularly for those with complex difficulties (and many would argue, for most people in general), this approach is woefully inadequate.

Take, for example, a diagnosis of borderline personality disorder (BPD). From the list of symptoms or traits of BPD given in the diagnostic manual DSM-5 (American Psychiatric Association, 2022, pp. 733–737), you could reasonably assume that a person with BPD will be intensely fearful of abandonment or rejection and typically have relationships which are unstable. However, this simple description does not tell us anything about why a person with BPD may be fearful of rejection, how they express or respond to that fear, or how their response impacts on their relationships.

This means that two people who have a diagnosis of BPD could in fact present quite differently. For example, someone who has experienced abuse and neglect as a child may have come to believe that other people will also treat them that way, and that to survive this you must manipulate people to get what you need and always maintain power and control. Conversely, another person with BPD may have been held to a high standard as a child and punished or rejected if they didn't meet those standards, leading them to believe that they must prove their value and please others to be loved, behaving in ways that suppress their own needs in favour of the needs of others. These two people will present differently and will need separate treatment targets to support them to gain the insight and skills to experience and interact with themselves and the world differently.

Taken a step further, although offenders with personality disorders have an increased risk of violent behaviour, most people with a personality disorder do not go on to commit serious offences or harm others (Coid *et al.*, 2006). The diagnostic criteria or symptoms of a personality disorder may include factors such as erratic fluctuations in mood, intense feelings of anger, or a tendency towards impulsivity, but they explain why a person may commit violence towards themselves or others in response to these impulses or emotions. Some violent acts may indeed be linked with impulsivity and intense emotions, but others are planned. It has been noted that patterns of offending and violence can be linked with different personality disorder presentations (see Chapters 2 and 13), and this is a useful tool or starting point in assessment for treatment. Nevertheless, a more in-depth formulation is essential to help us understand how and why a person's behaviour escalates to this level and how to address this and reduce risk.

How to formulate

Chapters 1, 2 and 13 present useful theories and research that can help to understand a person's personality and risk; these will not be repeated here in depth. The purpose of this chapter is to explain how to make use of these ideas in the formulation process.

The crucial aspect of a formulation is that it is more than a description of personality factors or behaviours: it must also provide an explanation for how and why these developed. This explanation should make use of psychological theory and evidence, it should be based on a thorough clinical interview and, ideally, reports or records from the patient's life (e.g. previous psychological or psychiatric assessments, court and prison records, social care reports) and psychometric measures (e.g. measures of personality and risk such as the MCMI-IV [Millon, Grossman and Millon, 2015], HCR-20 [Douglas et al., 2014] and PCL-R [Hare, 2003]). Some psychometric assessments are also useful as a measure of change and ideally would be repeated on at least a yearly basis as well as prior to discharge and incorporated into the formulation to reflect progress.

Within most traditional forensic services, the formulation is completed by a psychologist or psychotherapist alone and then shared with the team. However, it is much more useful to involve the whole TC and the resident themselves in the assessment process. With this patient group, it often takes time to develop rapport, and it can also take some time to settle into the TC and for the relevant behavioural, psychological and relational patterns to emerge. As a result, a six-month assessment period is recommended, which should include six to eight weekly sessions of clinical interviews by the psychologist or psychotherapist on the team, as well as an occupational therapist assessment of strengths and needs (see Chapter 11). This period is also necessary for the TC membership to get to know the individual and provide their observations, contributing to a fuller understanding of the patient rather than just relying on self-report. The final formulation document should then be created and written as a team, with input from staff of all disciplines.

Formulations are working documents and should be actively utilised and updated throughout treatment. They should also reflect the wider values and processes of a TC. As with anything in a TC, a formulation should not be 'done to' a patient, but 'done with'. Patients should be aware of and signed up to the assessment and formulation process from the point of accepting their place on the TC. Their own reflections and ideas about themselves should be actively encouraged and incorporated into the formulation and treatment targets; the final document should be shared with them.

> I very much appreciated my initial psychology assessment sessions: they helped to build up a picture of me. The process was thorough and not rushed or skimmed over".
>
> – Former Millfields patient
>
> "When I arrived, I saw a lot of people asking the right questions, wanting to know what I was feeling. That is such a nice thing for us because we hadn't had it for so long".
>
> – Former Millfields patient

This collaborative approach makes the formulation process more challenging. Complex psychoanalytic ideas will need to be explained in plain language so that they can be fully understood. Many of these ideas may also be hard for patients to hear, and work will need to be done to explain concepts in an empathic and sensitive manner, as well as to prepare the patient for hearing difficult feedback. Some patients may disagree with ideas in the formulation, and these views should be heard and included even if the disagreement remains. In this case, the view of the team and the view of the patient can be included together. If there is significant disagreement or defensiveness, this can be a challenging process which takes courage and patience from all sides to work through.

Formulations should be in a narrative form, but aspects of the formulation can also be summarised in diagrams using various theoretical models (e.g. cognitive-behavioural, dialectical-behavioural). At Millfields, we found it useful to use both formats to help staff and patients at all levels understand the ideas presented. Diagrams are most useful to help everyone understand present dynamics, as well as ways of responding that could break destructive patterns. On the other hand, narrative formulations are helpful for explaining theory and the hypothesised development of difficulties.

Millfields method for formulation

Millfields developed a structured formulation document to support the multidisciplinary formulation process. This included seven broad areas:

1. Early experience

In every formulation, the patient's early life experiences and how these may link to their difficulties should be described. Consideration should be given to who were the primary caregivers for the patient and the quality of these relationships, as well as parental mental health, substance misuse, or offending. Much research on adverse childhood experiences (ACEs) suggests that they have a significant impact on personality development, identity formation, and mental and physical health (Baldwin *et al.*, 2021; Bethel *et al.*, 2014; Bower and Baldwin, 2017; Reuben *et al.*, 2016). It is therefore crucial to think not only about particularly traumatic events, losses, neglect or abuse, but also social or environmental factors such as socioeconomic status or discrimination. It is not enough to simply list adverse experiences: deeper thought needs to be put into *how* these experiences have impacted this patient's psychological development: his emotional regulation, mentalisation, problem solving, social skills and the way that he experiences or perceives himself and others.

2. Core affects and conflicts

Formulations should always include psychological theory to help explain why the patient's difficulties have developed. In the case of Millfields, we drew on primarily psychoanalytic theories to consider the psychological defences and internal conflicts that may be relevant to a patient's difficulties and risk and therefore to their treatment targets. There are a great many theories to consider here, and this chapter will not be a comprehensive guide (see Chapters 1, 2 and 13 for more in-depth consideration on this topic). Many Millfields patients struggled with extremes in relating to themselves and others. For example, some could be fiercely independent with a sense of omnipotence and a tendency to maintain control through aggression or hostility, while others were more passive and dependent, and got their needs met through emphasising their vulnerability. Some patients repressed sexual desires (e.g. in a more 'schizoid' personality state), and others used sex as a way of coping, projecting vulnerability into others, or bolstering their sense of self-worth or efficacy. Many struggled with a sense of emptiness and struggled to have a sense of self, moulding themselves to the situation or resorting to borrowed or fantasised identities. Guilt and shame and how these emotions were managed were also frequent themes to consider, e.g. denial or deflection of responsibility, self-punishment and self-blame versus an often-fragile grandiosity and need for praise and admiration.

3. Organisation of the mind

Building on the previous section, the formulation should include further exploration of how the patient perceives and relates to himself and others, as well as his ability to manage emotional states. Within this, consideration should be given not just to his perceptions, experiences and beliefs regarding himself and others, but also to his capacity for healthy attachments and relationships, self-regulation, coping and social skills, and the quality and helpfulness of unconscious defences such as use of humour, splitting, projection, acting out, sublimation, etc. (Galatariotou, 2005).

4. Patterns of relating

This section brings the formulation squarely to the here-and-now and attempts to encapsulate the common experience the patient has in relating to others as well as how others relate to him. It is useful to consider how his experience of others (transference) differs from others' experiences of themselves when they are interacting with him (countertransference), as well as how his experience of himself differs from other people's experiences of him (Sandler, 1976). Writing out (or drawing out a diagram formulation) can highlight the dangers of projective identification (Ogden, 1982; Sandler, 1989). For example, the patient expects that staff members will be abusive, which results in him behaving defensively and aggressively towards them, leading to feelings of anger in the staff and increases the likelihood of them behaving in an uncaring or neglectful manner. Gaining this understanding can also help the patient and those around him to identify and break destructive relational patterns.

5. Risk

All aspects of the formulation will of course be relevant to risk, but for clarity and to ensure this aspect is fully covered for this population of patients, there should be a section of the formulation dedicated to risk. The index offence and other significant offending should be named and factors related to offending should be identified. Drivers for offending might include seeking control or revenge, bolstering self-esteem or funding substance misuse. Disinhibitors might include lack of empathy, callousness or hopelessness. Destabilisers are often present, such as drug use or mental illness. There is likely to be repetition of relationship patterns with key attachment figures from the past. Social or environmental context will be important (e.g. violence normalised or encouraged in a peer group). Finally, the role of specific personality pathology must be considered, such as narcissistic rage, sadism, identification with the aggressor, sexual preoccupation, core complex anxieties, impulsivity, or a pattern of suppression and explosion.

6. Potential difficulties in therapy

As the formulation is a guide for treatment, it should also address the barriers to engaging in or benefitting from treatment and, if relevant, working with and complying with required supervision and regimes (e.g. probation licences, exclusion zones, prison regimes). For example, some patients perceive their problems and offending as being the result of external factors, placing the blame on others or believing that their feelings, thoughts and behavioural responses are completely out of their control. These patients will need support to take responsibility for themselves and develop a more internal locus of control (Rotter, 1966). Others will struggle with a sense of hopelessness or lack of purpose; they will need help to envision a healthy, safe and meaningful life outside of hospital or prison (e.g. education, community links and relationships, stable housing and employment, etc.). Treatment cannot be forced, so consideration should also be given to whether the patient has enough openness to new ideas, and readiness and capacity for change.

7. Strengths

Last, but certainly not least, all patients have strengths, and these should be identified and harnessed to their benefit. Intelligence, work ethic, hobbies, talents,
interests, pre-existing positive relationships, ambitions or goals for the future, psychological strengths or sources of resilience and positive coping strategies could all
be areas of strength to highlight.

Example narrative formulation

Below is an example narrative formulation. This is a combination of multiple anonymised formulations and therefore does not refer to any actual person.

Example formulation letter

Dear Duncan,

You arrived in Millfields saying that you wanted to work on your mental
health, offending, relationships and self-harming. You and your psychologist
met together on eight occasions to explore your life experiences and their
meaning. The whole community has also got to know you better over the
past six months. This letter outlines our understanding thus far of your difficulties and how they relate to your early experiences and personality.

You described that your mother died soon after you were born, and you
have always felt this as a painful absence in your life. Looking back, you
think your father was also struggling with the loss of your mother, but as
a child you found him confusing and frightening and could not talk to him
about your feelings because he would get angry and violent. He often told
you that there is no point in talking about feelings and that you just need to
toughen up and get on with things.

We wondered whether these experiences may have left you with a sense
that your presence and feelings are unlikeable or overwhelming to others,
and that you should hide yourself away and not show emotions. You have
told us that you kept yourself to yourself and had few friends growing up.
You also told us you were sexually abused when you were 11 years old, by a
teacher who initially made you feel special but then took advantage of you.
Understandably, this made you more mistrustful of people who are meant
to care for or look after you. As you grew older and understood more about
what had happened, you felt increasingly ashamed and angry, but you tried
your best to hold this inside.

You also described developing an intense desire for a partner, for someone
you could trust fully and who would make you feel safe and loved. However,
when you did get into a relationship, you often feared and suspected that

---

your partner was cheating on you or intended to take advantage of you. You would keep your suspicions and emotions to yourself for months, but eventually you would explode in rage, and in these moments you could be violent. On one level, this shows a pattern of suppression and explosion that is relevant to your risk and has been damaging to your relationships with others generally. On another level, we wondered whether there is a conflict in you around closeness with others: when you feel alone you have an intense desire for closeness, but when you get close you fear being betrayed and hurt.

We can see the pattern that this conflict produces now, because you can go through intense periods of closeness with others and seeking care and support, but when you become anxious you reject support, isolate yourself and sometimes behave aggressively or self-harm. This can leave people around you feeling confused, angry, anxious, helpless, and it can result in your relationships breaking down, which makes your difficulties with loneliness, mistrust and anger worse.

You described how you have struggled with feelings of low mood and anxiety throughout your life, and that you have tended to rely on self-harm, alcohol and drugs to manage your emotions. You also said that you have at times become suicidal, particularly after relationships breaking down. We thought that your lack of early care has left you not knowing how to look after yourself and understand or manage your emotions.

One way you managed your simultaneous desire for and fear of closeness with others in the past has been through seeking out the services of sex workers. We wondered whether this type of intimacy helped you to meet some of your needs, whilst at the same time allowing you to feel in control and safe from rejection or harm. On the other hand, your repressed feelings of shame and anger also came out during some of these encounters, and you have been convicted of multiple violent, sexual assaults. These offences were prolonged and involved the use of weapons to threaten and restrain your victims.

We wondered whether, on some level, your offending may represent an attempt to place the vulnerable, victimised aspect of yourself into someone else (i.e. projection). This enabled you to feel like the powerful aggressor rather than the helpless victim. As your offences also occurred after relationship breakdowns, we also wondered if they were an expression of a desire for retaliation and revenge against your ex-partners, or even against those who abused you as child. You have also expressed a belief that sex workers expect sexual assaults and are not as affected as others by them, which allows you to justify your actions and cope with feelings of shame.

You have taken a significant step in applying to come to Millfields, but you also acknowledge that it is difficult for you to trust that you are in a safe environment, so you continue to keep many aspects of yourself hidden.

During your treatment, it will be important for you to connect with and explore the aspects of yourself and your experiences about which you may feel ashamed or vulnerable, such as the parts of you that led you to offend and the impact of this on your victims. We recognise that this can be challenging.

We have also seen many strengths during your time here so far. You are an intelligent man, and you have already made efforts to contribute to groups and meetings, providing balanced feedback to your peers. This can help you to build relationships that are healthy and mutually supportive. It is also positive that you have chosen to engage in treatment and have been honest about what could get in the way of your success.

We understand that there may be parts of this letter that you agree with, and parts that do not fit with how you view yourself. We encourage you to take some time to think about this, and hope that you can trust that the purpose of this formulation is to support you in your treatment and help you reach your goals. We also hope that you will share your thoughts about this formulation letter with us, and that once you are ready you can bring it and your treatment targets to a community meeting so that others can better understand you.

Best wishes,
The Millfields Team

Treatment targets

Each patient's treatment targets are derived from the formulation, which should also include their own goals. The targets should address all areas that are hypothesised to cause or maintain their difficulties, including mental distress, risk and barriers to progression within institutions and/or to life in outside custody. To ensure the treatment targets fully address all these areas, it can be helpful to follow the 'risk, needs, responsivity (RNR) framework' (Andrews and Bonta, 2010, pp. 45–55). 'Risk' broadly refers to the factors that contribute to risk of offending and violence. This can include psychological processes and ideas such as 'identifying with the aggressor' (Berger, 2014), as well as factors such as addiction or their social environment promoting and normalising violence. 'Need' is often linked to risk, but more clearly relates to factors that increase distress or reduce healthy functioning such as mental health conditions, difficulties forming and maintaining healthy relationships, or institutionalisation. Finally, 'responsivity' includes barriers to engaging and benefitting from treatment including issues with trust, self-sabotage or resistance to change.

As we are forming treatment targets from an in-depth formulation of a person, and they are expected to address all significant areas of risk, need and responsivity, these targets will inevitably be complex and broad. They serve as a useful guidepost for the general direction of travel in treatment, but on the other hand can feel overwhelming to the individual and make it difficult for him to know where to start.

As a result, it is important to work with each patient to help them develop specific 'SMART' (specific, measurable, achievable, relevant and time-bound) goals from each treatment target (Doran, 1981). These can then be monitored each month and developed further, giving patients a better sense of what they are working on and the progress they are making.

Example anonymised treatment targets and monthly goals

Below is an example list of treatment targets with corresponding monthly (ideally, SMART) goals for the fictional patient Duncan.

1 *Pattern of Suppression and Explosion (risk):*

Duncan has a pattern of hiding himself away, holding his thoughts and emotions in for as long as possible (suppression), then exploding in rage and sometimes violence when they become too much. This has led to violence against partners in the past and many relationship breakdowns. Duncan can use his treatment to explore why this pattern has developed and its consequences. He can also try out different ways of coping which could be healthier, such as communicating his emotions, fears and suspicions when they arise so that they can be addressed and resolved before they reach boiling point.

Monthly goal: Duncan will bring this treatment target for exploration in his small group at least three times this month.

2 *Relationships (need):*

Part of Duncan wants meaningful relationships and craves closeness, but another part of him avoids or sabotages relationships because he expects that others will harm or take advantage of him. Duncan can use his treatment to learn to develop trust in others and communicate and work through concerns, fears or conflicts as they arise.

Monthly goal: At least one time this month, Duncan will ask for support from the community meeting chair to raise a concern or conflict with someone else in the community meeting so that he can be supported to work through it in a helpful way.

3 *Sexual Offending (risk):*

Duncan has a history of violent and sexual offending with sex workers. It is important that Duncan explores the triggers and contexts for these offences (e.g. relationship breakdowns), his beliefs about sex workers and the psychological processes (e.g. projecting the vulnerable aspects of himself onto others, getting revenge or punishing past abusers) that contribute to his offending. It is also essential that he finds ways of managing his emotions and coping with triggers that will help to reduce his risk of offending in future.

Monthly goal: Duncan will volunteer to explore one of his offences in the offence-focussed group this week and will record the formulation in his notebook for future work.

4 *Emotional regulation (need):*

Duncan struggles to identify how he is feeling and to manage his emotions in ways other than suppression, self-harm, or substance misuse. He can use his treatment to learn how to name, communicate and manage his emotions in healthier ways.

Monthly goal: Duncan will make a list of things that he finds enjoyable, calming, or helpful when he is feeling distressed or angry.

5 *Communication and authenticity (responsivity):*

Duncan has a good ability to communicate assertively and sensitively when giving constructive feedback to others. However, he struggles when he needs to communicate about himself, particularly about issues which make him feel vulnerable or ashamed. It is essential that Duncan is able to work through this if he is going to get the most out of his treatment.

Monthly goal: Duncan will attend every Friday afternoon activity session this month for at least 30 minutes, and he will have a conversation with at least one person in that time about something that is personal to him.

TC involvement in formulation and treatment targets

[Millfields] helped me to understand my pathology (borderline and narcissistic), about my vulnerability and lack of consideration for others".
                                                    – Former Millfields patient

As detailed in Chapter 3, the living learning environment of the TC and the interaction of its members is the treatment. The expertise and knowledge of professional staff members is needed to develop and bring together all ideas regarding each patient, so that there is a comprehensive understanding and guide for the treatment. However, patients within the TC also have essential expertise in knowing themselves and relating to each other; their understanding and ability to work together will be essential for meaningful change. As a result, it is important that the formulation and treatment targets are shared not only with the patient himself, but also with the TC membership. This is usually done by the patient reading out his formulation and treatment targets in a community meeting, and then regularly bringing them for discussion in groups.

Many patients will feel anxious and reluctant to share such intimate aspects of themselves with the TC. They are not required to do this immediately on admission, particularly as the assessment and formulation process itself will take at least six months. This means that they are given time to get to know everyone in the TC and will have observed other patients sharing their own formulations and treatment targets (and, hopefully, the positive and useful responses to this). However, many will also probably have had more challenging interactions with some members of the TC and will still be working on developing trust and motivation to change. As a result, the sharing of the formulation and treatment targets requires courage, support and a willingness to take a positive risk. If a patient cannot take this step after receiving intensive support, this may be an indication that further treatment in the TC is not right for them at this stage.

Self-written formulation and future planning

A rite of passage within the TC occurs after at least 1.5 years in treatment, when each patient is given the opportunity to write his own formulation. The aim of this is to give him an opportunity to formally consolidate and record what he has learned about himself and internalised from the treatment process. Many patients have spoken about this being both an immensely challenging and highly useful part of the TC treatment experience, as it encourages them to take responsibility and ownership of their treatment and progress, builds confidence and empowers them to move forward towards a more meaningful and fulfilled future. It is also a document that can travel with them, reminding them of the progress they have made and what they are continuing to work towards (i.e. relapse prevention), as well as being a tool to communicate to others who may need to understand their difficulties and what could be helpful from others in supporting risk reduction and improving wellbeing for the future (e.g. probation officers, healthcare professionals).

References

American Psychiatric Association (2022) *Diagnostic and statistical manual of mental disorders (DSM-5-TR)*. 5th edn. text revision. Washington, DC: American Psychiatric Association.

Andrews, D.A. and Bonta, J. (2010) *The psychology of criminal conduct*. 5th edn. New Providence, NJ: Lexus/Nexus.

Baldwin, J.R., Caspi, A., Meehan, A.J., Ambler, A., Arseneault, L., Fisher, H.L., Harrington, H., Matthews, T., Odgers, C.L., Poulton, R., Ramrakha, S., Moffitt, T.E. and Danese, A. (2021) 'Population vs individual prediction of poor health from results of adverse childhood experiences screening', *JAMA Pediatrics*, 175(4), p. 385. https://doi.org/10.1001/jamapediatrics.2020.5602

Berger, S.S. (2014) 'Whose trauma is it anyway? Furthering our understanding of its intergenerational transmission', *Journal of Infant, Child & Adolescent Psychotherapy*, 13(3), pp. 169–181.

Bethell, C.D., Newacheck, P., Hawes, E. and Halfon, N. (2014) 'Adverse childhood experiences: assessing the impact on health and school engagement and the mitigating role of resilience', *Health Affairs*, 33(12). https://doi.org/10.1377/hlthaff.2014.0914

Bower, C. and Baldwin, S. (2017) 'Poverty, stress, and academic performance: ACE scores and the WSCC model in an urban district', *SSRN Electronic Journal*. http://dx.doi.org/10.2139/ssrn.3055140

Coid, J., Yang, M., Roberts, A., Ullrich, S., Moran, P., Bebbington, P., Brugha, T., Jenkins, R., Farrell, M., Lewis, G. and Singleton, N. (2006) 'Violence and psychiatric morbidity in a national household population – a report from the British Household Survey', *American Journal of Epidemiology*, 164(12), pp. 1199–1208. https://doi.org/10.1093/aje/kwj339

Division of Clinical Psychology, British Psychological Society (2011) *Good practice guidelines on the use of psychological formulation*. Available at: https://explore.bps.org.uk/content/report-guideline/bpsrep.2011.rep100 (accessed 30 January 2025).

Doran, G.T. (1981) 'There's a S.M.A.R.T. Way to write Management's goals and objectives', *Management Review*, 70(11), pp. 35–36.

Galatariotou, C. (2005). 'The defences', in Budd, S. (ed.) *Introducing psychoanalysis: essential themes and topics*. London: Routledge.

Hare, R.D. (2003) *The hare psychopathy checklist-revised*. 2nd edn. Toronto: Multi-Health Systems.

Millon, T., Grossman, S. and Millon, C. (2015) *MCMI-IV: Millon clinical multiaxial inventory-IV—Manual*. Bloomington, Minnesota: NCS Pearson.

Ogden, T. (1982) 'The concept of projective identification', in *Projective identification and psychotherapeutic techniques*. London: Jason Aronson.

Reuben, A., Moffitt, T.E., Caspi, A., Belsky, D.W., Harrington, H., Schroeder, F., Hogan, S., Ramrakha, S., Poulton, R. and Danese, A. (2016) 'Lest we forget: comparing retrospective and prospective assessments of adverse childhood experiences in the prediction of adult health', *Journal of Child Psychology and Psychiatry, and Allied Disciplines*, 57(10), pp. 1103–1112. https://doi.org/10.1111/jcpp.12621

Glasser (1979) 'Some aspects of the role of aggression in the perversions', in Rosen, I. (ed.) *Sexual deviation*. 2nd edn. Oxford: Oxford University Press.

Rotter, J.B. (1966) 'Generalized expectancies for internal versus external control of reinforcement', *Psychological Monographs: General and Applied*, 80(1), pp. 1–28. https://doi.org/10.1037/h0092976

Sandler, J. (1979) 'Countertransference and role-responsiveness', *International Review of Psycho-Analysis*, 3, pp. 43–47.

Sandler, J. (1987) 'The concept of projective-identification', in Sander, J. (ed.) *Projection, identification, projective identification*. London: Routledge.

Chapter 15

How to form a therapeutic alliance

Jack Blake, Dean Bristow, Miguel Acha Gimenez, Will Irvine and Alex Maguire

Introduction

To engage and benefit from the intensive treatment offered within a therapeutic community (TC) like Millfields, patients need to feel able to fully commit to a process that requires facing fears of vulnerability and failure. The development of a good therapeutic alliance between patients and staff is essential in this endeavour, not only because it builds the trust and support the patient will need to engage in therapeutic work, but also because it is part of the 'corrective experience' which leads to more lasting change in the way patients relate to themselves and others (see Chapters 3 and 10). There are many challenges in fostering a therapeutic alliance, both for patients and staff, and there are important distinctions in the qualities of the treatment alliance within a TC as opposed to more traditional psychiatric environments, much of which will be covered in this chapter.

What is a therapeutic alliance

The word 'alliance' has its roots in the old French word meaning 'wedding ring', so it implies a feeling of a union, something approaching a contract: a joining in a common endeavour. The origins of thinking around therapeutic alliance can be traced back to Freud (1913), in which he recognised the need for trust and collaboration in treatment. Bordin (1979) added to this, defining the 'working alliance' between therapist and patient as a three-part construct: (1) consensus on the goals of the intervention, (2) agreement about the tasks required in treatment, and (3) creation of a reciprocal bond between therapist and patient. Bordin further proposed that the first two components are dependent on the third, as the outcome of treatment is enhanced when there is trust and a shared belief that the treatment is relevant and efficacious.

The strength of the therapeutic alliance has been shown to be a reliable predictor of therapy outcomes, regardless of the modality employed (Ardito and Rabellino, 2011; Horvath and Luborsky, 1993). In practice, therapeutic alliance will inevitably ebb and flow over the course of treatment and, of necessity, ruptures and reconciliations can be expected and even helpful to strengthening the relationship over

DOI: 10.4324/9781032717302-15

time. As this process and the experience of a therapeutic relationship is internalised by the patient (in psychodynamic thinking, installing a 'good internal object'), it can help them to reevaluate how they see themselves and others, and therefore become less destructive in their ways of relating (Klein, 1923). A healthy and robust therapeutic alliance can over time lead to something healthy and robust being set up inside the patient themselves.

Building therapeutic alliances within a forensic TC

In a forensic TC, forming a therapeutic alliance is complicated by the pathology of the patients, their incarceration, the number of professionals involved, and the patients' involvement in each other's treatment. Residents in a TC must not only develop a therapeutic alliance with specific members of staff, but also with the whole community, including other patients and staff members from various disciplines. TC staff must therefore monitor not only their individual working relationship with patients, but also the overall therapeutic health and levels of trust and collaboration amongst all members. Measures of 'ward atmosphere' such as the Essen Climate Evaluation Schema (EssenCES; Schalast et al., 2008) can be helpful tools in assessing the safety and effectiveness of the TC environment.

To ensure an effective therapeutic alliance, the patient's motivation for change must align with the TC's ability to provide a safe and supportive enough environment in which to do so. All patients and staff must also understand and agree to engage with the TC model. At Millfields, any patient wishing to join the TC would be briefed by staff about the treatment and its requirements and would be asked to agree to this by signing a therapy contract prior to admission. This preparation is the first step in forming the working relationship, as it helps to define the goals and tasks for treatment.

Challenges to building a therapeutic alliance with offenders with personality disorder

Offenders with personality disorder have frequently had histories of trauma and exclusion, leaving them distrustful of others and fearful of revealing needs and vulnerabilities. Many have developed beliefs that violence, corruption or manipulation are the only ways to protect themselves and get their needs met in relationships (Sainsbury, 2022; see also Chapters 1 and 2). This way of relating has led to unhealthy relationships and offending behaviour and makes the formation of a therapeutic alliance particularly challenging. Within the TC, this can take the form of an inability to tolerate treatment with persistent disengagement or disturbance of groups, violating boundaries with staff or other patients, trafficking illicit substances onto the unit, or serious self-harm and high levels of distress. Conflicts can also arise particularly when there are secondary gains or misalignment of treatment goals, or inauthentic engagement.

To work with the challenges of forming a therapeutic alliance with personality disordered patients, it is essential to understand their attachment system (Holmes, 2014 – need page number). The patients rarely have healthy, secure attachments, patients such as those at Millfields have the highest proportion of those with disorganised attachment style. As children, they have experienced their caregivers, who are meant to keep them safe, as a source of fear or abuse (Schimmenti *et al.*, 2014). Having no other way of coping and being reliant on an unsafe person for their survival, their behaviour becomes increasingly dysregulated and aggressive. This in turn often exacerbates the abuse, leading to a cycle in which the child's sense of defectiveness and rejection is internalised, and they grow to expect this treatment in all of their relationships going forward.

Patients with personality disorder lack skills in emotional regulation and rely instead on supressing or projecting their emotions and fears into others. For those with antisocial personality traits in particular, feelings of fear and vulnerability are so threatening and intolerable that they push them into others, often by being frightening and aggressive themselves. This can mean that the patients who present as the most hostile, terrifying and persecutory, often have equally strong, but suppressed feelings of fear, sadness and longing for closeness and care in relationships. Thus, whilst they may be extremely rejecting and neglectful in their behaviour towards others, they will be equally sensitive to feeling rejected or neglected in return. These patients usually have little insight into this, unconsciously pushing people away and lacking understanding regarding their role in this.

The strain that this dynamic puts on the therapeutic alliance is considerable. These men are often unpleasant and frightening to be around, and professionals will understandably wish to distance themselves from them. Without the understanding of the psychological factors at play, staff members can simply see these people with personality disorder as 'bad' and their issues as 'behavioural', rather than how they may see other patients in mental health settings as 'mentally ill' and less responsible for how they behave as a result. Even staff who do have insight into what is happening will also require significant emotional intelligence and clinical skills to regulate their own emotional responses and countertransference and continue to try to build the therapeutic alliance in the face of often intense hostility.

Despite the treatment model practising a flattened hierarchy (see Chapter 3), parallels can be drawn between the patients' experiences of authority in the past and their experience of authority which must still exist within a forensic TC. Rightly or wrongly, these patients have in the past felt unfair persecution within the penal, education and social systems. Such experiences can interfere with the establishment of a therapeutic alliance with professionals who are associated with these systems. The patients may lack trust, feel unsafe and face conflicting values, as they may perceive aligning with the professionals in the TC akin to aligning with authority such as police, which many would find unacceptable.

Alternatively, some patients may have sought admission for secondary gains – seeing the TC as an easier alternative to prison and seeking the TC's hospital environment rather than the treatment on offer. These hospital benefits are considerable, including amenities that are nicer than most prisons, with en-suite bathrooms, no 'lock ups', access to gardens, leave outside hospital and more opportunities for outside visitors. However, many of these patients will discover that the demands of intensive treatment carry such an emotional burden that, without the motivation to engage, the amenities seem to come at too great a cost to continue.

Patients with a high level of psychopathic traits and who score higher on the Hare Psychopathy Checklist (PCL-22; Hare, 2003) may also struggle with motivation and effective and authentic engagement in treatment. This is because these men have a lower capacity for empathy and accessing their emotional experience, are highly reward seeking, and unlikely to be impeded by an emotionally driven conscience. Coupled with an often-sadistic nature, this can lead to entrenched patterns of cruelty, manipulation and dominance in relationships, and for those who are more skilled, this dynamic can be well hidden. These patients may appear to be engaging and can even induce powerful transference which can be perceived as engagement, but in reality will be attempting to deceive for corrupt personal gain.

Working with challenges to the therapeutic alliance

Offenders with personality disorder typically present their challenging behaviour by frequently testing treatment alliances through destructive acting-out behaviours (McGauley, 1997). Their response to caregiving is likely to be linked to their primitive defences and offending or offence-paralleling behaviours and can therefore be a key tool in formulating their difficulties (Yakeley & Meloy, 2010; see Chapters 1 and 2).

As the work in a TC is relational, staff play a vital role in how residents progress. Alongside the standard roles and responsibilities, staff must also become the safe container for anxieties and projections, as well as sources of a secure attachment, so that they can help the patient develop a good, introjected object. The repeated experience of a nurse, for example, as a reliable caring and understanding figure, even in the face of hostility, can build up a sense of something reliable, caring and understanding in the patient himself and help him to lower his destructive defences. This gradual and delicate process can alter the resources and mental map that the patient draws on when faced with problems or emotional difficulties and build a helpful expectation that the world does have good, trustworthy parts, as does the patient himself. This is no easy task when our patients are accustomed to punishment and incarceration rather than gaining an understanding of the origins of their criminality or destructive behaviour.

Due to the nature of our patients' psychopathology, patients are expected to struggle to give insight into their actions (Bion, 1959). When in an emotionally aroused state, particularly when the attachment system is activated, the resident's capacity to mentalise breaks down, and the ability for reflection diminishes (Fonagy and Bateman, 2008). Mentalisation refers to the ability of one to identify what someone else is thinking and feeling. Failures in this ability can lead to misinterpretation of the behaviour of others as threatening, and this can often lead to altercations wherein patients use aggression or violence that is disproportionate to any perceived provocation.

When considering why the patient acts in a particular way (for instance, shouting, verbal abuse, self-harming, or violence against property) staff must consider how and what historical patterns of behaviour are playing out, not only in terms of offending behaviour but also in professional relationships. Sometimes, the professional is not always experienced by the patient in the way that they intend. Instead, they are distorted and seen through the lens of early life experiences, perhaps as an untrustworthy social worker or teacher or an unsafe or rejecting parent. They will likely not be aware of this as a projection, and it is important to highlight the unconscious nature of this process and support increasing insight over time.

These dynamics are informed by their attachment scripts, whereby staff, who hold the position of caregiver and are symbolic of authority, are automatically considered untrustworthy, incompetent and neglectful, or hostile and abusive, based on the patients' experiences of others in the past. Understandably, patients who see staff members in this way will be hostile and distant themselves, looking out for and overreacting to any evidence that their assumptions are correct. This can be painful and offensive to staff, who will often feel compelled to avoid, punish or, conversely, indulge patients to prove them wrong. However, behaving in this manner only identifies with and reconfirms the patient's projections. Thus, without this awareness and purposeful interactions, perverse or abusive dynamics can be unconsciously enacted.

Setbacks, ruptures and reparations

Working with patients with personality disorder means that the therapeutic alliance will be challenged and tested, both consciously and unconsciously. The ruptures and setbacks this produces can be pivotal therapeutic opportunities, particularly for patients who may have a repeated history of relationship breakdown, but limited experience of repair and recovery. Unfortunately, ruptures can also at times be irreparable or too destructive to the TC to continue working with, and it is important to distinguish as quickly as possible when this is the case.

Many patients who have been in prison have participated in structured offending behaviour programmes. These programs often introduce the Cycle of Change (Prochaska and DiClemente, 1983), which set out seven stages in the process of change, from unawareness to consciousness of the problem, to eventual changes to overcome this. Whilst traditionally used for substance use problems, it can be applied more broadly to other maladaptive or destructive behaviours contributing to patient's difficulties. The stages are:

Precontemplation:	no conscious understanding of the problem, or denies the need for change.
Contemplation:	becomes aware of the problem and starts considering change
Preparation:	deciding to change; starting to take small steps or making a plan and gathering resources
Action:	actively changing and moving towards goals
Maintenance:	working to keep change going long-term
Lapse:	a small slip, temporarily returning to previous behaviour, from which preparation and action can be resumed
Relapse:	a more significant reversion to old behaviour, possibly back to pre-contemplation

At Millfields, this model was introduced to the patients during their initial 'Orientation to Therapy' group which they must complete before starting the small groups (see Chapter 3). This framework provides a shared way of looking at setbacks as part of the process of positive change.

This cycle can be helpful in identifying patient's readiness and motivation for change, as well as providing a framework for understanding what is required for change and preventing an 'all or nothing' mindset around this. It can act as an important reference tool for patients when they begin to experience inevitable difficulties in the therapeutic alliance or work more broadly, reframing these as lapses which can be worked on rather than a relapse, which can inspire hopelessness.

It is also important that staff have reasonable expectations of patients as they engage in treatment, and understand how to work with patients at all stages of change. Resistance to efforts to form a therapeutic alliance is inevitable and can be seen as patients testing the staff's intentions before they are able to feel safe enough to engage in the psychological treatment (Blumenthal, Wood & Williams, 2018, pp. 25–43). However, this process can be highly frustrating, stressful and confusing to staff who are unused to their caring intentions and actions being treated with suspicion or met with hostility and rejection. Clinical supervision and group reflective practice and staff support sessions are two important fora for this necessary work and, when used appropriately by staff, can help repair staff to formulate ways of understanding and repairing ruptures with patients (see Chapter 18).

Difficulties for many of our patients begin to arise on the ward where boundaries are set and enforced. Patients can experience this as punitive and maliciously withholding or restrictive, particularly where the transference becomes centred around abusive caregivers. These difficult feelings can induce antisocial defence mechanisms such as hostility, aggression, subversion or corruption which, left un-addressed, can become highly destructive to the TC.

The TC is the most powerful tool for addressing interpersonal difficulties and ruptures in therapeutic alliance. Formal therapy groups like community meetings, crisis meetings and small groups (see Chapters 3–5) allow patients to hear a variety of perspectives and reflections on the difficulties that have arisen and take some of the destructive power away from intense projective dynamics that often develop between just two people. Patients often find this process of group discussion challenging and threatening, particularly at the start of treatment. The group settings can heighten familiar feelings of persecution and paranoia, and some can fear that the issues or people being discussed may not be able to be contained safely within the group. However, this aspect of treatment is non-negotiable, as failure to implement it can have a detrimental effect on the whole group's therapeutic alliance to the TC.

Patients with personality disorder often experience internal splits and conflicts, with one part of them wanting to foster a good relationship with others, while another fearful part feels compelled to sabotage or corrupt the connection. TCs are set up to work with this ambivalence, particularly with the pillar of 'permissiveness' (see Chapter 3) which assumes that residents cannot change all at once and fosters progressive change over time. Nevertheless, some patients will be unable to lower their defences and the assaults on the TC can be too great to bear. It is important to balance the need for permissiveness with the need to maintain the therapeutic culture and safety of the TC (Norton, 1992; Rapoport, 1960).

Over the years, Millfields had many patients who 'dropped out' of treatment. While fluctuations in engagement and commitment are expected due to the pathology of these patients, once someone is identified as irreversibly disengaged, it is important to promptly transfer them back to prison or, if possible, a lower-intensity treatment environment in which engagement is more likely. This measure helps preserve the therapeutic alliance with other patients who can be influenced by or resentful of others who are not engaging authentically or who seem to be exempt from the rules of the TC.

Inevitably, it can be a fraught process to gauge when this point has been reached and there can be strong differences of opinion amongst the team. Permissiveness is a key pillar of the TC: allowing and expecting a certain amount of maladaptive behaviour from the patients, particularly in the early parts of treatment, without rushing to punishment which is often ineffective and triggers destructive patterns of behaviour. This allows each patients' difficulties to be expressed to and experienced by the community so they can be understood and worked on over time. However, a frequent dilemma in TCs is determining when a patient crosses the line of behaviour and has become too destructive to themselves and the TC. If a patient in this position is allowed to stay too long, trust in the TC as a reliable and consistent container can be eroded and the therapeutic alliance irretrievably damaged. Alternatively, if a patient is removed overly hastily, familiar feelings of persecution, exclusion and neglect can be triggered which can also be equally damaging to the therapeutic alliance.

> "Some patients were left in the unit for too long. They were extremely destructive to the whole running of the unit and fostered ill-feeling within both staff and patients".
>
> – Former Millfields patient

With all but the most extreme behaviours, there are seldom blanket rules for all eventualities. The same behaviours from different patients may take on different meanings depending on their underlying difficulties and experiences as well as their length of treatment and therefore expectation of progress, and thus each incident requires tailored thinking from the TC. The severely personality disordered patient can be drawn to finding the smallest grey area to use, unconsciously, to test boundaries, and seemingly small but numerous incidents can build up to an intolerable level. Conversely, a quite explosive but infrequent incident of property damage or verbal aggression may feel able to be worked with. With a patient population who can be highly attuned to a sense of injustice and favouritism, much of the day-to-day work of the TC can involve communicating why certain behaviours may be responded to in different ways depending on the context. Helping patients to understand this permissiveness and the rationale behind it is crucial to maintaining the therapeutic alliance.

Encouraging autonomy in the context of a non-toxic attachment

Haigh (2013) notes that "authority must always remain negotiable – authority is something which exists between people rather than in individuals or policies". The TC model of having a flattened hierarchy and an intentional structure of giving appropriate levels of responsibility and authority to patients is enormously helpful to patients who distrust traditional systems of authority and therefore struggle to form a therapeutic alliance. Their standard ego-defence styles, usually directed towards authority, are suddenly challenged by peers who have shared similar life experiences and perspectives. This creates a less threatening space in which to explore the heart of the individual's internal experiences and ways of relating, reducing the probability of maladaptive ways of relating.

For patients whose relationship with caregivers may have been characterised by neglect or abuse, autonomy can easily be equated with solipsism, or the view that they must only ever rely on themselves as nobody else can be trusted. Conversely, they may have experienced narcissistic primary attachment figures who could not allow them normal development of independence (Winner and Nicholson, 2018). Whilst achieving a healthy therapeutic alliance is a significant achievement for patients at Millfields, patients can understandably be uncertain how to also maintain a healthy sense of autonomy within that relationship. Particularly as discharge, representing an end of the therapeutic relationship, approaches, care must be taken to ensure the ending of the relationship is therapeutic rather than traumatic. This can be very difficult for patients who may not have experienced consistent care before or those with dependent personality traits.

To also foster a sense of responsibility and healthy autonomy, patients should be involved in as many of the decisions and discussions in the TC as possible. Typically, these men have had little control or supported independence during their early experiences with their parents, and this has followed through to schooling to prison environments which prioritise obedience and compliance over all else. As a result, involvement in the TC is often a novel experience for these patients.

When decisions are made collectively, staff can provide information and help patients in considering the pros and cons of different options, but the purpose should always be to empower patients to make their own informed decisions. In a secure forensic environment, risk and security concerns mean that not every decision is open for negotiation, but the difference remains that these requirements are communicated clearly and openly, and power is returned to the TC at the earliest opportunity. This principle of the TC has obvious overlaps with the thinking underpinning trauma-informed practice (The Institute on Trauma and Trauma-Informed Care, 2022). In trying to give the patients as much choice, collaboration and understanding as possible, we avoid retraumatising those who have a history of being victims of coercion or neglect. This allows them more chance to be able to avoid the fight or flight responses of trauma and learn new responses to interpersonal difficulty.

The way staff and senior residents listen and talk to patients is also key in developing autonomy. Through respectful and active listening and open questions, patients are supported to think for themselves rather than simply seek answers from staff. This can develop into a virtuous cycle, where patients are able to mentalise better in the presence of staff with whom they have developed a therapeutic alliance, as they have the experience of being supported and are encouraged to work with them. In time this leads the patient to internalise this good experience and develop the ability to own and retain their new perspectives and mentalising skills without support from particular members of staff. It is this process internalising the experience of the therapeutic alliance that allows patients to achieve lasting change and live a healthier and safer life beyond treatment and incarceration.

Conclusion

For patients to benefit from therapy, there must be a therapeutic alliance, and within a TC this must be inclusive of all members and embedded in the culture. There are inevitable challenges to forming a therapeutic alliance with offenders with personality disorder, and it is essential that this is understood and worked with. Some periods of rupture and breakdown of the therapeutic alliance are unavoidable, and these are important opportunities for therapeutic work to take place.

However, when the TA breaks down completely and a patient disengages from therapy, there comes a point where, not only is further therapeutic work impossible, but the patient's continued presence in the TC undermines the treatment for all.

Whilst forming strong and trusting bonds with staff is a crucial developmental step for the patients, the end goal is not to make them permanently reliant on staff for their development. By the end of treatment, the aim is for patients to have gained the skills and experiences which allow them to have relationships which balance healthy dependency and independence. The experience of the therapeutic alliance has been internalised, allowing the patient to continue this healthier way of relating even when the treatment is far in the past.

References

The Institute on Trauma and Trauma-Informed Care (2022) *Trauma-informed organizational change manual*. Available at: http://socialwork.buffalo.edu/trauma-manual (accessed 22.01.2025).

Ardito, R. and Rabellino, D. (2011) 'Therapeutic alliance and outcome of psychotherapy: historical excursus, measurements and prospects for research', *Frontiers in Psychology*, 2(270). https://doi.org/10.3389/fpsyg.2011.00270

Bion, W. (1959) 'Attacks on linking', *International Journal of Psycho-Analysis*, 40, pp. 308–315.

Blumenthal, S., Wood, H. and Williams, A. (2018) *Assessing risk: a relational approach*. Oxen: Routledge.

Bordin, E. (1979) 'The generalizability of the psychoanalytic concept of the working alliance', *Psychotherapy: Theory, Research & Practice*, 16(3), pp. 252–260. https://doi.org/10.1037/h0085885

Fonagy, P. and Bateman, A. (2008) 'The development of borderline personality disorder—a mentalizing model', *Journal of Personality Disorders*, 22(1), pp. 4–21. https://doi.org/10.1521/pedi.2008.22.1.4

Freud, S. (1913/1966). 'On beginning the treatment', in Strachey, J. (ed.) *The standard edition of the complete psychological works of Sigmund Freud*. London: Hogarth Press.

Haigh, R. (2013) 'The quintessence of a therapeutic environment', *Therapeutic Communities: International Journal of Therapeutic Communities*, 34(1), pp. 6–16. https://doi.org/10.1108/09641861311330464

Hare, R.D. (2003) *The hare psychopathy checklist-revised*. 2nd edn. Toronto: Multi-Health Systems.

Holmes, J. (2014) *John Bowlby and attachment theory*. 2nd edn. New York: Routledge.

Horvath, A. and Luborsky, L. (1993) 'The role of the therapeutic alliance in psychotherapy', *Journal of Consulting and Clinical Psychology*, 61(4), pp. 561–573. https://doi.org/10.1037/0022-006X.61.4.561

Klein, M. (1923) 'The development of a child', *International Journal of Psychoanalysis*, 4, pp. 419–474.

McGauley, G. (1997) 'The actor, the act and the environment: forensic psychotherapy and risk', *International Review of Psychiatry*, 9, pp. 257–264.

Norton, K. (1992) 'A culture of enquiry: its preservation or loss', *Therapeutic Communities*, 13, pp. 3–25.

Prochaska, J.O. and DiClemente, C.C. (1983) 'Stages and processes of self-change of smoking: toward an integrative model of change', *Journal of Consulting and Clinical Psychology*, 51(3), pp. 390–395. https://doi.org/10.1037//0022-006x.51.3.390

Rapoport, R. (1960) 'Community as doctor: new perspectives on a therapeutic community', *Tavistock Publications*, 19(2), p. 325. https://doi.org/10.1177/001789696101900213

Sainsbury, L. (2022) 'Trauma, personality disorder, and offending', in Willmot, P., & Jones, L. (eds) *Trauma-informed forensic practice*. New York: Routledge.

Schalast, N., Redies, M., Collins, M., Stacey, J. and Howells, K. (2008) 'EssenCES, a short questionnaire for assessing the social climate of forensic psychiatric wards', *Criminal Behaviour and Mental Health*, 18(1), pp. 49–58. https://doi.org/10.1002/cbm.677

Schimmenti, A., Passanisi, A., Pace, U., Manzella, S., Di Carlo, G. and Caretti, V. (2014) 'The relationship between attachment and psychopathy: a study with a sample of violent offenders', *Current Psychology: A Journal for Diverse Perspectives on Diverse Psychological Issues*, 33(3), pp. 256–270. https://doi.org/10.1007/s12144-014-9211-z

Winner, N.A. and Nicholson, B.C. (2018) 'Overparenting and narcissism in young adults: the mediating role of psychological control', *Journal of Child and Family Studies*, 27(11), pp. 3650–3657. https://doi.org/10.1007/s10826-018-1176-3

Yakeley, J. and Meloy, J. (2010) 'Psychodynamic treatment of antisocial personality disorder', in Clarkin, J.F., Fonagy, P., & Gabbard, G.O. (eds) *Psychodynamic psychotherapy for personality disorders: a clinical handbook*. Arlington: American Psychiatric Publishing.

Chapter 16

The process of change

Will Irvine, Alex Maguire and Celia Taylor

What do we know about change in this group?

In England, services for offenders with personality disorder such as Millfields come under what is known as the Offender Personality Disorder (OPD) pathway. The overarching goals of the OPD pathway are (a) to reduce serious sexual and/ or violent re-offending; (b) to improve the psychological wellbeing of people receiving the services; (c) to increase competence and confidence of staff; and (d) to increase the cost-effectiveness and efficiency of OPD services (National Offender Management Service and National Health Service England, 2015). The people at whom these services are aimed, the offenders themselves, would probably not disagree with these goals, but would set them in a much more personalised frame. Most of the patients coming to Millfields wanted to escape from themselves – from their painful, often disastrous relationships; from a sense of their life wasting away behind bars; and from inner misery, disappointment and shame. They were very much the 'treatment seeking', as opposed to the 'treatment rejecting' individuals distinguished by Tyrer *et al.* (2003), although they often found it difficult to articulate their longing for change.

In order to be able to offer these individuals genuine hope, it is important to ensure that our understanding of change in treatment is based on evidence and not simply loyalty to a particular model – such as the psychodynamic versus the cognitive-behavioural. In fact, as will be discussed later, it is likely that a variety of models will be needed to address these individuals' complex needs, so services must offer a 'big tent' approach that can incorporate that variety. Livesley (2012) has argued that different theoretical models are likely to be more useful during different phases. For example, symptoms might best be relieved (as opposed to 'cured') through a combination of cognitive-behavioural work and, if really required, medication. Interpersonal difficulties, however, are not likely to be responsive to medication and need to be addressed via psychological or relational interventions.

A meaningful process of change, however, also relies on the subjective experience of the participants. It has long been established that the quality of the therapeutic alliance is crucial to positive change being achieved in this group (e.g. Baier, Kline and Feeny, 2020). An interesting study by Sturm *et al.* (2021) analysed which components

DOI: 10.4324/9781032717302-16

of the therapeutic alliance make the biggest difference for a group of men undergoing mandatory probation supervision. They were: growing levels of trust in the probation officer's good intentions, and diminishing levels of what the authors called 'reactance', or the offender's perception of the probation officer as punitive. Improvements in both variables were significantly associated with reductions in later reoffending. Participants in a qualitative study of their experience of the OPD pathway (Jarrett et al., 2025) identified it as being important that a relational environment existed, in which clear feedback about their behaviour was given. This was a new experience for people who were used to setbacks where no cogent explanation was given. It is interesting to note that, while given a high rating, being on the receiving end of full and frank feedback is not necessarily an enjoyable experience. The study also identified encouragement by staff, a focus on strengths as well as difficulties, participation in decision-making and being given choices as highly valued. Offenders in a London-based prison OPD service told researchers (McMurran and Delight, 2017) that being treated with respect, feeling understood and gaining hope helped them to change.

General features of formal treatment

Personality disorder can be thought of as consisting of universal disturbances common to all patients, and specific features particular to each form or subtype of the disorder. These two core areas involve chronic disturbances in interpersonal relationships (e.g. Benjamin, 1993; Rutter, 1987, p. 267) and the failure to form a cohesive self-system or sense of identity and agency (e.g. Kernberg, 1984; Kohut, 1971). Such difficulties underly all the various manifestations of the disorder. They also pose great challenges to the therapeutic relationship, which is the main vehicle for change. Therefore, in order to achieve positive progress, formal interventions must attend to and address the challenges inherent in these disturbances. Various authors have proposed some key general features that should provide the foundation of any treatment, such as a clearly defined and structured approach that is based on developing an attachment between the patient and his therapists (Bateman and Tyrer, 2002). An over-arching therapeutic community (TC) model acts as a further vehicle for change, by providing open communication and the involvement and empowerment of the patients – doing with, rather than doing to (Haigh, 2013), with an emphasis on taking personal responsibility. These elements provide much needed consistency, thus preventing the eclectic nature of the approach becoming haphazard; and structure, thus containing the strong fluctuations of disturbance that are likely to be manifest during periods of change.

"It was helpful to have staff who would listen to you and put you on the right road, no judgement, patience and calmness. At the same time, it was helpful to have staff who couldn't have the wool pulled over their eyes".
– Former Millfields patient

Phases of change

The Millfields model incorporated a phased plan of change that began with the person's arrival in the unit and progressed through to the end of therapy. Being both eclectic and staged allowed the therapy to incorporate a number of inter-related treatment modalities, which operated both concurrently and consecutively. A key reason for this is that no single therapeutic approach is sufficient in itself to achieve a comprehensive, global change in personality: there needs to be a multifaceted approach to multi-determined problems. Furthermore, although many of these patients have difficulties in common, there are also individual nuances that will need to be addressed via a tailored approach, allowing adaptations depending on personality subtype or particular defences. Acknowledging each person as an individual in this way also enables him to feel recognised and understood.

The model presented here is not intended to be prescriptive, because the treatment of offenders with severe personality disorder requires both flexibility and creativity. What follows is, rather, a description of the likely general progression of a patient's treatment in favourable circumstances. As already mentioned, in reality there is inevitably some overlap and movement back and forth along a timeline, as difficulties emerge or re-emerge. In this sense, it can be called, a 'continuous corrective experience' (Livesley, 2007). It can be extremely useful to write a plan of his timeline with each patient, to serve as a yardstick, both for him and for the clinical team, of areas of progress and areas that are 'stuck' or have come adrift. Research can indicate to us which patients are particularly susceptible to this phenomenon (Mathlin *et al.*, 2021): unsurprisingly, they include people with psychopathic tendencies, but people with symptoms of a co-morbid psychosis can also become mired in confusion and stasis without appropriate treatment. The phased approach is also an important part of instilling hope that change is possible, when it might initially seem overwhelming or hopeless.

The Millfields phases of change is loosely based on a sequential approach, rooted in an understanding of the disorder (e.g. Livesley, 2012) and of what is needed for healthy emotional development (Haigh, 2013). The careful sequencing of interventions is designed to build the patient's capacity to face up to parts of himself that he has spent his life resisting or denying, eventually enabling him to tolerate talking about them. Indeed, verbalising emotions such as distress or rage is one of the main ways in which the tendency for violent acting out can be lessened (Norton and Dolan, 1995). This is, by necessity, a deeply uncomfortable and painful process because of the vulnerability it exposes. Newcomers are generally unable to manage the anxieties generated by this kind of self-exposure, without resorting to the unhealthy defence mechanisms which have held them together up to this point. To prepare patients for the work ahead, it is necessary to increase their window of tolerance.

As the patients spend more time in the community and trust builds, a virtuous cycle can develop whereby they risk sharing more vulnerable aspects of themselves, gain insight and even relief, and therefore trust in the process builds. This leads them to be able to explore their offending behaviour and the early relational traumas that are likely to lie underneath. It is worth noting that setbacks, lapses and crises are a natural part of this gradual progression. Indeed, how the community responds to setbacks can be a compelling factor in changing a patient's paranoid or nihilistic 'internal working model' of the world (Bowlby, 1969). If the response is compassionate, boundaried and inquisitive, keen to understand the motivation for a destructive act rather than condemn and punish, it will provide a rich opportunity for internal change. Finally, it is important to allow patients to change at their own speed, albeit with a firm 'nudge' if and when needed. We learned from experience that different individuals progress at very different rates in ways that are difficult to predict, and this fact should militate against service Commissioner demands for a uniform length of stay.

Attachment and containment

This initial stage is crucial, providing the basis for the success of any further work in the community. The goal here is to instil in the patient a basic level of safety, through establishing a transparent, consistent and dependable relationship. These patients have extremely low levels of 'epistemic trust'. This important concept has been defined as, "the ability to accurately identify specific others as trustworthy and, therefore, to rely on the information they convey as personally relevant and generalizable" (Fisher *et al.*, 2023, p. 2). A lack of epistemic trust impairs a person's ability and willingness to learn from others, so the entire staff team needs to make efforts to build that trust, not just through what they say, but also through how they behave. Interestingly, patients will accept necessary limits to transparency, or a human failure to follow up on a commitment, if a sincere and timely explanation is given.

In addition to low levels of internal epistemic trust, those admitted to the unit from prison were used to an environment where suspicion and guardedness were often necessary for survival. Arriving at a new place with different rules and expectations could be extremely disorientating, precipitating paranoia or anxiety about the sincerity of community members. Each new patient was therefore welcomed with a proactive effort to establish the unit as being a safe space for him. In practice, fears about the unfamiliar environment and especially the people in it, could persist for months. One patient, for example, wore his bath towel wrapped around his neck for many weeks, so afraid was he of being stabbed from behind. Later, he said:

> "I will remember learning and understanding my suffering and pain. Learning to feel emotions, to trust, to move forward. Without Millfields I probably would have been dead. Who I was before, I couldn't even have any of those conversations".
>
> – Former Millfields patient

Each new member of the Millfields TC was assigned a 'buddy': a senior, more longstanding patient member of the community, to act as a kind of peer mentor. The buddy would ideally be someone who has been able to make good use of the treatment programme and thus to inspire hope that change is possible. With staff, he was responsible for showing the newcomer round, helping him settle into his room and familiarising him with the basics of the daily timetable and rules of the unit. Members of the clinical team made conscious efforts to begin to establish a therapeutic alliance, contain feelings of vulnerability and provide encouragement.

A newly arrived patient would start attending community meetings from day 1, and he and all his peers were expected to disclose their index offences, in the interests of promoting the transparency mentioned above. This practice also conveyed a clear message that offending was what everyone had come to work on. Other interventions at this stage were focused on psychoeducation and familiarisation. The men would not yet begin work in small groups; instead, they would join the 'Orientation to Therapy' (OTT) group, usually with two or three other newcomers. In this group, patients were taught how and why they met the diagnostic criteria for personality disorder, the concept of the 'personal scientist' (essentially, curiosity and self-awareness), and some skills in emotion management and working in groups. Later, having learned from experience, we added modules on attachment and the impact of trauma, which were very helpful in helping the men understand the sources of damage in their lives.

The nascent relationships a newcomer began to form inevitably brought to the surface old patterns of connecting with others. This allowed the community to begin to understand him, and provided opportunities for an understanding response and corrective feedback, rather than more familiar retaliatory or punitive reactions. An important element of this stage was collaborating with the patient on writing his formulation and individual treatment targets. The co-creation of these was essential, as it invited him into an active role in his treatment. Included in this process was a psychodynamic risk assessment, which helped the staff begin to understand the meaning in the acts the patient was drawn to.

> "I met the teacher in my first week at Millfields, and I worked with her the whole way though. She got me my skills to develop and then go to college".
> – Former Millfields patient

Patients must also begin to learn how to give and receive feedback. This is likely to be a difficult experience at first, but navigating it without precipitating conflict was essential to being able to make the most of the group interventions of the TC.

Control and regulation

In order to be equipped to take part in intensive therapy, new patients needed to be able to manage overt distress in ways that were not damaging to themselves or to others. This phase began with addressing those areas that were most distressing and most easily (relatively) amenable to change, such as impulse control, anger management or self-harm. The interventions likely to alleviate these symptoms were based on cognitive behavioural therapy, which required less epistemic trust than later work. Sometimes, the response of the community very quickly led to resolution of these outward signals of upset; for example, knowing that a crisis meeting would be called to support someone who had cut himself in itself helped him to stop. The experience of being 'heard' and attended to helped to sow a seed of trust. The OTT group taught awareness of triggers for anger, shame and rejection; of distorted assumptions about others; of the links between problems, thoughts, feelings and actions; and the beginnings of an ability to self-sooth or distract without resorting to, for example, drugs or alcohol. If it was suspected that a mental health problem might require medication, this was explored collaboratively. It was not uncommon for some patients to have lived with significant depression for years, and they became much better able to take a meaningful part in the therapy when it was treated. Addictive tranquilisers or pain killers were not prescribed.

Exploration and communication

By this phase, the patient will be deeply involved in multiple therapy fora, which provide multiple opportunities to explore his difficulties on a daily basis, from different perspectives and with differing kinds of feedback, both experiential and verbal. Over time, we saw patients' tolerance of, and ability to reflect upon this feedback grow, as did their awareness of the needs and feelings of others. The broad focus in this phase is on addressing the person's lifelong internal and interpersonal difficulties, by noticing how they play out in the day-to-day life of the unit. Building on their formulation, the patients can then also begin to explore their schemas, their particular areas of vulnerability and their triggers. These are likely to emerge in their relationships within the community and so will naturally become a focus for thinking about in the groups. Listening to others describe the impact of their behaviour will enhance his capacity to mentalise. He will gradually begin to make links between how he is acting in the present and the harms he has done in the past. Highly relevant too are the harms that have been done to him, and he will tentatively begin to talk about and process childhood trauma and learn that in this area, he has much in common with his peers.

Involvement

As time went on, each patient was expected to play a bigger part in the life of the unit. Some found this more difficult than others, and a degree of flexibility for natural 'loners' is needed. However, those who had learned to prefer their own company benefitted especially from moving beyond their 'comfort zone' and developing skills in relating to others with confidence, consideration and thoughtfulness. Social capabilities we looked for included eating meals in the dining room and participating in the Friday afternoon social time. Eventually, many patients were able to organise or lead on unit events by taking on the role of Activities Co-ordinator. A few individuals tended to 'take over' and run things purely their own way – in which case, feedback about how to share and work co-operatively was valuable.

Offending behaviour

This phase by necessity overlapped considerably with the others, but each patient needed to have achieved a certain amount of change before he could begin to explore his most serious offending, and its core contributing factors such as shame, anger and vengefulness. The more senior residents undertook structured offending behaviour and substance misuse work, which they would then be asked to take to their small groups for emotional processing (Bull, Taylor and Minoudis, 2019). The offending behaviour groups tended to be small and to run for around a year, and the patients valued highly the containment they afforded and the sense of progress being made in self-understanding and awareness.

> "Kaizen [offender behaviour group] was fantastic. Learned about myself so much. The process really helped me to break things down, put together the jigsaw, see the patterns in my life with triggers, feelings. Going through those patterns cemented itself in my brain so it came naturally. I learned so much".
>
> – Former Millfields patient

Integration and synthesis

This final phase could also be called consolidation and generalisation, or the stage of strengthening a new identity and sense of agency. Toward the end of his stay, the patient would be expected not only to be a more confident and self-aware individual, but also to show it consistently in his daily actions and inter-actions. These fledgeling attributes will be manifest in the person's ability to become a buddy, chair the community meeting and become an informal 'elder' of the group, modelling change for others and helping newer residents navigate their difficulties. Some patients might take on unit representative, external teaching, spokesman or other roles of responsibility. They should have learned to manage their time, having achieved a balance between therapy, education, work and leisure.

Patients who were able to sustain their therapy to this phase of treatment would be faced with the difficult challenge of preparing for life after Millfields. This could mean a return to prison or discharge into the community; two distinctly different propositions evoking very different fears and hopes. The TC is likely to have provided an experience of safety, understanding and belonging, and it is understandably painful to have leave it.

> "This is the only home I've ever had. I've never felt safe anywhere in my life before".
>
> – Former Millfields patient

Creating 'over-dependence', however, is a recognised iatrogenic harm (Jones, 2007). It can indirectly contribute to a paradoxical increase in the risk of reoffending at the end of treatment, when the patient reacts badly to the separation, and so it needs to be avoided. The purpose of the TC is, of course, to prepare the men to be able to build better lives for themselves beyond it, wherever that might be. The final stage of treatment therefore entails a combination of loosening their ties to the community, so painstakingly built over time, and augmenting their capacity to take responsibility for their own goals and, fundamentally, their own lives.

An important part of the therapy at this stage is helping the patients manage their feelings of loss, fear, hope, relief and whatever other feelings are stirred up by the approaching ending. For the more dependent patients, the task can be to wean them off the support of the TC, encouraging their confidence in themselves. For others who are more impulsive or dependency-averse, the task might be to slow them down at this vital stage, guiding them to make use of the TC while they can, to avoid overextending themselves. For patients prone to self-sabotage, staff and peers can play a central role in helping him to monitor and share his impulses to disrupt the leaving process, before he reaches the stage of destructive acting out.

During this period, if appropriate, patients are likely to be granted increasing periods of leave in the community, initially escorted, but ultimately unescorted. This allows them to begin to make sense of the inevitable challenges and setbacks that close contact with the outside world throws up. If returning to the community, they might begin to set up work or training opportunities, giving them structure and purpose, but also a chance to build new relationships and communities based on what they have internalised in the TC.

> "I will remember learning and understanding my suffering and pain. Learning to feel emotions, to trust, to move forward. Who I was before, I couldn't even have any of those conversations".
>
> – Former Millfields patient

The final part of a patient's journey of change was his 'leaving do': an organised special event with food, drinks and speeches recognising his achievements and the changes he had made as a result of his hard work and persistence. Each leaver was given a scrapbook in which all staff and patient had recorded a message of support and hope for the future. It was something for him to take with him and remember his time in the unit by. For those returning to prison, it was recognised that therapy would continue elsewhere. For all, it was recognised that the process of emotional and personal development would very likely be lifelong.

References

Baier, A.L., Kline, A.C. and Feeny, N.C., (2020) 'Therapeutic alliance as a mediator of change: a systematic review and evaluation of research', *Clinical Psychology Review*, 82. doi: https://doi.org/10.1016/j.cpr.2020.101921

Bateman, A. and Tyrer, P. (2002) 'Effective management of personality disorders', *Advances in Psychiatry*, 10(5), pp. 378–388. https://doi.org/10.1192/apt.10.5.378

Benjamin, L.S. (1993) *Interpersonal diagnosis and treatment of personality disorders*. New York: Guilford Press.

Bowlby, J. (1969) *Attachment and loss, Vol. 1: Attachment*. London: Hogarth Press and the Institute of Psycho-Analysis.

Bull, C., Taylor, C. and Minoudis, P. (2019) 'The use of an accredited violence reduction offending behaviour programme in a medium secure personality disorder service', *Personality and Mental Health*, 13(3), pp. 190–194. https://doi.org/10.1002/pmh.145

Fisher, S., Fonagy, P., Wiseman, H. and Zilcha-Mano, S. (2023) 'I see you as recognizing me; therefore, I trust you: Operationalizing epistemic trust in psychotherapy', *Psychotherapy*, 60(4), pp. 560–572. https://doi.org/10.1037/pst0000501https://doi.org/10.1037/pst0000501

Haigh, R. (2013) 'The quintessence of a therapeutic environment', *Therapeutic Communities*, 34(1), pp. 6–15. https://doi.org/10.1108/09641861311330464

Jarrett, M., Trebilcock, J., Weaver, T., Forrester, A., Cambell, C.D., Khondoker, M., Vamvakas, G., Barrett, B. and Moran, P.A. (2025) 'The offender personality disorder (OPD) pathway for men in England and Wales: a qualitative study of pathway user views about services, perceived impact on psychological wellbeing, and implications for desistance', *Criminal Justice and Behavior*, 52(1), pp. 98–118.

Jones, L.F. (2007) 'Iatrogenic interventions with personality disordered offenders', *Psychology, Crime and Law*, 13(1), pp. 69–79. https://doi.org/10.1080/10683160600869809

Kernberg, O. (1984) *Severe personality disorders: psychotherapeutic strategies*. New Haven, CT: Yale University Press.

Kohut, H. (1971) *The analysis of the self: a systematic approach to the psychoanalytic treatment of narcissistic personality disorders*. Chicago: University of Chicago Press.

Livesley, J.W. (2007) 'The relevance of an integrated approach to the treatment of personality disordered offenders', *Psychology, Crime and Law*, 13(1), pp. 27–46. https://doi.org/10.1080/10683160600869734

Livesley, W.J. (2012) 'Moving beyond specialized therapies for borderline personality disorder: the importance of integrated domain-focused treatment', *Psychodynamic Psychiatry*, 40(1), pp. 47–74. https://doi.org/10.1521/pdps.2012.40.1.47

Mathlin, G., Freestone, M., Taylor, C. and Shaw, J. (2021) 'Offenders with personality disorder who fail to progress: a case control study using PLS-SEM path analysis', *JMIRx Med*, 2(4). https://doi.org/10.2196/27907

McMurran, M. and Delight, S. (2017) 'Processes of change in an offender personality disorder pathway prison progression unit', *Criminal Behaviour and Mental Health*, 27(3), pp. 254–264. https://doi.org/10.1002/cbm.2032.

National Offender Management Service and National Health Service England (2015) *The offender personality disorder pathway strategy*. Available at: https://www.giustizia.it/resources/cms/documents/b35d1fbb4f220cb6cd0fd341ea28db77.pdf (accessed 28.01.2025).

Norton, K. and Dolan, B. (1995) 'Acting out and the institutional response', *Journal of Forensic Psychiatry*, 6(2), pp. 317–332. https://doi.org/10.1080/09585189508409898

Rutter, M. (1987) Attachment and the development of social relationships in *developmental psychiatry*. Washington D.C: American Psychiatric Association Publishing.

Sturm, A., de Vogel, V., Menger, A. and Huibers, M.J. (2021) 'Changes in offender-rated working alliance in probation supervision as predictors of recidivism', *Psychology, Crime and Law*, 27(2), pp. 182–200. https://doi.org/10.1002/pmh.1606

Tyrer, P., Mitchard, S., Methuen, C. and Ranger, M. (2003) 'Treatment rejecting and treatment seeking personality disorders: Type R and Type S', *Journal of Personality Disorders*, 17(3), pp. 263–268. https://doi.org/10.1521/pedi.17.3.263.22152

Chapter 17

The importance of transitions and aftercare

Celia Taylor

Being part of something

An important part of arriving in a therapeutic community like Millfields is the formation of an attachment to the place. This is deliberately fostered: it is well-established in psychodynamic practise that the attachment between patient and therapist is pivotal in promoting change, and the nature of that attachment, especially if it is insecure or disorganised, will itself be a focus of the therapy (e.g. Levy *et al.*, 2018; Slade and Holmes, 2019). In the case of Millfields, the entire unit – the staff and patients within it, and even the building itself – became the attachment figure, in that it provided a sufficiently secure base for therapy to take place. This sense of safety and belonging was something that almost none of our patients had experienced before, so it could take quite some time before sufficient trust was established for the true work to begin. Some were never able to trust enough and therefore could not engage fully in therapy and had to move on: "the fear and shame of letting others know them was just too great" (Haigh, 2013). If this initial attachment phase is sufficiently successful, the patient will be able to use it as a springboard for embarking on the long, slow process of change. The process of change has been described by Livesley (2003) as a series of steps whereby the next one always builds on the last. They are: recognising and naming the problems; exploring them and their associated thoughts and feelings in depth; trying out alternative ways of responding to the world; and consolidating and generalising this learning. It is at this final stage that the questions arise, when is the right time to leave, and how is leaving best achieved?

Paradoxically, the formation of a successful attachment over a period of several years also makes it very difficult for the patients to move on. The longed-for state of freedom suddenly becomes a source of anxiety and threat, awakening old fears of neglect and abandonment. This state of ambivalence can lead to 'acting out' in ways that make discharge problematic. These often include aspects of regression to an earlier stage in therapy: reverting to disputes, incidents and rule-breaking leading to the loss of community leave. The consequence is often that no Parole Board or Mental Health Review Tribunal will consider the person ready for discharge, and no community-based mental health team – already reluctant to accept referrals

DOI: 10.4324/9781032717302-17

from the service – will accept him for ongoing care in the community. As noted by Riordan (2007), it is important to provide "a metaphorical anti-pyretic to quell {these manifestations} of gate fever". His recommendation is that we listen to, and try to understand, the anxieties being expressed.

The concrete mother and 'prisonisation'

We also need to bear in mind that, for many of these patients, custody has been preferable to life outside. One of the men at Millfields admitted that he would deliberately reoffend in order to be given another sentence: outside of prison, he was faced with a wife and children who were terrified of his drunken rages and for whom he was unable to provide, let alone connect with or support emotionally. For all this, he felt shame and self-loathing, because he realised he had 'become' his father. Inside prison he was fed and housed, and his schedule for the day was governed according to a strict timetable, with little room for latitude or independent thinking. This sense of safety conferred by prison has led to the institution being described as a 'concrete mother'. The term refers to an emotional and psychological function provided by custodial environments, and the care, however harsh, provided within them. The 'concrete mother' thus represents a failure of internalisation of the maternal – and, some would say, the paternal – function. As described by Bryan (2016), the prison (and any locked institution) gives warmth, food and shelter. It absolves the individual of the need to make decisions or fulfil his responsibilities. There is a clear hierarchy in which he knows his place, and the rules are clear, if inflexible. Furthermore, the prisoner/patient is removed from the chaos of his world, whether it be fraught relationships with partners, the obligation to care for children or parents, debt, drugs or gang involvement.

However, the very factors that make confinement on some level attractive, lead to institutionalisation. For many of our patients, leaving Millfields was made harder because of the sheer length of time they had been locked up – up to forty years in one case.

> My first leave was overwhelming, after not having leave for 25 years. Things like crossing the road made me nervous. I was worried I might get lost. So much had changed: Oyster (public transport) cards, self-checkouts at the supermarket. I slowly got used to it and did things like setting up a bank account. I got a smartphone, and the tutor taught me how to set up apps so I could use FaceTime with my family.

Haney (2003) has described the impact of long periods of incarceration as 'prisonisation'. It is important to note that these are the kinds of adaptation to prison life that anyone has to make in order to survive: they are not abnormal, but they do mean that these individuals face a particularly problematic transition "as they return to the free world" (Haney, 2003). The implication is that a great deal of support is needed, both as leaving approaches and for a long while afterwards. Haney summarises two important aspects of 'prisonisation' as the loss of capacity to take initiative or make one's own decisions; and the need for hypervigilance to violence: one has to cultivate a 'strong man' persona or face being exploited throughout one's sentence. The corollary to this is never to admit to vulnerability. Haney is writing about the United States, but lengthy prison sentences for serious offences are the norm in many countries. He cites an experienced prison adminis-trator as writing, "Prison is a barely controlled jungle where the aggressive and the strong will exploit the weak, and the weak are dreadfully aware of it".

Growing old, or at least middle-aged, in prison can also make a person feel he has missed out on many opportunities in his life, for example the chance to marry, have children, or find work. In practice, many of our leavers did achieve some of these goals, albeit later in life than would have been the case if they had not gone to prison. A few became seriously ill, and the patient who returned on a weekly basis as Expert By Experience died unexpectedly while undergoing a routine operation. This was a great shock to the others: in dreaming of a future of freedom, they had never considered such an outcome.

Imagining the future

As we have seen, when the moment of leaving approaches and those old fears of abandonment and neglect resurface, they prompt the conscious or unconscious impulse to sabotage the entire process. Preparing the patient for his departure so as to avoid or minimise gate fever should start, on a very practical level, prior to his arrival. Before admitting a patient to Millfields, we discussed with him his likely pathway out of the service. There were two broad possibilities: first, a premature end to treatment through his choice, or through ours if his behaviour became too destructive to himself or to others. Each individual knew before he arrived what kinds of behaviour we would not tolerate, and relatively few tested our limits to the point of ensuring their rejection. A signed agreement with the referring institu-tion to take the individual back meant that these limits were no empty threat. The second route to discharge was through successfully completing treatment within an approximate timescale.

Those past their tariff were given a chance at applying for a Mental Health Re-view Tribunal and then a Parole Board (both described in more detail below), while those with many years left to serve would be referred on to a specialist, prison-based Psychologically Informed Planned Environment (PIPE; Turley, Payne and Webster, 2013) for consolidation of their therapy. The patient moving into the com-munity especially could 'try out' different scenarios in his imagination, consider what he wanted in his life and where he wanted to live, and take some responsibil-ity for his future. This became important material for therapy: for example, patients would share and explore potentially life-changing decisions such as whether to seek out an estranged family member or child, and the risks of rejection. Positive emotional investment in the future also helped serve as a motivator in the therapy and in persisting with the difficult process of change because it was seen as worthwhile.

Leaving therapy

Ending treatment after two-and-a-half or three years in a therapeutic community is a significant loss. Not only do patients forfeit the secure spaces of therapeutic groups in which they share and process their experiences, but they are also going to have to give up their physical home. Most importantly, they have formed attachments with peers and staff, and these relationships must also come to an end. Bowlby (1969) theorised that the purpose of attachment is to mitigate loss. An irreversible separation from an attachment figure can be painful and frightening and thus lead to distress and a re-emergence of difficulties. The hope is that, by the end of his therapy, the patient will have internalised the maternal and paternal functions that the unit served for him during his stay, such that he feels he can survive and progress without it. It is important to emphasise, however, that learning the capacity to seek out help in a timely and proportionate manner is equally important. The sadness of leaving is not only difficult for the patients, but it is also difficult for staff. We can feel compelled to try to alleviate the patient's distress, for example by granting extensions to therapy. However, this does not necessarily help the patient to work towards a healthy ending and can instead encourage him to regress back into dependence. With this in mind, we have a responsibility to foster a sense of autonomy and help our patients to move forward.

> When I left, I never thought I was going to make it. I lost the place I was living, my home, all the memories. It was so hard. But I got through it. I'm doing what I'm supposed to, sticking to my appointments, being free, not committing crime, even scared to think that way about crime now.

At Millfields, the decision as to when to leave was arrived at collaboratively with the individual patient; though his peers would also contribute their views. We found that the leaving process was assisted by setting mutually agreed treatment goals early on in the patient's stay, via an initial in-depth assessment and formulation. Each person had perhaps five or six of these treatment goals, which were kept in focus through the course of the therapy: they were reviewed regularly and could be modified or added to as new information came to light. They were considered alongside annual assessments of the risk of reoffending, maladaptive personality traits or beliefs about crime or violence, and psychological wellbeing (the severity of anxiety, depression or PTSD, etc.). We also found it helpful to give the patients an approximate maximum length of time for their stay in the unit. We knew that those with the most severe psychopathology would have the slowest responses to treatment (e.g. Nordmo *et al.*, 2021), and that many would experience setbacks along the way. Indeed, learning how to manage these setbacks was an important part of consolidating learning and change. Taken in combination, however, these approaches served to keep it in each person's mind that the day for him to move on would eventually arrive. This awareness, in itself, helped to offset longings to stay indefinitely.

Decisions about readiness to leave also involve clinical judgement, and an important part of this is to see if the patient can generalise his learning. A previously violent patient at Millfields, for example, had to show he could refrain from violence within the unit, even under severe provocation, in order to be granted community leave. By refraining, we meant that he needed to show that he could navigate difficult relationships without resorting to bullying, controlling or intimidating others – all of these are 'offence paralleling behaviours' (see Chapters 7 and 13). His capacity to manage would then be further tested on community leave.

> The leave process took time, but eventually I go to go to the temple, college and the charity shop. This helped me with structure. Now I still have structure, I don't wander the streets like I did before prison. I know I need structure in life. The leave helped me work on my social skills too.

Interacting with members of the public can be highly challenging: we are inadvertently bumped into or pushed when amongst crowds of people, and others are sometimes deliberately rude or confrontational. At Millfields, we had to suspend the leave of a man who got into a serious shouting match on a bus, over a minor disagreement. In a community meeting, one staff member told the story of being spat at through an open car window. Most of the patients were incredulous to hear that they would be expected not to get involved in a confrontation if this happened to them. However, a serious offender, perhaps on a life licence with recall conditions, cannot afford to take that kind of risk. Other patients had to learn to decline offers of a drugs deal, to pass off-licences and pubs without going in, or to remain within the bounds of an exclusion zone. An interesting sign of progress was that some patients said they became reluctant to return to the unit at the end of their leave, as they were developing an increased sense of confidence with being out in the community.

We learned that some Millfields patients would act out just towards the end of their treatment, when plans were already being made for their discharge into the community or return to prison. Sometimes this was due to conscious or unconscious anxiety about leaving: many had formed a strong attachment to the Unit, its residents and its staff, often saying that this was the 'only stable home' they had ever known. No matter how much we tried to prepare each person for his move on to a new environment, fears of the past repeating itself always loomed large. Those returning to prison were all too used to being forgotten in a vast system where they had little to no power to ensure that their progress continued. The predominant fear of those moving into the community was that of being left 'all alone', essentially abandoned in life. Other, more usually unconscious anxieties included continuing guilt and the impulse towards self-punishment, a deep-rooted expectation of failure, and fear of disintegration without the containing, nurturing environment of the unit. It could be challenging to navigate this phase, but by and large we tried not to stop the forward momentum, but rather slow it down to allow these feelings to be expressed and worked through in the therapy.

Making an imagined future a reality

Practical considerations also play a part in deciding that a patient is nearing departure. Those who can be discharged into the community will typically be spending more and more time out on community leave, which should begin to be structured so as to incorporate aspects of the person's future outside the unit. Depending upon the individual, this might involve an application to supported accommodation, with visits to get to know the staff and the place that might become home, for a while at least. A patient might begin regular meetings with his probation officer or visit his future community forensic mental health team. If such meetings clashed with part of the therapy programme at Millfields, we might agree to the person missing a session, although never without prior discussion and not if essential work, for example on an aspect of his offending, needed to be completed. All these new beginnings and new experiences should be continuously fed back into the community meeting, for processing, constructive debate and learning.

Many patients tended to idealise their future life in the community. In this respect, unexpected events were often salutary and provided a chance to learn resilience. An example is provided by the Education sector, which is usually more tolerant of people with a criminal record than most. We successfully enrolled one patient in an IT course at a local college, which he was going to attend one day per week during his community leave. The enrolment process involved talking to a college tutor and disclosing his convictions for serious sex offending. However, on his very first day in class, he was unceremoniously asked to leave. It emerged that the college's senior management had just found out about him and baulked at what they felt was too high a risk to their reputation if others were to find out or something went wrong. The patient naturally felt both publicly shamed and unfairly rejected, and it took a lot of encouragement before he would resume his forays into the outside world. A local Sikh temple finally took him in, offering him a small job within their community in full knowledge of his past life. He continued attending for several years after his release, and it gave him a sense of belonging and purpose that was crucial to him building a meaningful and safe life outside of custody.

Patients should be encouraged to spend their last few months exploring with their small group what leaving would mean, especially on an emotional level. The other patients, through participating in this process, inevitably begin to think about what it would be like when their own turn comes. This is, of necessity, more limited in the case of patients who have to return to prison, usually because their sentence or tariff is too long for them to remain in treatment until release. However, whenever possible and in collaboration with the patient themselves, the return to prison should be to a specialist prison service, which in the United Kingdom is usually in the Offender Personality Disorder Pathway, such as a Therapeutic Community or a PIPE (Turley, Payne and Webster, 2013). This will lead to a referral and subsequent assessment by that service, giving the patient the chance to meet the team, ask questions and express fears about his potential future with them. The same process of exploration should be expected in his small group: what would leaving mean to him, especially on an emotional level? We found that much of the anxiety around leaving could be ameliorated if the patient could build a reality-based picture of his future, rather than leaving him with nebulous fears of being left to fend entirely for himself.

External scrutiny

If being discharged into the community, the patient will usually have to face consideration by an external panel as to whether he was both well enough and safe enough to leave the unit. In the United Kingdom, this mostly took the form of a Mental Health Review Tribunal, which is part of His Majesty's Court and Tribunal Service. In England, an independent panel hears applications from people detained under certain sections of the Mental Health Act (1983, amended 2007). In the case of restricted patients (i.e. subject to special controls by the Justice Secretary due to the level of risk they pose), which all Millfields patients were, the panel is chaired by an experienced high court judge, who is joined by a forensic psychiatrist and a lay member. The panel members ask the patient, in depth, what he has achieved in his treatment, how it has improved his mental health and how it has reduced the risk he poses to the public. It can be a formidable, hours-long experience, and the first time since their trial that they have had to face outside scrutiny by people who are, essentially, representatives of society. We used to remind our patients that this day would come when they sometimes said, angrily, "I'm not doing your treatment any longer"! The treatment was not, of course, for us.

A transferred prisoner can be granted a 'deferred conditional discharge' by the Tribunal, allowing him to stay in hospital awaiting a Parole Hearing; the wait might be for many months due to the backlog of cases in the criminal justice system. The Parole Board is another independent body whose job it is to determine if a convicted prisoner, even one who has been transferred to hospital, is safe to release. Public safety is the priority, rather than mental health or wellbeing, although the links between these factors are recognised. The panel's risk assessment is based on detailed evidence presented in a large dossier, and on evidence provided at the oral hearing. In more recent years, victims have also been allowed to make representations to the Tribunal and the Parole Board. We worked closely with both the patients and the probation service to determine appropriate licence conditions – which should be comprehensive but not needlessly punitive – and the likely warning signs that risk was increasing and recall to prison might be needed.

Saying goodbye

We found it helpful to mark a patient's departure via a leaving event or 'do'. One patient, often the person closest to the leaver, would volunteer to take the lead, with support from a staff member. The lead patient was provided with a scrapbook and squares of coloured card were handed out for everyone to write out their comments, memories, or encouragement to the person leaving. These were incorporated into the scrapbook along with photos and funny memes or cartoons, sometimes even decorated with glitter and the like. The cover usually had a picture of the unit and the person's name on it. The leaving 'do' involved setting aside a special time for a meal, or tea and cake, and a presentation of the scrapbook by the patient who had prepared it, with a short speech. Many others in the room, including staff, would also say a few words of encouragement and acknowledgement of the leaver's achievements. The leaver would then speak, usually taking a look back at his time in the unit as well as forward to whatever future awaited him. This could occasionally lead to tears, but no one scoffed at them. Members of the clinical team who were leaving were honoured with exactly the same kind of event (and, indeed, were expected to provide the same notice and time for processing of their ending as patients). The scrapbook served as an important memento of the time each person had spent in Millfields.

You don't choose your family

At Millfields, one of the most problematic areas pertaining to a future life in the community had to do with family members. For some, their relatives had long since severed all ties, or for children, contact had been forbidden by Children's Services. A few tried to track their relatives down, for example via the Salvation Army, but initiating contact required careful thought about timing and the potential response. For example, some patients decided it would be better to wait until after discharge, as 'proof of change' from the criminal the family had known and rejected. Others agonised about the possibility but could never gather the courage to make an approach, for fear of being rebuffed, possibly permanently.

> I'm very lonely – I don't have any real friends, all the old ones were criminals. I really miss having someone close to talk to. My sister's gone … she won't speak to me or call me … nothing.

Even when family ties had been successfully re-established, the past had left scars that needed to be worked through. Family therapy was a very valuable resource we could draw upon, but it was not always acceptable to both parties, or practicable, given work commitments or travelling distance. One man serving a life sentence for serious sexual offences had been in prison for thirty years before reconnecting with his father and sisters. He wanted to be welcomed back like a prodigal son, and to some extent he was. However, his offending had led to the family being chased out of their home by neighbours, and the shame and fear were etched into their memories. Meanwhile, both the patient and the family had done a lot of growing and changing – separately, not together – and were in some ways now strangers. The sister of another patient, an armed robber, agreed to take a few telephone calls from him, but had been let down too many times by his relapses into drug use to stay in touch after his release; she now had a disabled daughter to consider. He recently said of the situation, "she's gone", meaning with this connotation of death that she had disappeared from his life forever: "I've had to accept it".

After leaving

Life in the community after leaving the unit could be tough, and any tendency to idealise freedom was soon dispelled. One man was recalled within a week, after he got drunk and became aggressive. Later, he admitted that he had not been ready – in fact, "I was scared of being free". He had just barely recognised this internally at the time of his parole hearing but could not admit it openly. Another man was lonely and had no real friends: he profoundly missed the experience of having someone to talk to in depth. He also struggled with extreme poverty and having to appeal a rejection to his application for benefits.

> I'm an ex-armed robber. I know about cars and safes, and it's scary to sit here with pennies in my pocket knowing how I used to deal with that.

However, he had managed to stay away from drugs after a lifetime of abuse – no mean feat – and was doing voluntary work at a local drugs support service, advising current addicts and telling them his own story. He had also been given a prefilled Naloxone syringe, so that he could 'save someone's life' if they overdosed on opiates. Many patients and prisoners say, as he does, that they want to help young people to avoid following the path they got sucked into, and to 'give something back' to society. Interestingly, much of the literature on happiness derived from helping others suggests that it is maximised when the help is freely given, improves the giver's sense of competence, and results in a sense of human connectedness (Aknin and Whillans, 2021). At Millfields, we found that this could be one of the most powerful factors in a healthy ending and successful return to life in the community.

References

Aknin, L.B. and Whillans, A.V. (2021) 'Helping and happiness: a review and guide for public policy', *Social Issues and Policy Review*, 15(1), pp. 3–34. http://dx.doi.org/10.1111/sipr.12069

Bowlby, J. (1969) *Attachment and loss, Vol. 1: Attachment*. London: Hogarth Press and the Institute of Psycho-Analysis.

Bryan, A. (2016) 'Ethical dilemmas in the prison setting', *British Journal of Psychotherapy*, 32(2), pp. 256–273. http://dx.doi.org/10.1111/bjp.12219

Haigh, R. (2013) 'The quintessence of a therapeutic environment', *Therapeutic Communities: The International Journal of Therapeutic Communities*, 34(1), pp. 6–15. http://dx.doi.org/10.1108/09641861311330464

Haney, C. (2003) 'The psychological impact of incarceration: implications for post-prison adjustment', *Prisoners Once Removed: The Impact of Incarceration and Reentry on Children, Families, and Communities*, 33, p. 66.

Levy, K.N., Kivity, Y., Johnson, B.N. and Gooch, C.V. (2018) 'Adult attachment as a predictor and moderator of psychotherapy outcome: a meta-analysis', *Journal of Clinical Psychology*, 74(11), pp. 1996–2013. http://dx.doi.org/10.1002/jclp.22685

Livesley, W.J. (2003) *Practical management of personality disorder*. New York: Guilford Press.

Mental Health Act (1983) available at: https://www.legislation.gov.uk/ukpga/2007/12/contents

Nordmo, M., Monsen, J.T., Høglend, P.A. and Solbakken, O.A. (2021) 'Investigating the dose–response effect in open-ended psychotherapy', *Psychotherapy Research*, 31(7), pp. 859–869. http://dx.doi.org/10.1080/10503307.2020.1861359

Riordan, D. (2007) 'Gate fever', *Mental Health Nursing*, 27(4), p. 24.

Slade, A. and Holmes, J. (2019) 'Attachment and psychotherapy', *Current Opinion in Psychology*, 25, pp. 152–156. http://dx.doi.org/10.1016/j.copsyc.2018.06.008

Turley, C., Payne, C. and Webster, S. (2013) *Enabling features of psychologically informed planned environments*. London: National Offender Management Service.

Chapter 18

Staff selection, supervision, training and reflective practice

Jinnie Jefferies and Brittni Jones

Introduction

This book provides a guide for working with offenders with personality disorder and outlines the therapeutic community (TC) model of treatment. Nevertheless, this model cannot be delivered concretely or prescriptively, because a fundamentally relational approach relies on a nuanced understanding of the people being treated and a meaningful working relationship between individual residents and the staff and resident members of the TC. Any complex rehabilitative environment of this kind requires skilled and motivated staff to maintain the therapeutic culture and navigate the complexities and challenges that inevitably arise. Attracting, training, supervising, supporting and retaining the right people to work in these environments is therefore essential, and will be the focus of this chapter.

Who are the 'right people'?

The importance of having the 'right staff' was one of the most common themes in interviews with former residents at Millfields.

> "Some of the staff were there for me, as well as some of the other patients. It was a community and I'd never felt that before. I could open up and gain confidence. I could relate to the others, even though they had lived a very different lifestyle. I had never had that in my life ... we could talk to who we wanted to. The social therapists took the time, which was a huge bonus that I had never had in my life before. Here [in prison] the officers don't see you. Obviously, Millfields was much more comfortable, but here it's 'them and us'. In Millfields you could bring things up. You had a degree of autonomy, and we were equal – it was liberating. [But Millfields needed to] reduce the high turnover of staff and hire experienced social therapists. Brand new nursing staff helped lead to the Unit's demise. The racial differences between the nursing team and the rest of the staff helped to foster resentment".
>
> – Former Millfields patient

DOI: 10.4324/9781032717302-18

"Some of the nursing management knew that they had power over us patients and that they would be believed by the team over us. So I felt I could never cross them, I always had to be on their good side even though some of the stuff they did was just wrong ... it was like two different teams in two different hospitals. Professional staff downstairs blatantly lied about patients thinking they would never be believed because they had a mental illness".

– Former Millfields patient

"It was helpful to have staff who would listen to you and put you on the right road, no judgement, patience and calmness. At the same time, it was helpful to have staff who couldn't have the wool pulled over their eyes. In prison you are always judged and put to the side. You don't get honest and fair people. When you went to Millfields and you got treated differently, you realised that not everyone is bitter and twisted. That there are people in the system who are willing to help".

– Former Millfields patient

With the rise of trauma-informed practice (The Institute on Trauma and Trauma-Informed Care, 2022), there is increasing acknowledgement within healthcare and prison settings that effective rehabilitation of offenders requires awareness of the impact of their early experiences on their mental health and offending, and the need to work relationally to help them change or, at the very least, to not make them worse. However, this is a complex endeavour, and the reality is that most staff in these services will not have the skills and knowledge required to do this work safely and effectively from the start.

As a result, in most forensic services the therapeutic treatment is left to the single psychologist or counsellor on staff. This can provide a helpful therapeutic relationship in discreet sessions, but it is not possible for one person to create the therapeutic environment or culture that is required and outlined in this book, and that we argue is essential to the treatment of offenders with personality disorder. Additionally, TCs are relatively rare, so even clinically trained staff may not have the experience and knowledge they need to practise effectively within this model.

The people who make up a therapeutic environment or community, their working relationships with each other, and the culture they create, are the aim of the treatment as well as the treatment itself (see Chapter 3). As Rapaport put it, it is the "community as the doctor" (Rapaport, 1996). As a result, staff at all levels need to have the capacity and motivation to engage relationally. Since most staff cannot have all the knowledge and skills they require to do this from the beginning, services must be able to attract people who have the potential to develop these skills, and must provide focussed and specialist training, supervision and support to enable this growth.

Essential qualities in staff

The bare minimum for staff in a TC is that they must be willing to work within the model, participate in training, therapeutic activities and supervision, and interact with others in line with what they have learned. It is not negotiable that staff will follow the model rather than be obstructive or destructive, through either non-participation or active subversion (see Chapter 20). Although it is not a given, people who are motivated and interested in working relationally are also more likely to possess (or have the capability to develop) the emotional skills that will enable them to learn and fulfil their role effectively. These skills can roughly be divided into the following categories:

1. Reflective capacity

Reflective capacity or functioning, also often termed mentalisation, refers to the capacity to understand self and others in terms of mental states, or in other words to think about what others may be thinking or feeling and what is motivating their behaviour (Fonagy, 2016). Improving reflective capacity is almost always a treatment target for residents, as it is often their hostile interpretation or lack of consideration of the mental states of others that leads to violence and criminal acts. Their inability to work with others can also lead to treatment or supervision failures, mental health problems, social isolation and recidivism (National Health Service England and Her Majesty's Prison and Probation Services [HMPPS], 2020).

To help residents develop their reflective functioning, staff also need to have reflective skills. Firstly, they need to be able to put themselves in the shoes of the patient to understand his perspective and the ways in which this view is damaging or risky to him and to others. This is essential for developing a formulation, assessing and managing risk and developing a treatment plan. Secondly, within the therapeutic community or relational environment, effective treatment is reliant on experiential learning. This requires staff to recognise the learning opportunities and support the resident to take these up through reflection, exploration and modelling, all of which requires staff to have reflective functioning skills.

Case Example

Tom, a resident, asks Sara, a staff member he normally gets on well with, to help him access a restricted item, a blender, to make himself a smoothie. Sara is dealing with an urgent matter and, not considering Tom's request to be as important, asks him to wait. Tom explodes into rage, shouting at Sara that she is lazy and stupid, and punching the door to the nurse's station before walking away. Sara is shocked, angry and frightened, and thinks that Tom is just a horrible person who throws a tantrum when he does not get his way. She has the impulse to shout back at him and punish him through immediate restraint and seclusion.

Sara seeks support in managing what happened in her supervision and in a reflective practice group. Through these groups, she considers how Tom's behaviour links with his childhood, growing up with parents who neglected his needs, often leaving him hungry. The team thinks that perhaps this could make him more likely to experience being asked to wait as deliberate rejection or neglect, and this could trigger a reaction of panic and rage. Sara is encouraged by the team to see the incident as a learning opportunity for Tom and supported to think of ways to address it.

Sara approaches Tom when he is calm and asks what made him so angry, and he explains that he felt Sara was ignoring him because she doesn't like him, and it was not obvious to him that Sara had other things to do that were pressing. Sara and Tom agree to speak about the incident in community meetings and small groups. With the support of other community members, they reflect on wider themes of trust, communication, rejection sensitivity, frustration, anxiety around restrictions and dependency on others, and how all these issues relate to their life experiences, difficulties in relationships and offending.

2. Therapeutic relational skills

The example of Sara and Tom demonstrates a high degree of relational skills in a staff member. Like Sara, staff need to understand, value and proactively pursue opportunities to develop the therapeutic relationship with residents. If Sara had not been supported to do this with Tom, a likely consequence would have been an escalation of conflict not just between Sara and Tom, but between others in the unit who would feel compelled to choose sides, with Sara being hated by many for being lazy or callous and Tom being seen by others as aggressive, bullying and manipulative. Learning opportunities would have been lost, the rifts could be destructive to the entire unit, and eventually Sara could experience burnout, and Tom could lose his treatment place.

Due to their life experiences (and despite often longing to be close to others), most residents will not understand the value of relationships or will believe that it is impossible to develop trusting or meaningful connections with others. Many will have minimal relational skills and struggle to communicate effectively or understand perspectives other than their own. Others may have good relational skills but nevertheless will believe that others must be manipulated or corrupted to get what they want or need. It is therefore crucial that staff can work with this variety of presentation and model prosocial, meaningful and useful relationships, as well as the skills to manage conflict constructively rather than destructively.

Relationships can be challenging to maintain in general, so fostering therapeutic relationships with residents who are often actively destructive or abrasive in their interactions is a particularly difficult, often one-sided, endeavour, especially at the beginning of treatment. Staff must therefore understand that developing and maintaining therapeutic relationships is one of their central tasks and have some pre-existing skills to build on to achieve this. Members of staff will need skills in listening, assertive communication, negotiation, setting and maintaining boundaries in a non-punitive manner, and the ability to communicate empathy and insights gained through their reflective capacity. They will also need to have the capacity to regulate their own emotions and understand the need to allow time for all parties to calm down before being able to reflect on what happened. Training and support are essential in developing these skills, as will be detailed later in this chapter.

3. Resilience and capacity to make use of supervision

The example of Tom and Sara also demonstrates the high degree of resilience demanded of staff working in these environments. Our instincts as human beings are to avoid people who are unpleasant or potentially dangerous, and it is difficult to listen and show empathy towards those who seem incapable or unwilling to reciprocate. Feeling upset or angry with how we are treated can also take a toll, especially when we must continue to act therapeutically towards the person who has made us feel that way. Staff require resilience to rise to this challenge, but they also require support from colleagues as well as supervision and training. The essential elements of this will be covered in more detail later in this chapter.

Attracting and recruiting staff

Institutional environments are typically resistant to change and fixed in views about what staff should be hired for 'frontline' roles, prioritising qualifications and experience in security and medical procedures over therapeutic clinical skills. In prisons, this means that most staff are security focussed guards or officers, and in hospitals they are medically focussed social therapists or healthcare assistants and mental health nurses. As a result, the first step in recruiting an effective staff team is to work with higher level service managers to understand what is needed and why, and to gain their support, both in the selection process as well as in the de-selection of staff who turn out not to be a good fit. However, this can feel threatening and destabilising for those invested in a traditional service structure (see Chapter 20).

Some people who choose to work in hospitals or prisons do so because they want to work within a purely security or medically focussed role and have developed skills to do this effectively. These skills are important within services working with offenders, and roles focussed on security are required within forensic environments. However, staff with this singularity of focus will not be the right fit for a therapeutic community and will likely create more problems than they resolve, as they often do not engage therapeutically, damage trust with residents and are ultimately destructive to the wider culture. Senior managers of services need to understand this and be supportive of services when they do not want to take a 'bums on seats' approach to recruitment or staff retention, even in times of staff shortages and service pressures.

Services which endeavour to provide truly therapeutic environments need to be permitted to brand and promote themselves and the work they do so that they can attract people who have the skills and motivation to work in a relational model. For these people, TCs offer a valuable opportunity to engage in experiential learning and specialist training and supervision which will develop their therapeutic skills and knowledge and lead to personal and professional growth. This can be particularly attractive for people who aspire to progress in their careers towards psychotherapy, psychology or treatment programme work, and this should be expected and encouraged.

Staff selection

Even knowing what you are looking for in terms of staff and possessing the freedom and resources to recruit them, it can be difficult to determine whether a potential member of staff is right for the service from a traditional interview alone. Including senior residents in the interview process and asking questions which require staff to explain (and, ideally, demonstrate through roleplays) how they would respond to examples of challenging situations with residents are useful interview tactics. However, even the most thoughtful and comprehensive interview process may only find the members of staff who have pre-existing values and understanding of the skills needed, but who will still be unable or unwilling to engage in the full treatment model.

As a result, we recommend a more imaginative interview process which includes experiential elements. Many TCs offer days for professional visitors to attend and experience a community meeting as well as some unstructured time (e.g. lunch) with residents and staff. Visitors are also encouraged to participate in the community meeting and are given dedicated time at the end to feedback their experience. This model can be extended to be part of the interview process for new members of staff, giving them a clearer understanding of what will be expected of them, and the ethos and model of the service they will be joining. It also gives an indication of the interviewee's abilities and confidence in engaging relationally and in participating in the model through their feedback in the community meeting.

Millfields developed an interview process which included an experiential community meeting, a traditional interview with residents on the panel and questions developed by the TC membership, and roleplay scenarios. If resources are available, it would be ideal to work with the organisation's Human Resources team to make use of objective measures of reflective capacity and relational skills as part of the recruitment process. Perhaps the best 'test' is to agree a trial period for new starters, as sometimes their abilities or lack of them only emerge over time. Staff who are found to be unable to fulfil their role in the TC can move to more suitable and fulfilling roles elsewhere.

Training and supervision

Joining a TC can be bewildering for both residents and staff. Irrespective of former training, staff often feel deskilled, asking such questions as, "What is my role, how do I relate to residents, what is the treatment process and how does it work?" or "How do I manage my uncomfortable feelings and those that are experienced by the residents?"

To support staff and answer some of these questions, Millfields had a bespoke training adapted for them from the HMPPS accredited programme for staff working in Democratic Forensic Therapeutic Communities (2007). This training was delivered in two parts, consisting of three days each. All staff, regardless of seniority and prior qualifications, were required to attend, ideally completing part one within the first few months of starting work and part two within the first year.

Any TC training package should be designed to ensure that all staff have the knowledge and skills to fulfil their roles within the TC. The training should include didactic teaching on theory and practice, as well as experiential elements (e.g. role plays). It is also crucial that training is followed up with staff supervision and support groups as well as individual or small group clinical supervision with a qualified supervisor at a frequency of at least once a month. The training and supervision should cover at minimum the following: relationships/attachments, boundaries, understanding personality disorder, the therapeutic community model, psychological processes such as transference and projection, and conflict resolution.

Relationships/attachments

The first challenge for staff in a TC is to embrace the concept that change relies heavily on the relationships built between staff and residents. Within forensic services in hospitals and prison, this means shifting away from an emphasis on prescriptive care plans, medication and behavioural compliance.

Residents entering a TC are understandably distrustful of relationships. Some have a history of parental neglect and abuse, and of being moved between different institutions. These experiences will impact on their attachment styles, both historically and currently (Ainsworth, 1978; Bowlby, 1988/1995). As a result, staff need to understand the importance of creating a safe, secure relationship and to realise that their own way of responding to residents will be crucial during their time on a TC, to provide a 'corrective emotional experience' for those in their care (Raus and Auty, 2018; Shuker, 2010). The corrective emotional experience provides an opportunity for another person with whom there is a strong attachment to behave differently to that of the primary carer.

Developing strong attachments is not an easy task, as staffs' efforts are often rejected. It is therefore important for them to be provided with a space to express their anger, disappointment and frustration. They will also need to begin to understand that many residents, whilst longing for the care and the love they have never experienced, will also be fearful of vulnerability: they will fight against what is offered, or transfer their negative feelings towards parents and past authority figures on to staff. Other residents have a deep unconscious need to envy, spoil or steal what is good (Haigh, 2013).

Whilst understanding the importance of attachment theory and the concept of transference, many members of staff will struggle to maintain enough positive regard for those in their care, especially towards those who fight the process and reject their efforts to provide help. Driven, sadly, by destructiveness, many patients will attempt to provoke staff into joining them in spoiling the therapeutic relationship and potential for change. Staff in forensic services who are otherwise caring and level-headed, can find themselves agreeing with cynical views on patients or being unfairly punitive. With a high risk of burnout and empathy fatigue, staff need enhanced support to continue trying to understand and work effectively and fairly with residents who behave negatively.

Boundaries

Boundaries are a set of agreed rules and regulations which form a 'frame' or 'container' in which the work of the TC can take place safely, disturbances are tolerated and distress is held (Raus and Auty, 2018; Tyndale and Rosenberg, 2014). Agreed boundaries will be needed around role, time, place, space, gifts, services, security, clothing, language, disclosure and physical contact. They provide a template as to what is or is not allowed or tolerated, providing a sense of right and wrong.

In forensic TC settings, the rules of no alcohol or drugs, violence or sex are well understood, as these cause clear harm to self or others. Beyond the necessary physical boundaries however, there are also psychic boundaries, a concept of 'me and not me'. This is a method of separating out one's own energy, emotions and thoughts from those of others, and these boundaries help to manage projective identification, transference and peer pressures. Offenders in forensic environments have not only broken boundaries themselves but have also come from environments where their own boundaries have often been broken, or boundary keeping was poorly modelled. As a result, most residents in TCs will attempt to break or push boundaries, particularly those coming from authority figures.

Training for staff should focus on the importance of boundaries to keep individuals and the community safe, the need for consistency across the staff team and what processes are in place for when boundaries are broken. It is also important for the staff group to realise the impact on the patient group when they themselves break boundaries, even in small ways. When boundaries are not adhered to, TC's risk failure. Individual staff will often have different personal positions regarding boundary setting, some being too relaxed as to what they allow or too much personal information given, whilst others are too formal, too guarded. Staff who have less structured roles with residents often wonder what kinds of conversation they can have with patients, what is acceptable and how to deal with intrusive questions. Training and supervision should provide a space in which to consider these dilemmas and develop understanding.

Understanding personality disorders

One common reflection at Millfields from staff more used to working with mental illness, was that they felt they could be more tolerant and understanding of the resident's behaviour had they been given a diagnosis such as psychosis. Many from nursing backgrounds reflected that their training had given them little knowledge of personality disorders, leaving them feeling totally ill-equipped for working at Millfields. As a result, it is essential that staff are trained to understand personality disorder and the life experiences and factors that can lead to the development of difficulties (see Chapters 1, 2, 13 and 14).

The TC model

With TCs being a specialist, relational model that most staff will be unfamiliar with, it is essential that training and supervision help them to understand the TC and their role within it (see Chapter 3 for a comprehensive explanation of the TC model).

TCs have accrued to themselves great mystique and ever-increasing jargon. This is despite their inceptual history of patients helping each other through mutual understanding, rather than relying on professionals (McKenzie and Anthony, 2018). TCs are also often seen as 'cliquey' and difficult to join, and the previous professional experience of staff can feel devalued. The experience at Millfields was that staff from medical backgrounds (e.g. nurses) struggled with a sense of being de-skilled, not knowing how to apply their previous professional experiences, and how their previous roles could be adapted to the model of change. This could result in staff retreating into offices or behind the glass windows of the nursing station, restricting their input to ensuring that basic care plans were being followed, and leaving other forms of engagement to staff considered to be 'clinical' (e.g. psychologists, psychiatrists, social workers). It is therefore essential to demystify the work of TCs and to convey its concepts in a way that is relatable and accessible.

New staff in therapeutic communities can often feel intimidated by community meetings, not knowing what their role is, their purpose, how to contribute and how to find their voice. Whilst clinical staff are normally always present, sometimes staff who consider themselves 'non-clinical' will prioritise other activities, nominating one member of their team to represent them. Such questions as "Why is so much time spent on discussing apparently irrelevant issues rather than offences?"; "Why does it take so long to make decisions?"; and "Why do staff allow the community members to make what is clearly the wrong decision?" are frequently raised. Helping staff to understand what are often referred to as 'The Four Pillars' of a TC enables them to understand the purpose behind the model and engage in a meaningful way (see Chapter 3).

Frustration on the part of residents in TCs can also be shared by staff. For example, "Why was my concern or decision not supported"? There are two important issues here. Regarding the residents, it is not the decision but the process of decision-making that is important; this is their learning. Regarding staff, democratisation in a multidisciplinary staff team means that the voices of all those who have different interactions and thereby different experiences with the resident can and should be heard to inform decision-making.

Ultimately, however, the safety of the residents and public, and the functioning of the TC must be kept foremost in mind, and as such one's view or voice may be rejected on those grounds. Staff as well as residents often feel marginalised when their view is not adhered to, either because they are not in the majority or because overriding concerns about safety take precedence. Trying to help staff understand the importance of being involved in decision-making, and the difficulties that occur in the implementation goes some way to reducing the tension that often occurs.

Giving staff comprehensive training and supervision in the TC model can help to reduce concerns and anxieties around feeling deskilled or not knowing what to do in their new roles. Learning about group dynamics, such as the stages of groups, defence mechanisms and anti-group processes are also useful (see Chapters 5 and 20).

Psychological processes such as transference and projection

Residents of a therapeutic community, and members of small groups can represent people in their families of origin, raising strong emotions such as hostility and competitiveness. It is inevitable that, in time, residents will interact with staff and other members of the community in modes reminiscent of the way they interacted with parents and siblings. This dynamic provides an opportunity for 'unfinished business' to be worked through in a corrective way. Fixed, inflexible roles need to be explored and challenged, and new ways of behaving need to be encouraged.

Staff should be aware and observant of this dynamic, and familiar with the concept of transference: the displacement of feelings towards someone from the past onto someone in the present. The very fact that staff are perceived by the residents as figures of authority who have control over their lives makes them vulnerable to transferential feelings. Freud saw transference as a useful tool to recapture feelings from the past, often transferred onto the therapist – in the case of TCs, staff – which can provide rich opportunities for learning (Freud, 1914; Symington, 1986). Working in a forensic setting, transference in the model of change can lead to offence-paralleling behaviour. This can provide rich and essential opportunities for learning but also risk and even reoffending if not worked through competently (Daffern et al., 2007; Neville, Miller and Fritzon, 2007; Shuker, 2010).

During training and supervision, staff should be invited to explore the transferential feelings that might contribute to conflict with residents and learn ways of dealing with these in such a way that all remain safe. They are also encouraged to explore their own countertransference (feelings and thoughts evoked by the resident's behaviour) and how an understanding of these feelings might aid them (Lees, Haigh and Tucker, 2017). Of course, transference is not uniquely the prerogative of residents. Through training, staff also can come to realise that transference and countertransference are present in all relationships, not just those with residents, and that understanding and working with these processes may also help to resolve conflicts or misunderstandings in the staff team (Halton, 2019, pp. 11–18).

Understanding Rapoport's principles (2001) and Yalom's therapeutic factors (Yalom and Leszcs, 2005, pp. 19–52) helps staff to think about how they can contribute therapeutically to the TC. Staff can be supported to look out for opportunities to ask useful questions such as:

- "Has anyone had a similar experience (universality)?"
- "Perhaps you could share your journey (instillation of hope)?"
- "What does it feel like when you listen to how your feedback helped Tom (altruism)?"
- "Who does he remind you of (family re-enactment)?"

Staff can also look out for opportunities to increase group cohesiveness, such as pointing out unhelpful judgements or encouraging people in the group to relate to each other. These principles and skills help staff to find their voice in the community meeting and to have a sense of meaning and direction in their interventions.

Conflict resolution

When groups of people live and work together in such an intense way, interpersonal conflicts will inevitably occur. There will always be some friction amongst TC members and although such frictions may have a negative effect on the community, they are not necessarily something 'bad' or 'pathological' to be gotten rid of. Rather like states of crisis, conflicts can be viewed as normal in healthy relationships and, if properly managed, seen as an opportunity for learning and growth. However, considering the complex and almost infinite sources of various conflicts, conflict resolution is a formidable undertaking. It is helpful to understand that an individual with unrealised goals feels frustrated and that such frustration can lead to aggression, turning inwards as attitudes of hatred or outwards as verbal or physical violence; i.e. they must learn that they can survive the pain of failure. Ongoing reflective practice and supervision can also aid in formulating and working with conflicts.

Clinical supervision, reflective practice and staff support groups

The work of a TC is complex and personally challenging. Individual or small group supervision, reflective practice and staff support are essential ways of dealing with the clinical challenges as well as the difficult dynamics that can occur between residents and staff, but also between different staff members or staff and the organisation. These spaces enable members of the team to do their work more effectively and to reflect on this as well as on their relationships within the community. They are also seen as a continuation of training and learning.

At Millfields, individual or small group clinical supervision from a clinically trained member of staff was required for all staff at least once a month, with many less experienced staff having weekly supervision (as well as ad hoc supervision available as needed for all staff). Reflective practice and staff support groups were also held with all staff members together once a week, conducted by external facilitators experienced with the resident group and with TCs. The reflective practice group was focussed on helping staff to understand and formulate an individual resident's difficulties and come up with strategies for intervention and support. Conversely, staff support group was focussed on helping staff to manage their own responses to residents and to each other, and to gain support from colleagues. Supervision is a smaller space in which to focus on all these aspects as needed.

Perhaps not surprisingly, staff are not always clear on how to use supervision or reflective practice and staff support groups. It is therefore essential to help staff prepare for these spaces by thinking about what they need, their expectations, their learning styles, focusing on one need at a time and helping them understand that uncertainty is part of learning.

Different supervisors can use different models for supervision (e.g. Hawkins and Shohet's 7 Eye Process Model of Supervision [2012]), to help provide structure and aid engagement. Regardless of the model used, supervision and reflective practice will need to support staff to continually think at a deeper level about residents, and the links between their current presentation, their life experiences and their offending. This understanding in turn helps staff to feel less personally attacked by the behaviour of residents, and to act in a therapeutic manner towards residents to support them to change.

Evaluation and challenges

To keep the training fresh and to meet the needs of the staff, evaluation is critical. After each training module, participants should be asked to evaluate the training and their personal and professional experience of it. They should also be supported in supervision to measure their knowledge and skills against the TC competencies (The Consortium for Therapeutic Communities and Community of Communities, 2014).

Whilst most staff will find benefit in the reflective group and will welcome supervision, some will be wary of and resistant to it. These members of staff are likely to be from a nursing or security focussed background and will not understand or support the therapeutic model and the requirement of their role to participate. If this is highlighted as a problem by TC leadership, it could be taken as unfair and unconstructive criticism, particularly if higher levels of management share the misunderstanding. Equally, for staff who are on board with the model, there can be increasing levels of frustration and resentment at having to compensate for the lacking or counterproductive contribution from colleagues who are not. This can damage trust in the process, leave issues unresolved, and ultimately reduce the effectiveness of the TC for residents. These dynamics and challenges, as well as ways of addressing them, will be covered further in Chapter 20.

References

The Consortium for Therapeutic Communities and Community of Communities (2014), *TC Practitioner Competencies Framework*. Available at: https://www.therapeuticcommunities.org/wp-content/uploads/2014/11/TC-Core-Competencies-with-Preface-2014.pdf (accessed 30 January 2025).

The Institute on Trauma and Trauma-Informed Care (2022) *Trauma-informed organizational change manual*. Available at: http://socialwork.buffalo.edu/trauma-manual (accessed 22 January 2025).

Ainsworth, M., Blehar, M., Waters, E. and Wall, S. (1978) *Patterns of attachment*. Hillside, NJ: Erlbaum.

Bowlby, J. (1988/1995) *A secure base: clinical applications of attachment theory*. London: Routledge.

Daffern, M., Jones, L., Howells, K., Shine, J., Mikton, C. and Tunbridge, V. (2007) 'Editorial – refining the definition of offence paralleling behaviour', *Criminal Behaviour and Mental Health*, 17, pp. 265–273. https://doi.org/10.1002/cbm.671

Fonagy, P., Luyten, P., Moulton-Perkins, A., Lee, Y.W., Warren, F., Howard, S., Ghinai, R., Fearon, P. and Lowyuck, B. (2016) 'Development and validation of a self-report measure of mentalizing: the reflective functioning questionnaire', *PlOS One*, 11(7). https://doi.org/10.1371/journal.pone.0158678

Freud, S. (1914) 'Remembering repeating and working through (further recommendations on the technique of psycho-analysis II)', *The Standard Edition of the Complete Psychological Works of Sigmund Freud*, 12, pp. 145–156.

Haigh, R. (2013) 'The quintessence of a therapeutic environment', *Therapeutic Communities*, 34(1), pp. 6–15. https://doi.org/10.1108/09641861311330464

Halton, W. (2019) 'Some unconscious aspects of institutional life', in Obholzer, A.; & Roberts, V.Z. (eds.) *The unconscious at work: individual and organizational stress in the human services*. London: Routledge, pp. 11–18.

Hawkins, P. and Shohet, R. (2012) *Supervision in the helping professions*. 4th edn. Maidenhead: Open University Press.

Lees, J., Haigh, R. and Tucker, S. (2017) 'Therapeutic communities and group analysis', *Therapeutic Communities: The International Journal of Therapeutic Communities*, 38(2), pp. 87–107. https://doi.org/10.1108/TC-11-2016-0025

McKenzie, J. and Anthony, R. (2018) *Trust and change thinking points on therapeutic communities*. Hook: Waterside Press.

Neville, L., Miller, S. and Fritzon, K. (2007) 'Understanding change in a therapeutic community: an action systems approach', *The Journal of Forensic Psychiatry & Psychology*, 18(2), pp. 181–203. https://doi.org/10.1080/14789940601108439

Rapoport, R.N. (2001) *The community as a doctor: new perspectives on a therapeutic community (International behavioural and social sciences, classics from the Tavistock press)*. London: Routledge.

Raus, G.A. and Auty, J.M. (2018) 'The experience of change in a prison therapeutic community: an interpretative phenomenological analysis', *The International Journal of Therapeutic Communities*, 39(1). https://doi.org/10.1108/TC-11-2016-0024

Shuker, R. (2010) 'Forensic therapeutic communities: a critique of treatment model and evidence base', *Howard Journal of Crime and Justice*, 49(5), pp. 463–477. https://doi.org/10.1111/j.1468-2311.2010.00637.x

Symington, N. (1986) 'The clinical significance of transference' in *The analytic experience: lectures from the Tavistock*. London: Free Association Books.

Tyndale, A. and Rosenberg, V. (2014) 'The independent tradition', *British Journal of Psychotherapy*, 30(3), pp. 305–313. https://doi.org/10.1111/bjp.12096

Yalom, I.D. and Leszcs, M. (2005) *The theory and practice of group therapy*. 5th edn. New York: Basic Books.

Chapter 19

The impact of work on individuals, teams and organisations

Celia Taylor

Introduction

Study after study has found that people with personality disorder are generally thought of by clinicians as difficult to manage (e.g. Clarke *et al.*, 2015; Newton-Howes, Weaver and Tyrer, 2008), and less likely to improve with treatment (e.g. Beryl and Völlm, 2018; Black *et al.*, 2011). These repeated findings, however, do not explain the levels of hostility, judgementalism and sheer dislike that are still commonly found amongst clinicians (Chartonas *et al.*, 2017; Lewis and Appleby, 1988). Such feelings remain prevalent despite anti-stigma campaigns (e.g. Sampogna *et al.*, 2017), the widespread dissemination in the UK publications such as *Breaking the Cycle of Rejection: The Personality Disorder Capabilities Framework* (National Institute for Mental Health in England, 2013), and the exponential growth in treatment facilities for these patients in recent years (National Institute for Mental Health in England, 2003; Benefield *et al.*, 2015).

In order to offer the best possible care to this group of patients, it is important to try to understand the reasons behind such visceral expressions of dislike, which are even more exaggerated towards those who have committed serious offences. This includes examining what can happen in the relationship between would-be care giver and patient that can prove hurtful and damaging. These dynamics also affect some clinicians more than others, with the accompanying danger of them being acted out by the teams and organisations trying to provide services for them. Exploring the underlying factors in this process can help to determine the kinds of staff and settings that are more likely to be suited to the task of treatment.

How patients with severe personality disorder relate to care

As long ago as the 1950s, medical sociologist Talcott Parsons (1975) described the 'sick role', and the rights as well as the obligations of those allowed by society to assume it. Many of these hold good within mental health care, whereby professionals have a number of assumptions about how the patients in their care 'ought' to behave: they will present a psychological symptom or complaint to be solved; they

DOI: 10.4324/9781032717302-19

will take ownership of some aspects of their presentation; they will listen to and consider our views of their problem; they will work collaboratively with us to carry out our advice; they will endure any departures from the foreseen progress, including its speed, without undue distress or disturbance; and they will be able to deal with the consequences of ending their relationship with us. When we work with people with severe personality disorder, we soon learn that very few, sometimes none, of these assumptions hold true. For example, they might not understand or be able to express their profound and complex difficulties, either to themselves or to others. Their early life experiences make it unlikely that they will simply trust us, such that any suggested formulation, diagnosis or advice is disregarded or disputed. They do not deal well with frustration, but wish to be rid of their difficulties, with little understanding of the time needed to accomplish this. Even if they participate and find the work helpful, the ending is likely to be problematic, with regression, even re-offending, highly likely.

In examining our experience of caring for this group, then, it is most of all necessary to look at the origins of their difficulties in relating to others. Practically a defining feature is that they will have experienced severe harm at the hands of those who are meant to love and care for them at a very young age. The nature and degree of cruelty involved can be difficult to comprehend. An example we came across was that of a child being forced to eat off the floor, and alongside this degrading emotional abuse, being severely physically abused and having himself and his mother and siblings threatened with a machete by their father. As an adolescent, this child began to fear his father would end up killing them all in a drunken spree, and took matters into his own hands by stabbing his father to death as he slept. All this young person's knowledge, assumptions and expectations of the people in his world were built around a sadistic monster who presented an existential threat, and a terrified mother who could not protect them.

> "It was really important that I was never touched physically and restrained. Staff stood around me and talked to me, and that was really different".

Fonagy *et al.* (1997) have described how the child's ability to mentalise – or to consider what another person might be thinking – is inhibited and distorted by such experiences of an unpredictable or terrifying caregiver. The result is a baked-in, highly insecure attachment style, with the individual growing up to view the people in his world as inherently dangerous, made up either of victims or perpetrators, and thus developing a mind-set in which self-protection overrides empathy or altruism (see Chapters 1 and 2). Over time, aggression becomes a habitual defence, or the "internal organising influence in the construction of the self", such that pathological destructiveness replaces emotional relatedness (Fonagy, 2003). Anna Freud (1936) termed this the "identification with the aggressor". The child has introjected his experiences, such that his care giver's mode of being becomes part of his own personality and viewed as the only means of survival in a dangerous world. Gilligan (1997) describes how concomitant shame is also central to violent offending: "The 'self', starved of love, dies. That is how violence can cause the death of the self, even when it does not kill the body. Without feelings of love, the self feels numb, empty, and dead". The capacity for extreme violence is therefore rooted in experienced violence that has caused the death of self (De Zulueta, 2006).

Welldon (1991) reminds us that emotional deprivation is an important part of this developmental trajectory: early trauma inhibits the growth of the imagination and the ability to think symbolically rather than act mindlessly. As a result, our patients grow up lacking in interpersonal skills, lacking a sense of self-worth and lacking in any ability to form rewarding close relationships. A person operating at the psychopathic end of the spectrum will act instead from self-interest: he will be prepared to exploit, shame and deceive others with impunity (Narvaez, 2014). As Van den Berg and Oei (2009) point out, "to survive, which is what people with very unsafe attachments have to do, the obvious 'choice' is to enter into instrumental relations whose goal is the acquiring of power".

The impact on staff

We are now in a better position to ask, what does care mean to someone with severe personality disorder? Hinshelwood (2002) has described how a disordered response to care is at the core of severe personality disorder, so much so that it is, "the central feature of the condition to be understood". To people like the young person described above, all his experiences have proven to him that *help offered will be abusive*: he will "misread the signs and attribute cruelty, self-seeking dominance and neglect" to the actions of others – in this case, clinicians trying to help (Hinshelwood, 2002). Abuse is therefore detected in interactions with care givers in a most pervasive way. In addition, the patient will unconsciously exert pressure on the unwitting professional to fulfil aspects of the original faulty and damaging care-giving. And because the abused person has become the abuser, in retaliation, he will inflict abuse on those trying to help him. This can take the form of physical, sexual or psychological abuse. The first two of these are usually overt, although the lead-up to sexual abuse can be via a form of gradual encroachment on a staff member's boundaries that the less experienced will not always detect. We experienced this in Millfields with a male sex offender who had already succeeded, post-conviction, in seducing a prison officer and a woman working in the prison's education department. Psychological or emotional abuse, in the form of hurtful interpersonal assaults, is much more widely experienced, especially by nursing staff who spend long periods of time with patients, often without respite and with little or no clinical supervision in many services. Common examples of the 'onslaught' (Aiyegbusi and Kelly, 2015) include threats, self-harm, deception, formal complaints (Taylor, 2012), racism and the like.

At the heart of such assaults is a repudiation of the motives and expertise of the carer – his or her very professional identity and basis of self-esteem – and it can be very hard for us to take a step back to explore the meaning of the patient's communication. Instead, the patient who makes staff feel wretched is condemned as unworthy, purely malicious, hateful or frankly evil (Bowers, 2003), in whom no visible trace of the desperate help-seeker can be discerned. The impulse to control and punish the 'badness' becomes entrenched, with the patient, as a result, seeing that his assumptions about care are entirely justified. This risk is particularly high when an 'abuser' has unknowingly been recruited to be part of the clinical team. We sometimes see an alternative scenario in staff, born out of a hatred of being cast in the role of bad object and a need to preserve a sense of our professionalism as being wise and benevolent. Such individuals "deny the hatred engendered in response to the patient's transference hate ... and choose to provide a defensive form of love" (Celenza and Gabbard, 2007). Gabbard (1997) has termed this process a "disidentification with the aggressor". It predisposes the individual to boundary violations or a sentimentalised indulgence: as demonstrated by the second inquiry into the personality disorder service at Ashworth Hospital, which found that security had grown so lax that Fallon *et al.* (1999, p. 87) commented that it was "like giving children the keys to the sweet shop".

The impact on teams

Working on a "ward full of emotional, aggressive people" (Rodwell and Frith, 2024) has an undoubted impact on the functioning of whole teams. What *our patients* need from their clinical team is for those responsible for their care to communicate often and effectively, to get on well together, and to be clear about boundaries. What *we* need from working in this team is that we all know – and, crucially, buy into – our common purpose and work collaboratively towards achieving it, understand our individual role (and its limits) and feel valued. Unfortunately, clinical teams working with severe personality disorder are notoriously prone to splitting and conflict. Paradoxically, neither is a bad thing if it can be reflected upon and addressed maturely. In fact, they are almost inevitable, and part of the host organisation's role is to recognise this, understand it and actively support the structures and attitudes that will lead to a growing understanding of the patient and his journey. Splitting reflects the patient's failure in his thinking to bring together both positive and negative qualities of himself and others into a cohesive, real-world whole. The term derives from psychoanalyst Melanie Klein's work (1946) on personality development in young children, whereby the child's relation to the mother serves as the template for future relationships. When the infant is hungry, cold or in pain, and no immediate relief or comfort is offered, his reaction is to cry for relief. Klein's theory proposes that the infant believes he feels so dreadful because he is under external attack. In fact, this is a misattribution: the source of the problem is internal, not external, but this internal pain is denied, split off and projected onto an external 'source'. When mother is responsive and alleviates suffering, she is all-benign and safe; when she does not, she is all-malevolent and to be feared. Klein (1946) termed this defence mechanism the paranoid-schizoid state. If development proceeds normally, these paranoid anxieties and schizoid defences are largely superseded by a more integrated, balanced conception of others, although to some extent we all retain elements of the paranoid schizoid position, especially when under stress.

Staff teams experience splitting by their patients as 'black and white thinking' or 'idealisation and denigration', whereby some individuals are seen as wholly 'good' and some as wholly 'bad', with no middle ground. The danger is that the 'good' staff member will become lured into an unhealthy alliance with the patient, and into conflict with his or her colleagues who 'don't understand' the patient. Likewise, the rejected and condemned 'bad' staff member begins to feel that his or her colleagues have been naively duped. Despite this being an unconscious process in the patient, especially early on in treatment, responsibility for the conflict is then attributed to him, and he is accused of splitting the team. Patients can indeed respond selectively to staffs' differing interactive styles and/or his perception of the differing roles of members within the hierarchy of a team. However, avoiding the dynamic of how this can lead to conflict is the responsibility of the staff.

A split often triggers some team members to demand a firm approach to handling the offender, while other team members or agencies demand a more supportive approach. Splitting tends to be highly contagious, especially in demanding situations and under stress. Emotions become intense and people become rigid, causing impasse and escalating tension. Often rumours are spread about each side's statements or behaviour, and more and more people become involved. Staff who engage the most in this splitting dynamic do not realise it and often become 'high conflict' people, because they increase disputes in the team instead of resolving them. Colleagues take extreme, opposite, all-or-nothing positions about each other and especially about the 'high conflict' person. Others join in and start to act like a gang, even though they are usually reasonable people. From the outside it is hard to understand who is driving the problem, since several people have become emotionally hooked.

The conflict can also become personal, leading to criticisms of individual competence, intelligence, ethics, morality, etc. It can also be very hostile – not just a difference of opinion, but highly defensive and blaming. It often involves 'projection' onto the others: each 'side' starts to think of the others as being divisive and inappropriate – in ways that they are actually being divisive and inappropriate themselves. Whereas a functioning team can tolerate such divisions and find time to resolve real or apparent differences in staff opinions about a patient, dysfunctional teams get stuck in unpleasant polarised positions, or refuse to participate in attempts at resolution.

Other important signs of growing dysfunction in a team include: poor leadership, an inability to retain focus on the team's core purpose or primary task; the failure of a discipline's management hierarchy to provide both direct and indirect support for more junior staff; opting out of clinical supervision and reflective practice; an increased risk of boundary crossings and violations; staff acting punitively towards those in their care; and staff forming an 'anti-group' with an envious conscious or unconscious wish to destroy any good that the therapy is achieving.

Impact on organisations

The organisation that hosts the personality disorder service can be thought of as a complex, organised system of sub-groups and individuals, whereby a division of labour contributes to the fulfilment of the primary task (Durkheim, 1984). Examples of subgroups within forensic settings include the clinicians, security staff, human resources, managers, administrators, etc. Although each part of the system tends to be specialised, there is a high degree of mutual interdependence, and despite the individuals working within each role changing over time, the nature and function of role persists. Mental health and prison services can be thought of as just such complex systems, within which the particular personality disorder service is often experienced as the 'black sheep' of the family. The reasons are not hard to discern and have to do with difference: primarily psychologically-based treatment approaches are poorly understood in contrast to the medical model, and what is expected of the patients and staff is very different. Unlike the mentally ill, patients admitted to personality disorder services are high-functioning, do best with a flattened hierarchy within the staff group and between staff and their charges, and with an emphasis on responsibility-taking as the desired outcome. Medication is emphatically not the mainstay of treatment.

These differences pose an inherent threat to the authority of the institution that will not easily be tolerated by a management system that relies on control, especially of the perception of outside, regulatory bodies: achieving 'gold stars' has, arguably, become the primary task (Haslam, Ellis and Plumridge, 2022). This is in part because organisations that lie directly within the sphere of governmental influence are easy prey as targets for blaming and reputational death. Nevertheless, components of the organisation are still expected by society to perform two, somewhat contradictory primary tasks: the provision of care, but also the protection of society from its most dangerous members. When it functions well, these tasks are understood and fulfilled at all levels of the hierarchy, with self-correcting information and feedback flowing up as well as down.

The impact of accommodating personality disordered offenders within the organisation has a similar impact on its functioning as on individual practitioners and teams. These people have become patients or prisoners because they have acted on others in criminally sexual or violent ways. Inevitably, they will behave similarly in the secure environment – even if their acts are now tempered by external constraints – by subverting security, bullying or grooming others, or directly challenging rules and procedures (Ruszczynski, 2018). The response by management tends to be two-fold: first, there is conscious or unconscious fear: fear of one's professional competence and authority being challenged and exposed as lacking; fear of being duped or corrupted; and fear of reputational damage via serious incidents. Second, there is the impulse to "focus on the badness" (Hinshelwood, 2002) by clamping down on the subversion: visits are restricted, freedom of movement is curtailed, and access to the outside world prohibited. Thus, the organisation becomes the exemplar of punitive care that the patient expects. The danger is that of a vicious cycle being enacted, whereby the institution and the patients mutually abuse one another. Sometimes managers will repudiate the role of abuser, by enforcing a loosening of boundaries and becoming over-indulgent. In both instances, the space and capacity to think about the patient's communication has been lost: "the fate of those working with personality disordered patients is to feel abused, or omnipotently indulgent, or hostile and dismissive" (Ruszczynski, 2018).

As the organisation's management style becomes increasingly drawn into these dynamics, the knee-jerk, and hence mindless, reaction is also to find fault, and ideally, to blame others rather than themselves. Witch-hunting and scapegoating become rife, and it is hard to find support from colleagues in times of pressure to find a culprit. Blame being passed around is often a sign of 'systemic' failure. Conscious or unconscious hatred can become part of the institutional response, which manifests itself via sabotage, taking sides in a 'split' or turning a blind eye to poor practice and lack of professionalism. This could include allocating unsuitable staff to the service, especially at a more senior level where those below are most impacted; and supporting a destructive 'anti-group' (Nitsun, 1996) element, thus undermining the service's ethos and therapeutic task.

How to mitigate these impacts

The institution

It is useful to consider first how the institution can best preserve the integrity of the therapeutic task, because unless the institution survives intact, nothing else will. This might sound overly dramatic, but by their very nature, forensic personality disorder services can be the target of destruction by their patients and by senior managers, acting in a kind of unholy alliance. It is the responsibility of the latter to be actively committed to the service, and to contain and ameliorate the impulse of the former to destroy, in favour of preserving a space for thoughtful therapy. To be successful, the approach needs to be system-wide. Space and time must be carved out and protected for teams to receive training, staff support, clinical supervision and reflective practice. This means that staffing levels need to be adequate. Ideally, the more senior staff should be experienced, for which no amount of training can substitute. In practice, recruitment of people experienced in the care of these patients is difficult because there are few of them, in which case they can be sought out via external, specialist facilitation and consultation. It is not enough for senior managers to establish and defend these spaces: they need to be present, involved and open to questioning. As described in Chapter 3, there are helpful elements of the therapeutic community (TC) approach that open organisational dynamics up to inquiry. Thus, a core TC standard (Paget, 2008) is that all patients and staff can consider and challenge managerial processes and institutional dynamics. This obviously does not mean that policies and rules can be vetoed, merely that questions can be asked. Another core standard is that change is managed in a way that recognises the impact on patients and staff.

Those in charge of the organisation also need to be alert to the main ways that people with personality disorder can manifest their destructiveness. Often, this will be by subversion, usually of security and of the people responsible for maintaining it. There is an important balance to be struck between giving patients a voice and supporting staff in trying to do their jobs in the face of challenges, for example, to their authority or their knowledge of policies. Complaints must be understood (Taylor, 2012) and fairly investigated, without too much power being given to either party to undermine the other. Service user representation within the organisation is now universally recognised as desirable, but one lesson from the Fallon Inquiry (1999) was that the Ashworth Hospital Patients' Council had become dominated by individuals suffering from personality disorder as opposed to mental illness, to the detriment of the organisations functioning (see recommendation 2.29.7, p. 174).

As noted by Norton and Dolan (1995), institutions can consciously develop policies that will either remove or promote "the potential for these patients to learn from experience and to mature psychologically, to individualize". A vivid example can be drawn from the common institutional response to suicide attempts: we have experience of all clothes hangers and every kind of plastic bag being banned from being brought into the secure perimeter after incidents in which patients used them successfully to end their lives. It is also common for policy to dictate that every single possession must be removed from a patient's room that could possibly be used for acts of deliberate self-harm – resulting in a bare space devoid of comfort, since most items can be so used. While careful consideration does indeed need to be given to what patients can avail themselves of, such all-or-nothing responses tend to alleviate the institution of anxiety, while leaving the individual isolated and bereft.

Similar remarks can be made about intimidating and aggressive behaviour, which are usually dealt with via forcible restraint, and/or seclusion and/or sedation. Even the use of enhanced observations, while seemingly intended to offer close emotional support, can all too often simply mean following the individual around. Even quite senior staff can become wary of not implementing policies in blanket form, rather than judging individual situations. It is essential for all levels of the organisation to recognise the communication inherent in such acts, of conscious or unconscious emotions such as distress, pain and anger. The response can then be not just safe physical containment, but also emotional containment and encouragement for the patient to put his feelings into words rather than simply act them out.

A TC approach that can be readily adopted is that, following such incidents, a crisis meeting is held, whereby everyone meets together to hear the individual talk through his feelings, process them and receive supportive but also challenging feedback – both about his impact on others and how he might manage differently in future. The fact that some of this feedback will come from people who have been 'in the same boat" will give it extraordinary weight and validity. He will often think of himself as the 'victim' in relation to his actions, but as Norton and Dolan (1995) point out, "patients are enabled to develop psychological complexity only if they are shown, via the institutional response, a more complete and hence complex picture of themselves". Importantly, the typical institutional response of only wielding power and control is minimised.

Individual staff

Perhaps the first and most essential question for individual staff members to ask themselves is, "am I in the right place?" In other words, do they have sufficient liking for and interest in these individuals to want to help them? Clearly, it is an important issue for managers and recruiters to consider as well. The question can be thought of as an examination of the person's 'valence' in relation to the task. Lewin (2013), one of the founders of social psychology and the study of and organisational dynamics, described how we can have an overall positive or overall negative valence towards other individuals, events and situations, which make them more, or less, attractive to us in our lives. The factors that make up this valence can be internal: do I enjoy working with people with personality disorder; am I interested in their plight; can my personal moral framework balance out my aversion to what they have done with empathy for what they have suffered, and keep me alert to the dangers of unethical practice? And they can be external: am I committed to working in a team; to receiving and honestly reflecting on feedback; to constant learning with others about my patients and myself; to being questioned and to sharing my authority? Without these characteristics, individual staff members will probably not only dislike the work, but also suffer from it, both personally in terms of the 'onslaught' described above (Aiyegbusi and Kelly, 2015) and reputationally. We know, for example, that disliking patients is associated with higher levels of job stress, burn out and possible vicarious traumatisation (Freestone *et al.*, 2015; Kurtz, 2005). There is no shame in deciding that one is better suited to a different role, for example caring for the mentally ill or the learning disabled.

> "Some members of staff did not like how we worked in our ward ... they could not deal with PD patients. Reflective practice did not work to hold their emotions. All staff should have a psychology background and agree on how to work".

Bowers *et al.* (2003) studied the factors underlying and maintaining nurses' positive therapeutic attitudes to patients with severe personality disorder. They found the main influencers to be: having a psychological understanding of their behaviour; having a moral commitment (e.g. to professionalism); having an ability to identify with the patient as well as with his victim(s); and having effective self-management tools with which to contain their emotional reactions (e.g. separating the person from the behaviour). Nurses who "expressed a reluctance to stigmatise or label anybody challenged themselves to get to know the patient as a person with a rich personal history and unique characteristics, instead of angrily and summarily rejecting them at an earlier stage". Likewise, a commitment to preventing the recurrence of crime helped them to "put emotional reactions to past offences to one side and engage with the patient in order to make therapeutic progress". In addition, certain key events could have a profound influence upon an individual nurse's point of view, such as reading the case notes, being verbally abused, and suffering or witnessing a violent attack.

Perhaps the best place to start in terms of managing the impact of the work on us as individuals is by paying attention to our relationship with the patients, right from the beginning. Confusingly, these patients' hopes of us can be unrealistically high, completely absent or oscillating between the two extremes, so time must be spent in establishing a working alliance. These patients have a longing to be known and understood but, equally, fear of being seen, lest judged negatively and harshly for their vulnerability or deficits, which they hate in themselves and strive to avoid experiencing. Our attitude and behaviour will speak to them more loudly and memorably than our words: words can mean little to these patients, as they are associated with being misled or manipulated, and hence unreliable. Their internal working model predicts that what we say we will do is unlikely to happen. Knowing this forearms us to expect their mistrust, and to realise that they will need us to follow through with actions: an undertaking to do something must be kept if at all possible. If for some reason it cannot, a full and honest explanation should be given quickly. Likewise, if we do make a mistake – which is also inevitable in life – it is crucial to apologise at the earliest opportunity. This will be a new experience for the patient and will garner much respect. The patient should be enlisted as a collaborator in the work, in which both are free to inspect and criticise, preferably, in a constructive manner. This will be alien territory, so we should anticipate the setbacks that will inevitably happen, by talking about the possibility in advance and how both parties would hope to achieve a resolution. Contracts can be helpful, but these patients have a knack of finding grey areas that can be exploited.

They are also likely to test out the genuineness of our intentions, as well as our capacity to be tolerant of them and their acts of 'self-expression'. Those forms of self-expression that will have an adverse impact on us can be thought of as 'active' and 'passive'. The active ones are the 'loud' acts that involve shouting, swearing at or even threatening us. The passive ones are more 'silent': not attending individual meetings or groups, persistent lateness, keeping quiet, or evading important but painful and shaming topics. It pays to be aware of apparently 'positive' responses that might be intended to charm, or even groom, us – for example, expressions of excessive praise of our wonderful efforts, which are the 'best ever' received, yet without providing evidence. We all wish to be liked and praised, and working with severe personality disorder offers no quick successes, so it can feel slow and unrewarding. Frustration at this lack of progress is hard to deal with, so any positive response can feel like an oasis in a desert. It is hard to question positive feedback regarding our own input, but retaining a curious and scientific attitude is important: if praised, we can say thank you but ask for evidence, or at the very least maintain our understanding that we are being put on a pedestal.

The combination of our frustration about the lack of speedier progress and their testing out of our reliability can draw us out of our role. Where this is temporary and recoverable, it is termed a 'boundary crossing', and where it is sustained and irrecoverable, a 'boundary violation'. Because of the arduous and protracted nature of much of the work, crossings are not unusual, but they need to be recognised as such: we must understand the limits of our role and when we have strayed or been pulled out of it. Most of us will be drawn into boundary crossings at one time or another: they are not 'sins', and both parties have usually contributed, not just the patient. As such, they are more worthy of understanding than punishment. Common crossings are being lax with timekeeping or revealing a little too much personal information. There is usually disagreement within teams about where exactly to draw the line in this regard, so the topic should be reviewed often.

On the other hand, boundary violations usually involve a professional relationship degenerating into a personal one, with disclosure of our own emotional problems or sexual contact. Epstein and Simon (1990) have pointed out the essentially exploitative nature of such boundary violations, which tend to have components of self-deception and a narcissistic need to feel special. A useful rule of thumb is to ask oneself in any situation, "am I saying/doing this to help the patient in his treatment, or for myself?" and, "would I be comfortable talking about it in reflective practice or to my clinical supervisor?" It is important to note that the over-zealous enforcement of boundaries will easily offend these patients, for example rebuffing their overtures in a critical or cold manner. If asked where we live or whether we have children, it is far better to respond with deflection or humour than by saying "that's inappropriate". Better still, the opportunity can be used to teach social skills and the navigation of other people's privacy.

Miller and Maier (2002) have pointed out a particular kind of boundary violation that tends only to happen in forensic or custodial services, in which the patient 'manipulates and coerces' the clinician to carry out his will – for example, to smuggle in a smart phone or drugs. In this instance, the power dynamic has been reversed and the patient has exerted control. This may be the culmination of a process of grooming in which a member of staff who commits increasing boundary crossings or violations is then blackmailed to bring in contraband or be exposed. Alternatively, staff members who are unsuitable for this type of work may willingly deal in banned items for financial gain. This type of behaviour from staff is highly destructive to the patients as well as to the reputation and morale of the staff team.

Finally, individual staff can be susceptible to burnout (Chandler, Newman and Butler, 2017), or growing feelings of cynicism, lack of a sense of personal accomplishment and emotional exhaustion. Those who are unprepared for the rigours of the work (regardless of age or experience) or have concurrent stress, are at extra risk of it. It may reveal itself slowly, with decreasing job satisfaction and possibly a growing use of alcohol or even drugs in an attempt to cope. Relationship problems with a partner, friends or family can ensue, with anxiety or depression emerging. Taking time off work, not wanting to be there, increasing sickness or lateness can all be signs, singly or together. If we recognise them in ourselves or have them pointed out to us, it is important to confide without delay in someone we trust: a friend, colleague, supervisor or manager. A change in role or even job might be needed for those badly affected.

The clinical team

As described by Bateman and Tyrer (2002), treatments known to have some efficacy in personality disorder have certain features in common, tending to be well-structured; devote considerable effort to enhancing engagement; have a clear focus; be theoretically highly coherent to both therapists and patient; be relatively long-term; encourage a powerful attachment relationship between patient and therapist; and be well-integrated with other services available to the patient. Large studies of team functioning (e.g. Borrill *et al.*, 2000; Katz and Kirkland, 1990) have found that the wards with the least violence are run according to predictable routines with a good amount of contact between patients and staff, wide-ranging therapy programmes, a cohesive staff group and visible, committed leadership. The responsibility for achieving and maintaining these conditions belongs to the clinical team as a whole: no one individual can fulfil the goal. The tendency of patients with severe personality disorder will be to push back against or undermine coherence so, in order to remain on task, the team must, collectively, be aware of and manage the impact of the work on its functioning. In order to achieve this, the team must be made up of sufficiently collaborative individuals with the right 'valence' – as described above – with a good understanding of, and adherence to, the clinical model, and with enough experience to mentor and influence its newer members.

As we have seen, splitting and conflict will be almost inevitable, and it will be a part of the daily work to shore the team up against their impact. The best way of mitigating conflict is to cultivate a team view that differences of opinion are, in fact, valuable: each person's perspective gives us a new perspective on the patient, which, through discussion, can bring us to a better understanding of him as an integrated, whole person – something which he on his own has been unable to achieve. Differences of opinion are more difficult to reconcile when it comes to deciding the appropriate response to a patient who has 'acted out' in a destructive way. This will usually be via a breach of the rules or boundaries, which often prompts a clamour for 'consequences', without which the target of the acting out, and his or her closest colleagues (usually in the same discipline), will feel let down by the rest of the team. Because of the constant pull towards either punitiveness or towards over-indulgence, the team should try to agree, in advance, and preferably in consultation with the patients, what the appropriate, proportionate consequence is to the most common forms of rule-breaking. A useful way of tempering disappointment in those whose views are not given preference is to hold a 'trial' of a particular approach for, say, three months and then review together its success or otherwise.

Teams can be cruel and unforgiving of individual members whom they perceive to have broken the rules, for example via a boundary crossing. Again, this impulse needs to be resisted in favour of empathy and thoughtful exploration in reflective practice. This approach can even be powerfully modelled to the patients in a community meeting, with the staff member openly questioning his or her own actions. This takes some courage, and colleagues must be present and supportive. The goal is to head off a true, serious boundary violation, but if one is about to occur or has already occurred, decisive action must be taken for everyone's sake. This will usually involve the wider institution stepping in with a suspension, relocation or a disciplinary investigation. Discussion is usually prohibited in order not to prejudice the outcome, which can directly undermine the team's need to process and learn from what has happened. Nothing, however, prevents us from discussing the impact of such an event on us, individually and collectively.

Another challenge to the clinical team will be whether it can preserve consistency and coherence, as the tendency of the patients will be to undermine the integrity of the model, and preserving it will require daily effort. External events can contribute; for example, during the COVID pandemic and during building works, it became difficult to run our usual therapy programme of community meetings and small groups at Millfields. The solution was emphatically not to jettison it, but rather to arrive at the best possible compromise and run as much of it as we could. We usually had a two-week, partial break over the Christmas and Easter holidays in that we only kept the community meetings going, and it was very interesting how many patients admitted that they missed their small group: structure is containing for these individuals. Adshead (1998), writing about the usefulness of attachment theory in our treatment of these patients, has noted that, for those with histories of failed attachment, "confiding in someone, telling one's story and being listened to are potent modulators of anxiety". Thus, structure and consistency in themselves are important components of the secure base.

The preservation of structure and consistency applies equally to the need for the team as a whole to attend staff-only spaces set up for their benefit: this includes training, clinical supervision, staff support (looking at team and organisational dynamics), reflective practice and the like. Senior clinicians are important role models in this regard. Despite the near-universal acknowledgement that such spaces are essential, a lack of attendance is not uncommon, and as it undermines their function and effectiveness for the whole group, it is worth trying to understand why. We learned that those implacably against going, and line managers who tacitly or actively legitimise them, tend not to be suitable for the work and provide fertile ground for the establishment of an 'anti-group' (Nitsun, 1996). This perception receives some support in a paper by Hollander and Einwohner (2004) who noted that, when defined by conscious intent, resistance can be 'oppositional' rather than a defence against anxiety (as per classical psychodynamic thinking). Buus et al. (2018) interviewed a series of non-participants and found that some gave practical, 'legitimate' reasons for not attending, e.g. low staffing levels, while others admitted deliberately rejecting the opportunity. There was an overlap in the two groups when underlying intent was explored, with the practical reasons masking private rejection. Amongst the main reasons for deliberate absence were fear of exposing personal and intimate feelings, lack of trust in colleagues, pre-existing conflict and bad past experiences of feeling unheard or even bullied. In other words, although the reasons for avoidance are complex, it is worth recognising that these groups can themselves create severe anxiety. The answer is not to permit avoidance, but rather to plan with the facilitator how these dynamics might best be addressed. One solution we identified, together with a very experienced external facilitator, was to focus discussion on clinical matters surrounding individual patients, as a safe way into a deeper look at team dynamics.

References

Adshead, G. (1998) 'Psychiatric staff as attachment figures: understanding management problems in psychiatric services in the light of attachment theory', *The British Journal of Psychiatry*, 172(1), pp. 64–69. http://dx.doi.org/10.1192/bjp.172.1.64

Aiyegbusi, A. and Kelly, D. (2015) 'This is the pain I feel!' Projection and emotional pain in the nurse–patient relationship with people diagnosed with personality disorders in forensic and specialist personality disorder services: findings from a mixed methods study', *Psychoanalytic Psychotherapy*, 29(3), pp. 276–294. http://dx.doi.org/10.1080/02668734.2015.1025425

Bateman, A. and Tyrer, P. (2002) *Effective management of personality disorder*. London: Department of Health.

Benefield, N., Joseph, N., Skett, S., Bridgland, S., d'Cruz, L., Goode, I. and Turner, K. (2015) 'The offender personality disorder strategy jointly delivered by NOMS and NHS England', *Prison Service Journal*, 218, pp. 4–9.

Beryl, R. and Völlm, B. (2018) 'Attitudes to personality disorder of staff working in high-security and medium-security hospitals', *Personality and Mental Health*, 12(1), pp. 25–37. http://dx.doi.org/10.1002/pmh.1396

Black, D.W., Pfohl, B., Blum, N., McCormick, B., Allen, J., North, C.S., Phillips, K.A., Robins, C., Siever, L., Silk, K.R. and Williams, J.B. (2011) 'Attitudes toward borderline personality disorder: a survey of 706 mental health clinicians', *CNS Spectrums*, 16(3), pp. 67–74. http://dx.doi.org/10.1017/S109285291200020X

Borrill, C.S., Carletta, J., Carter, A., Dawson, J.F., Garrod, S., Rees, A., Richards, A., Shapiro, D. and West, M.A. (2000) *The effectiveness of health care teams in the National Health Service*. Birmingham: University of Aston in Birmingham.

Bowers, L. (2003) *Factors underlying and maintaining nurses' attitudes to patients with severe personality disorder: final report to National Forensic Medicine Health R & D*. City University: Department of Mental Health Nursing.

Buus, N., Delgado, C., Traynor, M. and Gonge, H. (2018) 'Resistance to group clinical supervision: a semi-structured interview study of non-participating mental health nursing staff members', *International Journal of Mental Health Nursing*, 27(2), pp. 783–793. http://dx.doi.org/10.1111/inm.12365

Celenza, A. and Gabbard, G.O. (2007) 'Analysts who commit sexual boundary violations: a lost cause?, *Focus*, 5(4), pp. 483–492. http://dx.doi.org/10.1177/00030651030510020201

Chandler, R.J., Newman, A. and Butler, C. (2017) 'Burnout in clinicians working with offenders with personality disorder', *Journal of Forensic Practice*, 19(2), pp. 139–150. http://dx.doi.org/10.1108/JFP-01-2016-0004

Chartonas, D., Kyratsous, M., Dracass, S., Lee, T. and Bhui, K. (2017) 'Personality disorder: still the patients psychiatrists dislike?, *BJPsych Bulletin*, 41(1), pp. 12–17. http://dx.doi.org/10.1192/pb.bp.115.052456

Clarke, S., Taylor, G., Bolderston, H., Lancaster, J. and Remington, B. (2015) 'Ameliorating patient stigma amongst staff working with personality disorder: randomized controlled trial of self-management versus skills training', *Behavioural and Cognitive Psychotherapy*, 43(6), pp. 692–704. http://dx.doi.org/10.1017/S1352465814000320

De Zulueta, F. (2006) *From pain to violence: the traumatic roots of destructiveness*. New Jersey: John Wiley & Sons.

Durkheim, E. (1984) *The division of labor in society*. 2nd edn. New York: Macmillan.

Epstein, R.S. and Simon, R.I. (1990) 'The exploitation index: an early warning indicator of boundary violations in psychotherapy', *Bulletin of the Menninger Clinic*, 54(4), p. 450.

Fallon, P., Bluglass, R., Edwards, B. and Daniels, G. (1999) *Report of the committee of inquiry into the personality disorder unit, Ashworth Special Hospital*. Cm 4194. London: HMSO.

Fonagy, P. 2003. 'The developmental roots of violence in the failure of mentalization.' In *A matter of security: the application of attachment theory to forensic psychiatry and psychotherapy*, edited by Parker, M.; & Morris, M. London: Jessica Kingsley Publishers.

Fonagy, P., Target, M., Steele, M. and Steele, H. 1997. 'The development of violence and crime as it relates to security of attachment.' In *Children in a violent society*, edited by Osojsky, J. New York: Guilford Press.

Freestone, M.C., Wilson, K., Jones, R., Mikton, C., Milsom, S., Sonigra, K., Taylor, C. and Campbell, C. (2015) 'The impact on staff of working with personality disordered offenders: a systematic review', *PloS One*, 10(8), p. e0136378. http://dx.doi.org/10.1371/journal.pone.0136378

Freud, A. (1936) Identification with the aggressor. *The ego and the mechanisms of defence*. London: The Hogarth Press, pp. 117–131.

Gabbard, G.O. (1997) 'Challenges in the analysis of adults who were sexually abused as children', *Canadian Journal of Psychoanalysis*, 5, pp. 1–25.

Gilligan, J. (1997) *Violence: our deadliest epidemic and its causes*. New York: Grosset/Putnam.

Haslam, M.B., Ellis, S. and Plumridge, M. (2022) 'It's not you; it's us!': the relevance of mental health team psychodynamics to the care of individuals with complex emotional needs', *British Journal of Mental Health Nursing*, 11(2), pp. 1–7. http://dx.doi.org/10.12968/bjmh.2021.0033

Hinshelwood, R.D. (2002) 'Abusive help–helping abuse: the psychodynamic impact of severe personality disorder on caring institutions', *Criminal Behaviour and Mental Health*, 12(S2), pp. S20–S30. http://dx.doi.org/10.1002/cbm.2200120604

Hollander, J.A. and Einwohner, R.L. (2004) 'Conceptualizing resistance', *Sociological Forum*, 19, pp. 533–554.

Katz, P. and Kirkland, F.R. (1990) 'Violence and social structure on mental hospital wards', *Psychiatry*, 53(3), pp. 262–277. http://dx.doi.org/10.1080/00332747.1990.11024508

Klein, M. (1946) 'Notes on some schizoid mechanisms', *The International Journal of Psychoanalysis*, 27, pp. 99–110.

Kurtz, A. (2005) 'The needs of staff who care for people with a diagnosis of personality disorder who are considered a risk to others', *The Journal of Forensic Psychiatry & Psychology*, 16(2), pp. 399–422. http://dx.doi.org/10.1080/14789940500098475

Lewis, G. and Appleby, L. (1988) 'Personality disorder: the patients psychiatrists dislike', *The British Journal of Psychiatry*, 153(1), pp. 44–49. http://dx.doi.org/10.1192/bjp.153.1.44

Miller, R.D. and Maier, G.J. (2002) 'Nonsexual boundary violations: sauce for the gander', *The Journal of Psychiatry & Law*, 30(3), pp. 309–329. http://dx.doi.org/10.1177/009318530203000302

Narvaez, D. (2014) *Neurobiology and the development of human morality: Evolution, culture, and wisdom (Norton series on interpersonal neurobiology)*. New York: W.W. Norton & Company.

National Institute for Mental Health (2003) *Personality disorder: no longer a diagnosis of exclusion*. London: NIMH(E).

National Institute for Mental Health in England (2013) Breaking the cycle of rejection: the personality disorder capabilities framework. National Institute for Mental Health in England.

Newton-Howes, G., Weaver, T. and Tyrer, P. (2008) 'Attitudes of staff towards patients with personality disorder in community mental health teams', *Australian & New Zealand Journal of Psychiatry*, 42(7), pp. 572–577. http://dx.doi.org/10.1080/00048670802119739

Nitsun, M. (1996) *The anti-group: destructive forces in the group and their creative potential*. London: Routledge.

Norton, K. and Dolan, B. (1995) 'Acting out and the institutional response', *Journal of Forensic Psychiatry*, 6(2), pp. 317–332. http://dx.doi.org/10.1080/09585189508409898

Paget, S. (2008) *The development of core standards and core values for therapeutic communities*. Royal College of Psychiatrists.

Parsons, T. (1975) 'The sick role and the role of the physician reconsidered', *The Milbank Memorial Fund Quarterly. Health and Society*, pp. 257–278. http://dx.doi.org/10.2307/3349493

Rodwell, D. and Frith, H. (2024) 'A ward full of emotional, aggressive people': social climate and interpersonal relationships in forensic settings caring for patients with borderline personality disorder. *International Journal of Mental Health Nursing*. http://dx.doi.org/10.1111/inm.13308

Ruszczynski, S. (2018) 'Thoughts from consulting in secure settings: do forensic institutions need psychotherapy?' in *Psychic assaults and frightened clinicians*, edited by Gordon, J.; & Kirtchuk, G. London: Routledge, pp. 85–95.

Sampogna, G., Bakolis, I., Evans-Lacko, S., Robinson, E., Thornicroft, G. and Henderson, C. (2017) 'The impact of social marketing campaigns on reducing mental health stigma: results from the 2009–2014 time to change programme', *European Psychiatry*, 40, pp. 116–122. http://dx.doi.org/10.1016/j.eurpsy.2016.08.008

Taylor, C. (2012) 'Complaints as a tool for bullying', *The Therapeutic Milieu Under Fire: Security and Insecurity in Forensic Mental Health*, 34, p. 63.

Van den Berg, A. and Oei, K. (2009) 'Attachment and psychopathy in forensic patients', *Mental Health Review Journal*, 14(3), pp. 40–51. http://dx.doi.org/10.1108/13619322200900020

Welldon, E.V. (1991) 'Psychology and psychopathology in women – a psychoanalytic perspective', *The British Journal of Psychiatry*, 158(S10), pp. 85–92. http://dx.doi.org/10.1192/S0007125000292052

Chapter 20

Complex but common pitfalls

Celia Taylor

Patient mix

All therapeutic communities (TCs) – arguably all inpatient/resident personality disorder services – function best with a mixed group of patients, in the sense that it is enormously helpful for there always to be a few senior residents who occupy the position of 'culture carriers'. These are those individuals who have been in the community for a sufficiently long period (how long will differ from person to person) that they have largely 'bought into' and endorse the shared endeavour. They do not have to be 'perfect' patients, but are capable, most of the time, of demonstrating a commitment to the therapy, upholding the rules and boundaries, and articulating the ups and downs of their quest for a better, safer life. Again and again, newcomers to Millfields eventually told us of the significant influence a long-standing resident had upon him, by demonstrating that change is possible:

> "I got a lot from X: him feeling not understood resonated with me. It gives you confidence when you see others being truthful. I learned about myself and how wedded to secrecy I was. Also, how I was unable to connect with my feelings and emotions. I didn't want to talk about myself. I learned how to mirror others. Also, how to question myself and see myself from another perspective".

Even more impressive is to see such an individual trip up in some way, and then to participate in the process whereby he gets back on his feet. The structure so common in mental illness services, with separate 'rehab wards', is therefore to be avoided.

Senior residents

The essential attribute of the senior resident is that he is ready to take more responsibility for his actions, past and present, and to consider their impact on others. He will have begun to develop a sense of his own agency and to use his

DOI: 10.4324/9781032717302-20

new skills, which enable him to make different choices – such as thinking before acting in an impulsive or damaging fashion (Pickard, 2014). He will also be ready to accept the opportunities for empowerment (Haigh, 2013) offered by the TC, without misusing them or succumbing to corrupting influences. These include acting as Chair or Vice Chair of the community meeting, Activities Coordinator and the like: roles that are challenging but upon which the work of the community depends. Senior residents are also willing to contribute in practical ways, such as writing service literature, hosting visitors' mornings or editing a newsletter.

> "I also had the chance to do other things that gave me a sense of purpose, especially in the anti-racism working group. I was trusted. Doing teaching with X. These things improved my sense of worth from a point that was low, low down".

Over time at Millfields, we developed more and more such opportunities. One of the most prized was being invited to work with the staff team to keep the unit safe. For example, any patient could request a crisis meeting, but to avoid this becoming a vehicle for merely airing grievances, we invited the Chair and Vice Chair to consult more widely with the patient group and to come back to us for discussion and a final decision on whether and when to hold the meeting.

It is important to remember that senior residents should not be idealised: they will still have problems, but they tend to manifest in subtler ways. One man, for example, 'took over' all the notice boards in the unit, organising what was displayed where, and designing notices in his own chosen, elaborate font. As Chair of the community meeting, we observed that he would allow certain people to speak whilst suppressing the voices of others. He felt he was contributing – and in many ways, he was – but eventually everyone else, staff included, felt they had lost a certain freedom of expression. His need to exert control was reflected in his index offences, which included false imprisonment of someone he wanted to have under his 'complete control and submission'.

Whether because of their benefit to the community or fear of moving on, it can be tempting to keep senior residents in the unit for as long as possible, but needless to say, their own interests and their future lives must take priority. Chapter 17 will address the complex task of navigating the joys, fears and sadness of leaving.

The destabilising patient

The corollary to the senior resident is the highly volatile and destabilising or corrupting patient. Examples of such behaviour that we encountered in Millfields included physical attacks, repeated sexualised verbal abuse of staff (both fortunately few and far between), destruction of valued community property such as the TV in the lounge, repeatedly throwing drinks over the day area, false allegations, smuggling in drugs, or absconding from community leave. A small, well-functioning group of senior residents can help to discourage such acting out before it begins, probably before staff are even aware of its potential occurrence. If it does happen, they can provide forthright feedback in the community meeting that 'hits home' and earns respect, more effectively we can. In this sense, they provide a containing function for the community. But no group of men striving to confront their own difficulties can be expected to do so for long periods in the face of continual, infuriating efforts to undermine their work. We should not forget that they must live with the perpetrators' constant provocations day and night, and might find it extremely difficult to resist succumbing to habitual ways of responding, be it by aggressive retaliation or collusion.

"Understanding Myself
I'm so sick, I want to stop kicking myself
When I was homeless I didn't see a light, I was kicked out many years ago
I forgot how it felt not to be on my own
The pain, the misery make me crazy
Nobody is faultless, I feel worthless, I also see kindness".
                                                   – Former Millfields patient

---

Before taking the decision to remit such a patient, it is important to consider what might underlie his behaviour: he will often be communicating an important message. Soon after the arrival of one very young man in Millfields Unit, it became evident that he would do whatever was needed to be secluded before nightfall. This pattern of disturbance disrupted the peaceful sleep of the entire ward, and there were bitter complaints from the other patients. It gradually emerged through sensitive exploration by night staff, that the evenings were when his abuser would enter his room. He first came to the attention of social services when he was a toddler and was once found locked in a closet while his mother slept. The seclusion room was the only place he felt safe: no one could get in. Ironically, voluntary seclusion was not a concept that policy writers ever imagined, but he knew how to achieve his goal of feeling safe.

On the other hand, sometimes it is important to recognise when remission is essential. A man who could only tolerate the unit briefly had been convicted of reckless Arson, probably as a suicide bid. Within days, he showed acute hypersensitivity to what he experienced as egregious failures of care: his medication was not given as soon as he requested it, and another patient received his clothing grant more quickly than he. He was unable to tolerate even the smallest delay in meeting his needs without becoming enraged. After a fellow patient asked him in a kindly manner, "Are you all right?", he became preoccupied with the thought that this man was bullying him and threatened to throw boiling water in his face unless he was sent back to prison immediately. His demand was taken seriously and acted upon: in his mind (although he could not articulate it), to lower his highly aggressive defences, as was required in the therapy, would be to expose himself to the threat of psychic and/or physical annihilation. The prospect was both unbearable and untenable. After he left, in his bedroom was found hidden, stolen supplies of sugar, coffee and biscuits, representative of his vain efforts to fulfil his need for care himself.

Another patient self-harmed so often and so severely that nursing staff were escorting him out to hospital on a near-daily basis. Since three escorts plus a driver were needed for each trip, these demands on their time disrupted the therapy programme and smooth running of the unit. Despite his obvious needs, we were forced to find an alternative service in order to maintain the integrity of everyone else's treatment.

> "Anytime anyone was affecting the therapy of others, that made me angry and bitter. It was the duty of staff to move them out. Too many of the staff wanted to see the good in everyone".
>
> – Former Millfields patient

Passive behaviour can also undermine the ethos of the community, such as 'going on strike' and refusing to attend the therapy programme. One man did this after a staff member mentioned details about his index offence in a community meeting, before he had been able to bring himself to talk about it. Deeply humiliated, he refused to attend any more therapy, and kept this up for a considerable period despite a formal, written apology. Eventually, another service was found for him. After this experience, we developed a protocol for all the community, including staff, on what would be kept confidential and what would not. Whilst we did not agree that a resident's index offence should be kept confidential (in fact, all residents were themselves expected to disclose their index offence from the start; discussed in Chapter 3), it was important that residents were signed up to this process on arrival and that staff recognised the need for sensitive handing of details particularly early in treatment.

Some examples of 'opting out', however, require patience and understanding. We usually had one or two individuals who stayed away from the Pavilion social events on a Friday afternoon – or 'organised fun' as one caustically described them. Therapy will not convert a natural 'loner' into an extravert, but over time, he can usually be persuaded to attend on special occasions, e.g. the 'leaving do' for a member of staff he thinks particularly highly of.

The psychopath

Perhaps the patient type to be most cautious about is those with pronounced or extreme psychopathic tendencies. Freud (1928) stressed the coexistence of pathological narcissism and cruel aggression in these individuals, while Cleckley (1941) described them as initially appearing engaging and kind; too late, one discovers the empty, pretend quality, and the lack of affection or guilt, behind the 'mask'. Such attributes are often (but not always) an emotional adaptation to very severe childhood abuse, whereby mentalising capacity has been distorted (Fonagy and Bateman, 2008) and the world construed as so dangerous that self-protection and self-interest become a means to survival (Van den Berg and Oei, 2009). Clinicians can have strong, negative countertransference reactions to these individuals, sometimes amounting to intense dislike (Searles, 1979). Symington (1980) has described how the psychopath can evoke 'our own primitive sadism', resulting in either condemnation or punitiveness. Another possibility is getting drawn into collusion, or a wish to rescue, via a process that has been called 'disidentification with the aggressor' (Gabbard, 2000): "The therapist is determined to prove that he is completely unlike the abusive parents, and that he can compensate for the tragic past".

Such features suggest that these individuals will not only be resistant to treatment, but also likely to corrupt the service in ways that are very damaging – often by deception, abuse and exploitation of staff and/or other patients, rather than overt violence. Heroic responses to appeals for help – which will be very convincing – or falling for an illusory treatment alliance should be avoided because of the harm that can, and usually will, follow: "the psychopath despises the person who holds onto the illusion that he is good" (Meloy and Reavis, 2007).

> "He was extremely destructive to the whole running of the Unit and fostered ill-feeling within both staff and patients. He would say sorry, but he despised people".
>
> – Former Millfields patient

Another risk such patients introduce is that of fomenting serious conflict within the team, which can be impossible to unravel unless everyone has the capacity and willingness to engage in honest self-examination with his or her colleagues, in a reflective practice group. Disagreements commonly arise in the context of widely differing experiences of the patient: one sub-group of staff witnesses the abusive bully, another the small, beginning steps he is taking to think about and understand himself. Explicitly framing the clash as about different parts of the patient, and not about the naivety of colleagues, is a useful way of defusing it and encouraging thoughtfulness. Even this might fail, however: "It is {often} thought that all can be resolved if everyone's role is clear and that by 'talking through', harmony can be reached. This may work in the absence of a psychopath, but not when one is present in the group" (Symington, 1980). In Millfields Unit, we took care to admit only one or two such patients at any one time, with less extreme features of psychopathy and who we felt might be amenable to therapy. It has been argued that the capacity to feel anxiety might well be a positive sign of treatability, since it indicates dissatisfaction with life and thus acts as a motivator for change. It also indicates that the individual has to some small degree internalised a good object in childhood (Meloy and Yakeley, 2007), which can form the basis of a nascent positive therapeutic alliance.

Staff mix

The success of any secure personality disorder service will also rest upon the professional characteristics of its staff. It can be difficult when running a service within a somewhat rigid NHS structure, to avoid the conventional mental health ward team structure, usually consisting of one or more members of each discipline working strictly within their professional roles. Our experience was that most individuals, with additional training, supervision and support, could adapt well to their parallel role within the TC. The same applied to unqualified social therapists, who technically belonged to the nursing group but were aiming for a career in psychology or psychotherapy. Some mental health nurses, however, found the necessary adjustment difficult or impossible. Almost all undergraduate degree courses tend to cover much the same content on mental illness, with little teaching about, or practical experience of, patients suffering from personality disorder. It has even been argued that 2018 changes in the UK pre-registration training curriculum have made things worse: "mental health nursing skills and qualities such as connection, genuine advocacy and therapeutic-use-of-self have been undervalued and under-represented by new education standards" (Connell et al., 2022). Paradoxically, there was "a move away from a … person centred approach, towards a model constructed on quantifiable competencies in physical health assessment and intervention" (Connell et al., 2022). This direction of travel illustrates the current, widespread emphasis on measurable standards, at the expense of less tangible but just as valuable, human relational skills. Mental health nurses are thus, through no fault of their own, woefully under-equipped for working with this patient group. That some excel is, in our experience, usually due to personal attributes of integrity, lack of defensiveness, sensitively upheld boundaries and responsiveness to role models. A fuller discussion about recruitment can be found in Chapter 18.

It is essential for all staff, perhaps especially nursing, to choose to work with personality disorder, rather than be allocated by managers who themselves have no direct experience of such services. Nursing staff who find themselves unexpectedly placed, with no prior consultation or preparation, in a setting with patients who are both "distressed and highly distressing in the actions they undertake" (Adshead, 2002), are likely to feel overwhelmed and, eventually, angry. It is not insignificant that nurses working in the Ashworth Hospital personality disorder unit, which was the subject of not one but two public inquiries after scandals coming to light, had the most negative attitudes compared to those working in similar services in other high secure hospitals (Bowers, 2005, p. 34). They, but not the others, had been 'allocated' to the task rather than choosing it voluntarily. Although specialist training has generally been shown to improve attitudes and confidence (Beryl and Völlm, 2018), the Millfields specifically adapted TC training had little impact on those most highly defended against forming authentic relational bonds with our patients. This is a version of the core anxiety identified by Isabelle Menzies Lyth (1960), and perhaps reflects the intense conscious and unconscious dislike that has already been noted: "In Millfields, the patient-nurse relationship was the closest in terms of hours spent together, and in terms of transference-countertransference exchanges: this was where the patients' most problematic ways of relating were often played out" (Taylor and Blake, 2024). All the evidence suggests that the emotional toll of engaging, in a humane, sympathetic way, with personality disordered offenders is exhausting (Freestone *et al.*, 2015). The most guarded individuals will retreat behind the wall of their professional identity and simply avoid contact, even when their role requires it.

The term 'anti-group' refers to a faction that can develop amongst patients within a psychotherapy group, which, split off from the healthier whole, functions to bring about the group's destruction – unless, that is, the 'anti-group' is recognised and contained (Nitsun, 1996). This description also fits well the propensity for splits and sub-groups to form in clinical teams working with personality disorder, which is one reason why structures such as staff support, reflective practice and clinical supervision are considered mandatory. Expressions of dislike by 'allocated' as opposed to 'voluntary' frontline staff can grow over time from the subtle (e.g. "Oh, you're a 'PD'") to the forthrightly sadistic and unprofessional (e.g. shouting, "sending them to Coventry" [ignoring them and denying care], overt disgust, "let him kill himself" and treatment sabotage). The first Ashworth Hospital inquiry (Blom-Cooper et al, 1992) identified outright physical abuse of patients by a highly destructive 'anti-group' of staff that had been permitted to prevail. It is essential that the lead clinician – albeit with consultation – be afforded the authority to address an anti-group before irrevocable damage is done. It is not beneficial for individual staff members to be left within its pernicious influence, or to continue working in a role he or she is unsuited to.

Alternative approaches to the conventional mental health nursing role are worth considering, for example, the psychosocial nursing model pioneered at the Cassel Hospital (e.g. Chettiar, 2012), with its specific training. This approach explicitly embodies the 'therapeutic use of self', by which the nurse works alongside the patient to understand, process and integrate his internal and external worlds. In a TC, this often takes place in 'living-learning' situations, or through sharing everyday activities. It explicitly mitigates the somewhat artificial milieu prevalent on mental health wards, where rules of no self-disclosure, social distance and explicit hierarchy inhibit authenticity in relationships.

Oversight by the host organisation

What is meant here by the 'host organisation' is the hospital or prison within which the forensic personality disorder service is situated, with all that that implies: it will be subject to a raft of over-arching standards, policies and procedures, as well as to a pervasive culture or ethos. In our experience, it is crucial for not only the host organisation but also the wider system of regulation both to understand and to be willing to work to sustain the task. However, as noted by Cooper (2001), in these days of inspections and ratings, the foremost *conscious* worry of almost all organisations is about what might go wrong: no one wants to be left 'holding the baby' when a scandal breaches the threshold of media and political awareness. It is a realistic concern: over the past decade, a major failing of an NHS mental health service has been investigated almost every year. The fear of disgrace is especially intense for the managers, commissioners and regulators who have oversight of a service for high-risk offenders with personality disorder: this is the group of patients most likely to corrupt staff and subvert the institution (e.g. Blom-Cooper *et al.*, 1992; Fallon *et al.*, 1999). In this sense, a degree of anxiety is justified, and serves to heighten awareness of very real risks.

In today's NHS, however, there are powerful incentives for managers, commissioners and regulators to maintain a narcissistic defence, in order to be part of what could be called a 'virtuous circle' of positive regard. Nowadays, the highest forms of good include avoiding serious incidents *at all costs* and garnering approval from external bodies such as the Care Quality Commission (CQC) and NHS England. These factors were noted to be pervasive almost a decade ago by Robert Francis (2013) in his report on the Mid Staffordshire NHS Foundation Trust, when he identified "an institutional culture which ascribed more weight to positive information about the service than to information capable of implying cause for concern". In such a culture, services for those with personality disorder will become less and less attractive to an uninformed or inexperienced host organisation, and vulnerable to being undermined, consciously or unconsciously. This can be achieved passively (by avoidance and shunning), and actively (e.g. via counterproductive hiring and staffing practices, hostility and partisanship). During the process, a blind eye can be turned to the genuine identification of difficulties, which will always arise with this patient group, and to thoughtful solutions – for example by ignoring expert advice and paying narrow, under-inclusive attention to whistleblowing complaints, thus evading an authentic recognition of the whole picture.

Very few overseers, however senior, will have a knowledge and understanding of the complex psychological pathology we encounter in personality disorder, let alone its treatment and risk management. Furthermore, antipathy remains widespread: few patients attract such conscious, sometimes intense, dislike as these: little has changed since Lewis and Appleby (1988) wrote their classic paper, *Personality disorder: the patients psychiatrists dislike*. The authors described 'pejorative, judgemental and rejecting' attitudes, including that they are 'undeserving of NHS resources'. These factors will be a source of conscious and unconscious shame, and thus provoke avoidance unless proactively countered by reaching out for regular formal and informal involvement. A negative mindset can be found in most disciplines, perhaps particularly amongst nurses (Beryl and Völlm, 2018). Proponents often remark that these patients are in control of their behaviour, unlike those with a mental illness (Markham and

238 Treating High-Risk Offenders with Personality Disorder

Trower, 2003). It is not difficult to understand that patients who are both 'in control' and commit terrible crimes, can come to be seen as deliberately 'bad' and are thus reviled.

> "Staff inconsistency was a constant negative distraction. If they had never worked with PD patients, this could dictate how they treated them. Stigma from the wider hospital was quite pervasive".
>
> – Former Millfields patient

Once stigmatising attitudes are given tacit 'permission' or licence, openly expressed denigration can become the norm and thus absorbed into the institutional culture. Staff in the wider institution then feel able to voice their contempt openly. Individuals with personality disorder can, for example, be described as 'PD thugs' without fear of sanction, and staff involved in their treatment denigrated as 'care bears' – a slight that is commonly heard within prisons. Such attitudes, and the underlying ethos, are then passed on to new employees during induction and training events, with the inherent message being one of shunning and disowning. Inevitably, such attitudes filter through to the patients themselves, with highly detrimental effects. It has been noted that, for the mentally ill, stigma is often internalised, leading to the person incorporating shame into his very sense of self (Dinos *et al.*, 2004) and hence to a poorer self-esteem and loss of a sense of agency. Feelings of antipathy are likely to lead even experienced forensic mental health practitioners to over-estimate dangerousness (Blumenthal *et al.*, 2010); in other words, to base their judgements on 'gut feelings' (Hale, 2018).

In practice, such strong, negative reactions are a source of shame: out-with specialist support, reflection and exploration, they are likely to remain unacknowledged. They then tend to be acted out as contempt and hatred, with blame being passed down towards colleagues or whole staff teams for their patients' behaviour (Moore, 2012). Responsibility is disavowed by the very individuals appointed – and paid – to assume it. This road can lead to outright abuse (e.g. Fallon *et al.*, 1999). The risks are especially high when clinical supervision policies are not adhered to or enforced, and early signs of unethical behaviour are left unaddressed. Another impulse is to get rid of this kind of patient altogether. If services are to be protected from destruction, therefore, it is essential that those responsible for their oversight understand these processes and how to build robust defences against them.

At a deeper level, the very nature of these individuals is at play: "unconsciously, it is the function of the psychopathic patient to attempt to destroy the institution and its therapeutic purpose. Equally and paradoxically, it is the function of the institution to prevent him from succeeding, for his sake (Hale and Dhar, 2008)". Institutional failure in this regard can be understood in terms of projective identification: "an aspect of the patient's self is split off and attributed to another, with the recipient unconsciously stimulated into ... enacting the projected impulse" (Hale, 2020). In other words, staff, both frontline and managers, identify with the psychopathic part of the patient and themselves carry out the demolition.

It has been argued that "the institution as a whole offers the most significant possibility for treatment and is in essence the primary therapeutic agent" (Ruszczynski, 2018). It is not usually possible to choose the individuals responsible for oversight of a service, but ongoing work should be attempted to inform, educate and build a collaborative relationship. Attention should be paid not only to clinical practice, but also to essential elements such as security, record-keeping and learning from incidents. Reflecting on how highly perverse and dangerous patients impact their entire environment requires staff to sustain their capacity to think. A lesson learned from the Fallon inquiry (1999) was that this can be greatly enhanced by external, psychodynamically informed consultation from someone familiar with these influences, but whose mind is less disrupted by them (Ruszczynski, 2018).

References

Adshead, G. (2002) 'Three degrees of security: attachment and forensic institutions', *Criminal Behaviour and Mental Health*, 12, pp. S31–45. http://dx.doi.org/10.1002/cbm.2200120605

Beryl, R. and Völlm, B. (2018) 'Attitudes to personality disorder of staff working in high-security and medium-security hospitals', *Personality and Mental Health*, 12(1), pp. 25–37. http://dx.doi.org/10.1002/pmh.1396

Blom-Cooper, L., Brown, M., Dolan, R. and Murphy, E. (1992) *Report of the committee of inquiry into complaints at Ashworth Hospital volume 1*. Stationery Office.

Blumenthal, S., Huckle, C., Czornyj, R., Craissati, J. and Richardson, P. (2010) 'The role of affect in the estimation of risk', *Journal of Mental Health*, 19(5), pp. 444–451. http://dx.doi.org/10.3109/09638231003728083

Bowers, L. (2005) *Dangerous and severe personality disorder: reactions and role of the psychiatric team*. Routledge.

Chettiar, T. (2012) 'Democratizing mental health: motherhood, therapeutic community and the emergence of the psychiatric family at the Cassel Hospital in post-Second World War Britain', *History of the Human Sciences*, 25(5), pp. 107–122.

Cleckley, H.M. (1941) *The mask of sanity: an attempt to reinterpret the so-called psychopathic personality.* St. Louis: The C.V. Mosby Company.

Connell, C., Jones, E., Haslam, M., Firestone, J., Pope, G. and Thompson, C. (2022) 'Mental health nursing identity: a critical analysis of the UK's nursing and midwifery Council's pre-registration syllabus change and subsequent move towards genericism', *Mental Health Review Journal*, 27(4), pp. 472–483. http://dx.doi.org/10.1108/MHRJ-02-2022-0012

Cooper, A. (2001) 'The state of mind we're in: social anxiety, governance and the audit society', *Psychoanalytic Studies*, 3(3–4), pp. 349–362. http://dx.doi.org/10.1080/14608950120103640

Dinos, S., Stevens, S., Serfaty, M., Weich, S. and King, M. (2004) 'Stigma: the feelings and experiences of 46 people with mental illness: qualitative study', *The British Journal of Psychiatry*, 184(2), pp. 176–181. http://dx.doi.org/10.1192/bjp.184.2.176

Fallon, P., Bluglass, R., Edwards, B. and Daniels, G. (1999) *Report of the committee of inquiry into the personality disorder unit, Ashworth special Hospital.* Cm 4194. London: HMSO.

Fonagy, P. and Bateman, A. (2008) 'The development of borderline personality disorder – a mentalizing model', *Journal of Personality Disorders*, 22(1), pp. 4–21. http://dx.doi.org/10.1521/pedi.2008.22.1.4

Francis, R. (2013) *Report of the Mid Staffordshire NHS Foundation Trust public inquiry: executive summary* (Vol. 947). The Stationery Office.

Freestone, M.C., Wilson, K., Jones, R., Mikton, C., Milsom, S., Sonigra, K., Taylor, C. and Campbell, C. (2015) 'The impact on staff of working with personality disordered offenders: a systematic review', *PloS One*, 10(8), p. e0136378. http://dx.doi.org/10.1371/journal.pone.0136378

Freud, S. (1928) 'Dostoevsky and parricide', *International Journal of Psychoanalysis*, 1945, 26, pp. 1–8. http://dx.doi.org/10.1075/llsee.31.04fre

Gabbard, G.O. (2000) 'Hatred and its rewards: a discussion', *Psychoanalytic Inquiry*, 20(3), pp. 409–420. http://dx.doi.org/10.1080/07351692009348897

Haigh, R. (2013) 'The quintessence of a therapeutic environment', *Therapeutic Communities: The International Journal of Therapeutic Communities*, 34(1), pp. 6–15. http://dx.doi.org/10.1108/09641861311330464

Hale, R. (2018) Gut feelings. In *Containment in the community: Supportive frameworks for thinking about antisocial behaviour and mental health* (eds A. Rubitel, D. Reiss): 187–202. Karnac Books. http://dx.doi.org/10.4324/9780429473210-10

Hale, R. (2020) 'Autonomic countertransference: the psychopathic mind and the institution', *The International Journal of Forensic Psychotherapy*, 2(2), pp. 101–112.

Hale, R. and Dhar, R. (2008) 'Flying a kite-observations on dual and triple diagnosis', *Criminal Behaviour & Mental Health*, 18, p. 145. http://dx.doi.org/10.1002/cbm.694

Lewis, G. and Appleby, L. (1988) 'Personality disorder: the patients psychiatrists dislike', *The British Journal of Psychiatry*, 153(1), pp. 44–49. http://dx.doi.org/10.1192/bjp.153.1.44

Lyth, I.M. (1960). Social systems as a defense against anxiety. *Human Relations*, 13, pp. 95–121.

Markham, D. and Trower, P. (2003) 'The effects of the psychiatric label 'borderline personality disorder' on nursing staff's perceptions and causal attributions for challenging behaviours', *British Journal of Clinical Psychology*, 42(3), pp. 243–256. http://dx.doi.org/10.1348/01446650360703366

Meloy, J.R. and Reavis, J.A. (2007) Dangerous cases: when treatment is not an option. *Severe personality disorders: major issues in everyday practice* (eds J.B. Van Luyn, S. Akhtar, J. Livesley). London: Cambridge University Press, pp. 181–195. http://dx.doi.org/10.1017/CBO9780511544439.012

Meloy, J.R. and Yakeley, J. (2007) Antisocial personality disorder. In *Gabbard's treatments of psychiatric disorders* (ed. G.O. Gabbard). American Psychiatric Publishing.

Menzies, I.E. (1960) 'A case-study in the functioning of social systems as a defence against anxiety: a report on a study of the nursing service of a general hospital', *Human Relations*, 13(2), pp. 95–121. http://dx.doi.org/10.1177/001872676001300201

Nitsun, M. (1996) *The anti-group: destructive forces in the group and their creative potential*. London: Routledge.

Pickard, H. (2014) 'Responsibility without blame: therapy, philosophy, law', *Prison Service Journal*, 213, p. 10.

Ruszczynski, S. (2018) Thoughts from consulting in secure settings: do forensic institutions need psychotherapy? In *Psychic assaults and frightened clinicians* (eds John Gordon and Gabriel Kirtchuk). Routledge, pp. 85–95. http://dx.doi.org/10.4324/9780429478604-6

Searles, H.F. (1979) *Countertransference and related subjects: selected papers*. Madison, CT: International Universities Press, Inc.

Symington, N. (1980) 'The response aroused by the psychopath', *International Review of Psychoanalysis*, 7, pp. 291–298. http://dx.doi.org/10.4324/9780429472237-8

Taylor, C. and Blake, J. (2024) 'Millfields unit: unveiling the factors behind its closure and examining the mechanisms responsible', *The International Journal of Forensic Psychotherapy*, 6(1), pp. 24–35. http://dx.doi.org/10.33212/ijfp.v6n1.2024.24

Van den Berg, A. and Oei, K. (2009) 'Attachment and psychopathy in forensic patients', *Mental Health Review Journal*, 14(3), pp. 40–51. http://dx.doi.org/10.1108/13619322200900020

Index

For Product Safety Concerns and Information please contact our EU
representative GPSR@taylorandfrancis.com
Taylor & Francis Verlag GmbH, Kaufingerstraße 24, 80331 München, Germany

9 781032 709215